Search Engine Optimization

FOR

DUMMIES®

Search Engine Optimization FOR DUMMIES®

by Peter Kent

WILEY

Wiley Publishing, Inc.

Search Engine Optimization For Dummies®

Published by
Wiley Publishing, Inc.
111 River Street
Hoboken, NJ 07030-5774

WILEY

About the Author

Peter Kent is the author of numerous other books about the Internet, including the best-selling *Complete Idiot's Guide to the Internet* and the most widely reviewed and praised title in computer-book history, *Poor Richard's Web Site: Geek Free, Commonsense Advice on Building a Low-Cost Web Site*. His work has been praised by *USA Today, BYTE, CNN.com, Windows Magazine, Philadelphia Inquirer,* and many others.

Peter has been online since 1984, doing business in cyberspace since 1991, and writing about the Internet since 1993. Peter's experience spans virtually all areas of doing business online, from editing and publishing an e-mail newsletter to creating e-commerce Web sites, from online marketing and PR campaigns to running a Web-design and -hosting department for a large ISP.

Peter was the founder of an e-Business Service Provider funded by one of the world's largest VC firms, Softbank/Mobius. He was VP of Web Solutions for a national ISP and VP of Marketing for a Web applications firm. He also founded a computer-book publishing company launched through a concerted online marketing campaign.

Peter now consults with businesses about their Internet strategies, helping them to avoid the pitfalls and to leap the hurdles they'll encounter online. He also gives seminars and presentations on subjects related to online marketing in general and search engine marketing in particular. He can be contacted at consult@iChannelServices.com, and more information about his background and experience is available at www.IChannelServices.com.

Dedication

For Melinda, a good friend in difficult times

Author's Acknowledgments

I'd like to thank a number of people for their help with this book. First, my mentor, colleague, and Technical Editor, Micah Baldwin of Current Wisdom (www.CurrentWisdom.com), who kept me focused and on target. I'd also like to thank Acquisitions Editor Terri Varveris, whose assistance was critical in getting my idea from proposal to contract, and Project Editor Paul Levesque, who kept me on the straight and narrow. And, of course, the multitude of Wiley staff involved in editing, proofreading, and laying out the book. Finally, I'd also like to thank my friend and one-time boss Mike Higgins, who's an example to us all (though for exactly what I'm not sure).

Publisher's Acknowledgments

We're proud of this book; please send us your comments through our online registration form located at `www.dummies.com/register/`.

Some of the people who helped bring this book to market include the following:

Acquisitions, Editorial, and Media Development

Project Editor: Paul Levesque

Acquisitions Editor: Terri Varveris

Senior Copy Editor: Kim Darosett

Technical Editor: Micah Baldwin

Editorial Manager: Kevin Kirshner

Permissions Editor: Carmen Krikorian

Media Development Specialist: Travis Silvers

Media Development Manager: Laura VanWinkle

Media Development Supervisor: Richard Graves

Editorial Assistant: Amanda Foxworth

Cartoons: Rich Tennant (`www.the5thwave.com`)

Production

Project Coordinator: Adrienne Martinez

Layout and Graphics: Jonelle Burns, Andrea Dahl, Denny Hager, Stephanie D. Jumper, Michael Kruzil, Jacque Schneider, Julie Trippetti

Proofreaders: Laura Albert, Andy Hollandbeck, Carl W. Pierce, Dwight Ramsey, Brian H. Walls, TECHBOOKS Production Services

Indexer: TECHBOOKS Production Services

Publishing and Editorial for Technology Dummies

Richard Swadley, Vice President and Executive Group Publisher

Andy Cummings, Vice President and Publisher

Mary C. Corder, Editorial Director

Publishing for Consumer Dummies

Diane Graves Steele, Vice President and Publisher

Joyce Pepple, Acquisitions Director

Composition Services

Gerry Fahey, Vice President of Production Services

Debbie Stailey, Director of Composition Services

Contents at a Glance

Table of Contents

Part III: Adding Your Site to the Indexes and Directories 171

Introduction

······································

Welcome to *Search Engine Optimization For Dummies*. What on earth would you want this book for? After all, can't you just build a Web site, and then pay someone $25 to register the site with thousands of search engines? I'm sure you've seen the advertising: "We guarantee top-ten placement in a gazillion search engines!" "We'll register you in 5,000 search engines today!"

Well, unfortunately, it's not that simple. (Okay, fortunately for me, because if it were simple, Wiley Publishing wouldn't pay me to write this book.) The fact is that search engine optimization is a little complicated. Not brain surgery complicated, but not as easy as "give us 50 bucks, and we'll handle it for you."

The vast majority of Web sites don't have a chance in the search engines. Why? Because of simple mistakes. Because the people creating the sites don't have a clue what they should do to make the site easy for search engines to work with, because they don't understand the role of links pointing to their site, and because they've never thought about keywords. Because, because, because. This book helps you deal with those becauses and gets you not just one step, but dozens of steps ahead of the average Web site Joe.

About This Book

This book demystifies the world of search engines. You find out what you need to do to give your site the best possible chance to rank well in the search engines.

In this book, I show you how to

- ✔ Make sure that you're using the right keywords in your Web pages.
- ✔ Create pages that search engines can read and will index in the way *you* want them to.
- ✔ Avoid techniques that search engines hate — things that can get your Web site penalized (knocked down low in search engine rankings).
- ✔ Build pages that give your site greater visibility in search engines.
- ✔ Get search engines and directories to include your site in their indexes and lists.

✔ Encourage other Web sites to link to yours.

✔ Keep track of how well your site is doing.

✔ Use pay-per-click advertising and shopping directories.

✔ And plenty more!

Foolish Assumptions

I don't want to assume anything, but I have to believe that if you're reading this book, you already know a few things about the Internet and search engines. Things such as

✔ You have access to a computer that has access to the Internet.

✔ You know how to use a Web browser to get around the Internet.

✔ You know how to carry out searches at the Web's major search engines, such as Google and Yahoo!.

Of course, for a book like this, I have to assume a little more. This is a book about how to get your Web site to rank well in the search engines. I have to assume that you know how to create and work with a site, or at least know someone who can create and work with a site. In particular, you (or the other person) know how to

✔ Set up a Web site.

✔ Create Web pages.

✔ Load those pages onto your Web server.

✔ Work with HTML (HyperText Markup Language), the coding used to create Web pages. In other words, you're not just using a program such as Microsoft FrontPage — you, or your geek, understand a little about HTML and feel comfortable enough with it to insert or change HTML tags.

I don't go into a lot of complicated code in this book; this isn't a primer on HTML. But in order to do search engine work, you or someone on your team needs to know what a TITLE tag is, for instance, and how to insert it into a page; how to recognize JavaScript (though not how to create or modify it); how to open a Web page in a text editor and modify it; and so on. You have to have basic HTML skills in order to optimize a site for the search engines. If you need more information about HTML, take a look at *HTML 4 For Dummies*, 4th Edition, by Ed Tittel and Natanya Pitts (Wiley).

How This Book Is Organized

Like all good reference tools, this book is designed to be read "as needed." It's divided into several parts: the basics, building search-engine-friendly Web sites, getting your site into the search engines, what to do after your site is indexed by the search engines, search engine advertising, and the Part of Tens. So if you just want to know how to find sites that will link to your Web site, read Chapter 13. If you need to understand the principles behind getting links to your site, read Chapter 12. If all you need today is to figure out what keywords are important to your site, Chapter 4 is for you.

However, search engine optimization is a pretty complex subject, and all the topics covered in this book are interrelated. Sure, you can register your site with the search engines, but if your pages aren't optimized for the search engines, you may be wasting your time! You can create pages the search engines can read, but if you don't pick the right keywords, it's a total waste of time. So I recommend that you read everything in this book; it will make a huge difference in how well your pages are ranked in the search engines.

Part 1: Search Engine Basics

In this part, I provide, yep, the basics — the foundation on which you can build your search-engine-optimization skills. Which search engines are important, for instance? In fact, what *is* a search engine? And what's a *search directory?* And why am I using the term *search system?* In this part, you find out the basics of sensible site creation, discover how to pick the keywords that people are using to find your business, and discover how to do a few quick fixes to your site.

Part 11: Building Search-Engine-Friendly Sites

Do you have any idea how many sites are invisible to the search engines? Or that, if they're not invisible, are built in such a way that search engines won't see the information they need in order to index the site in the way the site owners would like?

Well, I don't know an exact number, but I do know it's most sites. If you read Part II, you will be way ahead of the vast majority of site owners and managers. You discover how to create techniques that search engines like and avoid the ones they hate. You also find out about tricks that some people use — and the dangers involved.

Part III: Adding Your Site to the Indexes and Directories

After you've created your Web site and ensured that the search engines can read the pages, somehow you have to get the search systems — the engines and directories — to include your site. That's hard if you don't know what you're doing. In this part, you find out which search systems are important, how to register, and how to find other search engines and directories that are important to your site. You also find out why registering sometimes doesn't work, and what to do about it.

Part IV: After You've Submitted

Your work isn't over yet. In this part of the book, you find out why links to your site are so important and how to get other sites to link to you. You discover the shopping directories, such as Froogle and Shopping.com. I also explain the multibillion-dollar search engine advertising business. You find out how to work with the hugely popular Google AdWords and Overture pay-per-click programs . . . *and* how to buy cheaper clicks. You also discover paid placement and other forms of advertising.

Part V: The Part of Tens

All *For Dummies* books have the Part of Tens. In this part, you find ten really powerful search engine strategies. You also find out about ten common mistakes that make Web sites invisible to search engines, and ten services that will be useful in your search engine campaign.

Part VI: Appendix

Don't forget to check out the appendix, where you'll find information on copyright laws.

Icons Used in This Book

This book, like all *For Dummies* books, uses icons to highlight certain paragraphs and to alert you to particularly useful information. Here's a rundown of what those icons mean:

A Tip icon means I'm giving you an extra snippet of information that may help you on your way or provide some additional insight into the concepts being discussed.

The Remember icon points out information that is worth committing to memory.

The Technical Stuff icon indicates geeky stuff that you can skip if you really want to . . . though you may want to read it if you're the kind of person who likes to have the background info.

The Warning icon helps you stay out of trouble. It's intended to grab your attention to help you avoid a pitfall that may harm your Web site or business.

Don't forget to visit the Web sites associated with this book. At www.dummies.com/go/seo, you find all the links in this book (so you don't have to type them!), as well as a Bonus Chapter on how to power up your search engine skills. At www.SearchEngineBulletin.com, you find the aforementioned links along with additional useful information that didn't make it into the book.

Part I
Search Engine Basics

The 5th Wave   By Rich Tennant

"This is amazing. You can stop looking for Derek. According to an MSN search I did, he's hiding behind the dryer in the basement."

In this part . . .

The basics of search engine optimization are surprisingly, um, basic. In fact, you may be able to make small changes to your Web site that make a huge difference in your site's ranking in the search results.

This part starts with the basics. I begin by explaining which search engines are important. You may have heard the names of dozens of sites and heard that, in fact, hundreds of search engines exist. You'll be happy to hear that the vast majority of search results are provided by no more than nine systems, and three quarters of all the results come from a single company.

You also discover how to make some quick and easy changes to your Web site that may fix serious search engine problems for you. On the other hand, you may discover a significant (and common) problem in your site that must be resolved before you have any chance of getting into the search engines at all, let alone ranking well.

This part of the book also includes basic information on how to create a Web site that works well for both visitors and search engines, and you find out about one of the most important first steps you can take: carrying out a detailed keyword analysis.

Chapter 1

Surveying the Search Engine Landscape

. . . .

In This Chapter

▶ Discovering where people search

▶ Understanding the difference between search sites and search systems

▶ Distilling thousands of search sites down to about a dozen search systems

▶ Preparing your search strategy

. . . .

Vou've got a problem. You want people to visit your Web site; that's the purpose, after all, to bring people to your site to buy your products, or learn about them, or hear about the cause you support, or for whatever other purpose you've built the site. So you've decided you need to get traffic from the search engines — not an unreasonable conclusion, as you find out in this chapter. But there are *so many* search engines! There are the obvious ones, the Googles, AOLs, Yahoo!s, and MSNs of the world, but you've probably also heard of others — HotBot, Dogpile, Inktomi, Ask Jeeves, Netscape, EarthLink, LookSmart . . . even Amazon provides a Web search on almost every page. There's Lycos and InfoSpace, Teoma and WiseNut, Mamma.com, and Web-Crawler. To top it all off, you've seen advertising asserting that for only $49.95 (or $19.95, or $99.95, or whatever sum seems to make sense to the advertiser), you too can have your Web site listed in hundreds, nay, thousands of search engines. You may have even used some of these services, only to discover that the flood of traffic you were promised turns up missing.

Well, I've got some good news. You can forget almost all the names I just listed — well, at least you can after you've read this chapter. The point of this chapter is to take a complicated landscape of thousands of search sites and whittle it down into the small group of search systems that really matter. (Search sites? Search systems? Don't worry, I explain the distinction in a moment.)

If you really want to, you can jump to the end of the chapter to see the list of search systems you need to worry about and ignore the details. But I've found that, when I give this list to people, they look at me like I'm crazy because they've never heard of most of the names, and they know that some popular search sites aren't on the list. This chapter explains why.

What Are Search Engines and Directories?

The term *search engine* has become the predominant term for *search system* or *search site,* but before reading any further, you need to understand the different types of search, um, thingies, you're going to run across. Basically, you need to know about four thingies:

- **Search indexes or search engines:** These are the predominant type of search tools you'll run across. Originally, the term *search engine* referred to some kind of search index, a huge database containing information from individual Web sites. Google's vast index (`www.google.com`) contains over 3 *billion* pages, for instance. Large search-index companies own thousands of computers that use software known as *spiders* or *robots* (or just plain *bots* — Google's software is known as *Googlebot*) to grab Web pages and read the information stored in them. These systems don't always grab all the information on each page or all the pages in a Web site, but they grab a significant amount of information and use complex algorithms to index that information. Google, shown in Figure 1-1, is the world's most popular search engine.

- **Search directories:** A *directory* is a categorized collection of information about Web sites. Rather than containing information *from* Web *pages,* it contains information *about* Web *sites.* The most significant search directories are owned by Yahoo! (`dir.yahoo.com`) and the Open Directory Project (`www.dmoz.org`). (You can see an example of the Open Directory Project, displayed in Google, in Figure 1-2.) Directory companies don't use spiders or bots to download and index pages on the Web sites in the directory; rather, for each Web site, the directory contains information such as a title and description. The two most important directories, Yahoo! and Open Directory, have staff members who examine all the sites in the directory to make sure they are placed into the correct categories and meet certain quality criteria. Smaller directories often allow people submitting sites to specify which category should be used.

Here's how to see the difference between Yahoo!'s search results and the Yahoo! directory. Go to `www.yahoo.com`, type a word into the Search box, and click the Search button. The list of Web sites that appears is what Yahoo! calls the Yahoo! Search results, which are currently provided by

Google. But notice the Directory tab at the top of the page; or, underneath some of the search results, you see a line that says something like _More Sites about: Arthritis._ Click either the tab or link, and you end up in the Yahoo! Directory. (You can go directly to the directory by using `dir.yahoo.com`.)

✔ **Non-spidered indexes:** I wasn't sure what to call these things, so I made up a name: non-spidered indexes. A number of small indexes, less important than the major indexes such as Google, don't use spiders to examine the full contents of each page in the index. Rather, the index contains background information about each page, such as titles, descriptions, and keywords. In some cases, this information comes from the meta tags pulled off the pages in the index. (I tell you about meta tags in Chapter 2.) In other cases, the person who enters the site into the index provides this information. A number of the smaller systems discussed in Chapter 10 are of this type.

✔ **Pay-per-click systems:** Some systems provide pay-per-click listings. Advertisers place small ads into the systems, and when users perform their searches, the results contain some of these sponsored listings, typically above and to the right of the free listings. Pay-per-click systems are discussed in more detail in Chapter 15.

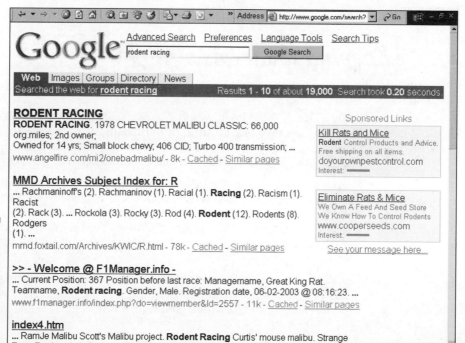

Figure 1-1:
Results from Google, the world's most popular search engine.

Figure 1-2:
Google also
has a
search
directory,
but it doesn't
create the
directory
itself; it
gets it from
the Open
Directory
Project.

Keeping the terms straight

Here are a few additional terms that you see scattered throughout the book:

✔ **Search site:** A Web site at which you can search through some kind of index or directory of Web sites, or perhaps both an index and directory. (In some cases, search sites allow you to search through multiple indices.) Google.com, AOL.com, and EarthLink.com are all search sites.

✔ **Search system:** An organization that possesses a combination of software, hardware, and people that is used to index or categorize Web sites — they build the index or directory you search through at a search site. Google is a search system, but AOL.com and EarthLink.com are not. In fact, if you go to AOL.com or EarthLink.com and search, you actually get Google search results.

Google and the Open Directory Project provide search results to hundreds of search sites. In fact, most of the world's search sites get their search results from elsewhere (see Figure 1-3).

✔ **Search results:** The information returned to you (the results of your search) when you go to a search site and search for something. Remember that in many cases, the search results don't come from the search site you're using, but from some other search system.

Why bother with search engines?

Why bother using search engines? Because search engines represent the single most important source of new Web site visitors.

You may have heard that most Web site visits begin at a search engine. Well, this is not true. It was true several years ago, and many people continue to use these outdated statistics because they sound good — "80 percent of all Web site visitors reach the site through a search engine," for instance. However, in 2003, that claim was finally put to rest. The number of search-originated site visits dropped below the 50-percent mark. Most Web site visitors reach their destinations by either typing a URL — a Web address — into their browsers and going there directly or by clicking a link on another site that takes them there. Most visitors do not reach their destinations by starting at the search engines.

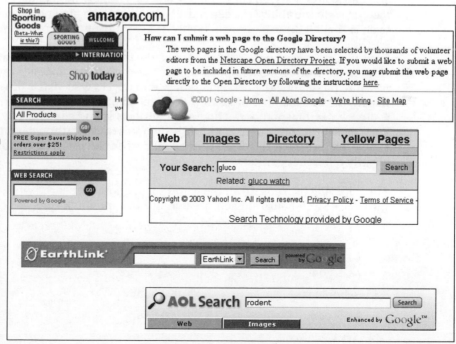

Figure 1-3: Look carefully, and you'll see that many search sites get their search results from other search systems.

However, search engines are still extremely important for a number of reasons:

- ✔ At the time of writing, almost 50 percent of site visits begin at the search engines. Sure, it's not 80 percent, but it's still a lot of traffic.

- ✔ Of the over 50 percent of visits that don't originate at a search engine, a large proportion are revisits — people who know exactly where they want to go. This is not new business; it's repeat business. Most *new* visits come through the search engines, making search engines the single most important source of new visitors to Web sites.

- ✔ Some studies indicate that a large number of buyers begin at the search engine. That is, of all the people who go online planning to buy something or looking for product information while planning a purchase, perhaps over 80 percent start at the search engines.

- ✔ The search engines represent a cheap way to reach people. In general, you get more bang for your buck going after free search engine traffic than almost any other form of advertising or marketing.

Where Do People Search?

You can search for Web sites at many places. Literally thousands of sites, in fact, provide the ability to search the Web. (What you may not realize, however, is that all these sites search only a small subset of the World Wide Web.)

However, most searches are carried out at just a small number of search sites. How do the world's most popular search sites rank? That depends on how you measure popularity: the percentage of Internet users who visit a site (audience reach); the total number of visitors; the total number of searches carried out at a site; or the total number of hours that visitors spend searching at the site. Each measurement provides a slightly different ranking, though all provide a similar picture, with the same sites appearing on the list, though some in slightly different positions.

The following list runs down the world's most popular search sites, based on the total search hours at each site during a one-month period, as compiled in a 2003 Nielsen/NetRatings study:

Google.com	18,700,000 hours
AOL.com	15,500,500 hours
Yahoo.com	7,100,000 hours
MSN.com	5,400,000 hours
AskJeeves.com	2,300,000 hours

InfoSpace.com	1,100,000 hours
AltaVista.com	800,000 hours
Overture.com	800,000 hours
Netscape.com	700,000 hours
EarthLink.com	400,000 hours
LookSmart.com	200,000 hours
Lycos.com	200,000 hours

Remember, this is a list of search sites, not search systems. In some cases, the sites have own their own systems. Google provides its own search results, but AOL and MSN do not. (AOL gets its results from Google, and MSN's results come from Yahoo! — at least at the time of this writing.)

The fact that some sites get results from other search systems means two things. First, the numbers in the preceding list are somewhat misleading. They suggest that Google has around a third of all the search hours. But Google also feeds AOL its results — add AOL's hours to Google's, and you've got almost *two thirds* of all search hours. Clearly the Google search system is far more important than the Google search site. In fact, the Google search system also feeds three more systems on this list — Ask Jeeves, Netscape, and EarthLink — and many smaller sites that don't appear on this list. Some estimates put Google's share of the Web's search results as high as 60 or 65 percent.

The second thing to understand is that you can ignore some of these systems. At present, for example, and for the foreseeable future, you don't need to worry about AOL.com. Even though it's probably the world's second most important search site, you can forget about it. Sure, keep it in the back of your mind, but as long as you remember that Google feeds AOL, you need to worry about Google only.

When you get to the search sites that appear below Lycos in the preceding list, the sites become dramatically less important. Google, according to this chart, has almost 100 times the search hours spent at Lycos. And the first 11 sites on this list combined have 265 times the search hours of Lycos. (However, as I explain in a moment, this list doesn't include some important search *systems*.)

Now reexamine the list of the world's most important search sites and see what you remove so you can get closer to a list of sites you care about. Check out Table 1-1 for the details.

Table 1-1		Big-Time Search Sites
Search Site	*On the List?*	*Description*
Google.com	Yes	Google's the big kid on the block. Lots of people search the Google index on its own search site, *and* it feeds many sites. Obviously Google has to stay on the list.
AOL.com	No	Fuggetaboutit — AOL gets search results from Google (although it manipulates them slightly, presenting them in a different way from the same search at Google itself) and from the Open Directory Project.
Yahoo.com	Yes	Yahoo! is one of the world's largest search sites, and feeds a variety of other sites. Yahoo! bought several important sites and systems over the last few years, in particular AltaVista, AlltheWeb, Inktomi, and Overture (a pay per click system), so not only does it feed results to these, but those results are passed through to sites that had relationships with these feeders, such as LookSmart, About, HotBot, Lycos, and various others. In addition, Yahoo! currently feeds MSN, one of the world's top search sites (though sometime soon, perhaps late in 2004, this feed will stop). So, all in all it's very important, so keep it on the list.
MSN.com	No	At the time of writing, MSN gets results from Yahoo! (though it will have its own search engine, probably in the second half of 2004); remove it from the list.
AskJeeves.com	Yes	Ask Jeeves gets its search results from Teoma, but because it owns Teoma, I refer to the search system throughout the book as Teoma/Ask Jeeves (and keep it on the list of important search systems). It also gets search results from Google and the Open Directory Project. Teoma/Ask Jeeves feeds results to many other search sites, too.
InfoSpace.com	No	InfoSpace runs "metasearch" systems that pull data from other search systems, so it's out.

Search Site	On the List?	Description
AltaVista.com	No	AltaVista gets its search results from Yahoo!, so you can forget about it.
Overture.com	No	Overture is primarily a pay-per-click (PPC) system, without its own non-advertising search system, so it gets its non-ad results from Yahoo!.
Netscape.com	No	Netscape gets results from Google and the Open Directory Project (Netscape owns the Open Directory Project, though). Netscape is pretty much a clone of Google, so there's no need to keep it on the list.
EarthLink.com	No	Another Google clone, EarthLink gets all its results from Google and the Open Directory Project, so it's out too.
LookSmart.com	No	LookSmart is another PPC system. It does feed some other search sites — Lycos, WiseNut, CNET, and others — but it gets non-ad results from Yahoo! and Zeal (and maybe, soon, from Grub), so you can drop it from the list.
Lycos.com	No	Lycos gets results from Yahoo!, so you can remove it from the list.

Based on the information in Table 1-1, you can whittle down your list of sites to three: Google, Yahoo!, and Ask Jeeves. These search sites are all important, and Google is also an important search system, feeding three quarters of the world's search results to AOL, Netscape, EarthLink, and many other search sites. Teoma/Ask Jeeves is an important search-system feeder, too, providing results to many smaller search sites.

Okay, so you visited one or two of the sites that you just crossed off and found that you *can* submit your Web site to the index at that site. What's going on here is that the search site is selling paid inclusion into the search system that feeds it. (I talk about paid inclusion in Chapter 9.)

Some important *systems* are not important *sites*.

Finally, you may want to add Zeal; this system feeds LookSmart, which feeds Lycos (Yahoo! also feeds LookSmart, by the way), WiseNut, and a variety of other search sites.

Now add the most important feeder systems to a "new and improved" chart. The chart becomes a combination of the three important search sites that maintain their own search systems — and, in a couple of cases, feed others — and a couple of feeder systems: the Open Directory Project (which is very important), and Zeal. Table 1-2 shows the chart in all its glory.

Table 1-2	The Search Systems to Watch
Search Site/System	*Description*
Google.com	This is the world's most important search site and the most important feeder system.
Yahoo.com	Yahoo.com doesn't feed anyone, but it's still the world's second most important search site.
Teoma/Ask Jeeves	Not only is this an important search site, but the search system also feeds sites such as About.com, Mamma.com, and many others.
The Open Directory Project	This is not much of a search site — few people have even heard of it — but it's a helluva search system, feeding Google, AOL, Ask Jeeves, Netscape, EarthLink, Lycos, and almost 400 other sites. (You can find it at www.dmoz.org.)
Zeal	Zeal feeds LookSmart (in fact LookSmart owns Zeal), but only for noncommercial sites. However, LookSmart also gets search results from Yahoo!, so Zeal isn't terribly important.

You can get an idea of this complex Web of relationships in Figure 1-4.

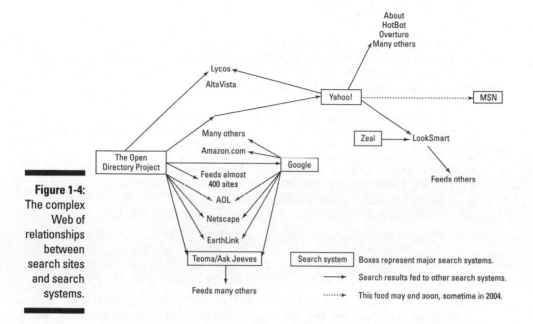

Figure 1-4:
The complex
Web of
relationships
between
search sites
and search
systems.

Aren't I missing some sites?

Some of you may be thinking, "Aren't you missing some sites? What happened
to HotBot, Mamma.com, WebCrawler, Dogpile, and all the other systems that
were so well known a few years ago?" A lot of them have disappeared or have
turned over a new leaf and are pursuing other opportunities. For example,
Northern Light, a system well known in the late 1990s, now "provides search
and content integration solutions for enterprises and individuals." In other
words, it sells search software. And in the cases in which the search sites are
still running, they're mostly fed by other search systems. Mamma.com, HotBot,
and MetaCrawler get search results from Teoma/Ask Jeeves, for instance.

Also, recent changes over at Yahoo! modified the landscape somewhat. Yahoo!
owned FAST/AlltheWeb, Inktomi, and AltaVista, but got its search results from
Google. Mid 2004, however, Yahoo! began using search results gathered by its
own spiders, ending the relationship with Google, and now uses those search
results to feed Inktomi, AltaVista, and AlltheWeb. Inktomi, for instance, used to
feed MSN, but now MSN gets its results from Yahoo! (at least for the moment;
MSN will soon stop using Yahoo! results and use its own data).

Multiple feeds

Are you getting confused yet about how all the major search systems are related? Don't worry; the picture will become clearer. A complex Web of relationships between the major search systems exists. Here's a rundown of different types of search-result feeds:

- **Primary:** Not surprisingly, a primary feed is one in which a search system feeds the most important results to a search site. The primary feed at AOL.com, for example, comes from Google.

- **Secondary:** Secondary feeds, sometimes known as *backfill,* are ones in which a search system feeds to a search site results that may or may not appear; in some cases, secondary feeds appear if the primary feed is unable to find good matches for a search.

- **Directory:** Some search sites combine both an index and a directory. Yahoo!, for instance, spiders the Web to build an index, but builds its own directory. Google, on the other hand, builds its own index but gets directory results from the Open Directory Project.

- **PPC:** PPC (pay-per-click) results are basically ads — search results that appear because the Web site owners are willing to pay each time someone clicks the link. Google provides PPC results to many sites, including AOL, Netscape, Ask Jeeves, and Amazon. Yahoo! gets its PPC results from Overture, a company it recently purchased. For more on PPC, see Chapter 15.

What the Future Holds — The List Expands

The centerpiece of this chapter is the handy-dandy list of top-flight search sites and systems, some of which you may never have heard of. Trust me; they're either important search sites or feed important sites or many smaller sites. In case you missed it, here are these sites and systems more or less in order of importance:

- Google
- Yahoo!
- The Open Directory Project
- Teoma/Ask Jeeves

Why is the Open Directory Project — not exactly a household name — so high on the list? The Open Directory Project feeds Google, AOL, Ask Jeeves, Netscape, EarthLink, Lycos, and many more. And why's Zeal on the list? Actually, I couldn't decide whether to leave it on the list or not. It's not terribly important, but it does provide a way for non-commercial sites to get into LookSmart, and LookSmart feeds a variety of smaller sites.

By the way, just a few months ago this list was larger. I've had to remove AltaVista, Inktomi, and AlltheWeb, because when Yahoo! began running its own search engine (rather than getting results from Google), it consolidated its other search properties, using the new search-engine index for all these systems. Inktomi, for instance, still feeds LookSmart but the data actually comes from Yahoo!

This list is likely to change soon. My prescient predictions are summarized in the following list:

✔ **MSN dumps Yahoo!.** Currently, MSN.com doesn't appear on the list because its search results come from Yahoo!. But Microsoft has begun building its own index and will soon be in the search engine business, which is too important for Microsoft to ignore. MSNBot, as it's known, is traveling around the Web as you read this. It's quite likely that MSN will be a hugely important search site with its own search system feeding results.

The result? The list of important search sites and search systems has now expanded by one *very* important system. Furthermore, Microsoft owns five of the world's top 17 Web sites (MSN.com, Passport.com, Microsoft.com, MSNBC.com, and Hotmail.com), all of which will be fed search results from the new Microsoft system. And when the next version of Windows ships in 2006, the search engine will be built into the operating system — you'll be able to search your hard disk for files and e-mails, search for the content within spreadsheets and documents, and search the Web, all from the same place.

✔ **Grub comes alive.** Grub (www.grub.org) is an interesting project that may, one day, be very important. Owned by LookSmart, Grub plans to build a massive index of billions of pages by using distributed computing — people around the world using their spare computing downtime to crawl the Web for Grub. However, one thing working against Grub is that it's owned by LookSmart, which simply isn't doing very well. Even though Grub results may feed LookSmart, LookSmart isn't really feeding many other search sites, and seems to be losing influence over time. It's hard to compete with the three monsters, Google, Yahoo!, and MSN.

✔ **Nutch takes off.** I think Nutch (www.nutch.org) may also become important at some point. It's an open-source project that plans to create a huge, multibillion-page index and make it available to anyone who wants it. At the time of writing, it's in the early stages, but it has the backing of some important people and may turn into something significant. On the other hand, it may not.

Visit www.SearchEngineBulletin.com for the latest news on the MSN, Grub, and Nutch developments. I'll let you know how to get indexed in the appropriate places.

Reviewing the Final List — Search Systems You Really Need

When push comes to shove, you need to care about only a handful of search systems right now. You should care about them because if you can get your site listed in these search systems, you will be in the systems that provide search results to almost all Web searches! And, the winners are . . . (drum roll please):

✔ Google

✔ Yahoo!

✔ The Open Directory Project

✔ Teoma/Ask Jeeves

✔ Zeal (if you have a noncommercial Web site)

I didn't add possible up-and-comers like Grub and Nutch to this list — I'll leave them in the "may become important one day, better keep your eyes on them, but it ain't imminent" list for now. But that leaves one more important search site that will be significant soon, if not by the time you read these words:

✔ MSN

That's not so bad, is it? You've just gone from thousands of sites down to six. And out of those, just three systems are really significant: Google, Yahoo!, and the Open Directory Project.

You'll also want to work with some other search systems, as you find out in Chapters 9 and 10. In some cases, you need to check out specialty directories and indexes related to the industry in which your Web site operates. But the preceding systems are the important ones for every Web site.

Google alone provides almost 75 percent of all search results. Get into *all* the systems on the preceding list, and you're in front of probably over 95 percent of all searchers. Well, perhaps you're in front of them. You have a chance of being in front of them, anyway, if your site ranks highly.

Determining Your Plan of Attack

Now you know what you're facing. You can more or less forget those thousands of search sites and focus on no more than nine search systems. The next step is to figure out how to get your Web site into these search systems and, more importantly, in front of the people using those systems to search the Web. Here's what you need to do:

- ✔ **Do the keyword analysis.** To rank high in the search engines, you better first determine what you want to pop up as a high-ranking search result in a particular search engine. In other words, you have to decide for which keywords and keyword phrases you want to rank. You can take a wild guess, but in my experience working with clients, you'll almost certainly fail to pick all the right keywords. A keyword analysis is the best way to select keywords and decide which you should target. See Chapter 4 for the lowdown on how to do this analysis.

- ✔ **Create readable pages.** If you want your site to appear in the search engines, you have to create pages that the search engine spiders or bots can read. (This isn't an issue for the search *directories,* but if you expect a searchbot to read your site, the pages have to be readable.) You might be surprised to hear that millions of pages on the Web cannot be read by search engines. For the lowdown on how to determine whether your Web pages are being read by the search engines, see Chapter 2; to find out how to fix the problem if they're not, see Chapter 6.

- ✔ **Create keyworded pages.** Having readable pages is just a start. Next you have to put the keywords into the pages — in the right places and in the right format. See Chapter 5 for details.

- ✔ **Register with the search systems.** When your pages are ready to be indexed, you need to let the search systems know where those pages are and get the search systems to include the pages in their indexes and directories — sometimes a harder task than you might expect. You can get into the search systems various ways, as described in detail in Chapters 9 and 10.

_____

> ✔ **Get other sites to link to your site.** Check out Chapters 12 and 13 to find
> out how the number and type of links pointing to your site affect how
> high you rank in the search engines.

The preceding strategies are the basics, but you may want to — or even need
to — go further. Here are a few additional techniques that I cover in detail in
this book:

> ✔ **Register with other places.** You may also want to register at specialized
> sites that are not important in the big scheme of things but may be impor-
> tant for your particular business. See Chapter 11.
>
> ✔ **Register with the shopping indexes.** If you're selling a product, it's a
> good idea to register with the shopping indexes. Although these indexes
> don't match the big search systems in volume of searches, they're still
> important. This is covered in Chapter 14.
>
> ✔ **Use pay per click.** You can get noticed in the search engines two ways.
> You can use natural search — that is, get ranked in the search engines
> without paying — or you can use pay per click. Many companies go
> straight to pay per click — a system by which you get ranked well but
> pay each time someone clicks a link to your site — and bypass natural
> search entirely. This is not a good idea, but at some point, you may want
> to use pay per click in addition to natural search — see Chapter 15.

Gathering Your Tools

You need several tools and skills to optimize and rank your Web site. I talk
about a number of these in the appropriate chapters, but I want to cover a
few basics before I move on. It goes without saying that you need basic
Internet knowledge, a computer connected to the Internet, and a Web site.

In addition, you need to have a good working knowledge of HTML *or* access
to a geek with a good working knowledge of HTML. Which path should you
take? If you don't know what HTML means (HyperText Markup Language),
you probably need to run out and find that geek. HTML is the code used to
create Web pages, and you need to understand how to use it to optimize
pages. Discussing HTML and how to upload pages to a Web site is beyond the
scope of this book. But if you're interested in finding out more about HTML,
check out *HTML For Dummies,* 4th Edition, by Ed Tittel and Natanya Pitts, and
Creating Web Pages For Dummies, 6th Edition, by Bud Smith and Arthur Bebak
(both published by Wiley).

You also need two great little tools, even if you plan to use a geek to work on
your site. They're simple to install and open up a completely new view of the
Web. The next two sections spell out the details.

The Google Toolbar

Go to toolbar.google.com, and download and install the Google Toolbar, shown in Figure 1-5. I refer to this fantastic little tool in various places throughout this book because it provides you with the following useful features:

- ✔ A way to search Google without going to www.google.com first
- ✔ A quick view of the Google PageRank, an important metric that I explain in Chapter 12
- ✔ A quick way to see if a Web page is already indexed by Google
- ✔ A quick way to see some of the pages linking to a Web page

The toolbar has a number of other useful features, but the preceding features are the most useful for the purposes of this book.

Figure 1-5:
The Google and Alexa Toolbars provide useful information for search engine campaigns.

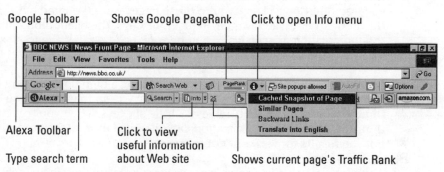

The Alexa Toolbar

Alexa is a company owned by Amazon.com. It's been around a long time, and millions of people around the world use the Alexa Toolbar. Every time someone uses the toolbar to visit a Web site, the toolbar sends the URL of the page to Alexa, allowing the system to create an enormous database of site visits. The Alexa Toolbar can provide traffic information to you — you can quickly see how popular a site is and even view a detailed traffic analysis, such as an estimate of the percentage of Internet users who visit the site each month.

Work with the Alexa Toolbar for a while, and you'll quickly get a feel for site popularity. A site ranks 453? That's pretty good. 1,987,123? That's a sign that hardly anyone visits the site.

You can find the Alexa Toolbar, shown in Figure 1-5, at www.alexa.com. Look for a Free Toolbar link in the main navigation bar at the top of the page.

Understanding the Limitations

Before you get started, I want to quickly explain the limitations of search engine optimization: what's possible and what's likely.

You've probably received spam e-mails guaranteeing you top-ten positions for your Web site in the search engines. You've probably also seen claims that you'll be ranked in hundreds or thousands of search engines. Most of this flood of commercial e-mail is nonsense, background noise that creates a picture that is entirely false. So here are the facts.

Sometimes it's easy to get a very high position in the search systems. But usually it isn't. I did one job for a client that went incredibly well. He wanted to be positioned in Google for six important key phrases. I built some pages, ensured that Google knew where those pages were (you find out how to do this in Chapter 9), and waited. In just four days, the client didn't just have a top-ten position or even just a number-one position, but the top *two* positions for five of the six key phrases.

But this situation is unusual. Typically, getting a high position isn't that easy. You try a couple of techniques, but they don't seem to work. So you try something else, and maybe you achieve a little success. Then you try another thing. Search engine optimization can often be labor intensive, and you may not see results for weeks, if not months.

Although the way that search engines work is based on science, search engine optimization is more art than science. Why? Because the search engines don't want outside parties to know exactly how they rank sites. You have to just experiment. Ranking a site can be very difficult, and tremendously laborious. After all, why should it be easy? There is huge competition, so it *can't* be easy. If it were easy for your site, then it would be easy for your competitors' sites, wouldn't it? And, after all, there can only ever be one number one.

Chapter 2

Your One-Hour Search-Engine-Friendly Web Site Makeover

· ·

In This Chapter

▶ Checking whether your site is in the search engines

▶ Choosing keywords

▶ Examining your pages for problems

▶ Getting search engines to read and index your pages

· ·

A few small changes can make a big difference in your site's position in the search engines. So rather than force you to read this entire book before you can get anything done, this chapter helps you identify problems with your site and, with a little luck, shows you how to make a significant difference through quick fixes.

It's possible that you may not make significant process in a single hour, as the chapter title promises. You may identify serious problems with your site that can't be fixed quickly. Sorry, that's life! The purpose of this chapter is to help you identify a few obvious problems and, perhaps, make some quick fixes with the goal of really getting something done.

Is Your Site Indexed?

It's important to find out if your site is actually in a search engine or directory. Your site doesn't come up when someone searches at Google for *rodent racing?* Can't find it in the Yahoo! Directory? Have you ever thought that perhaps it simply isn't there? In the next several sections, I explain how to find out if your site is indexed in a few different systems.

Some of the systems into which you want to place your Web site are not household names. If I mention a search system that you don't recognize, page back to Chapter 1 to find out more about it.

Google

I'll start with the behemoth, Google. Open your browser and load a page at your site. For now, start with your site's home page, although you can use this technique for any page, and then follow these steps:

1. **Click the i icon on the Google Toolbar.**

   I'm assuming that you're using Internet Explorer and have, as I suggest in Chapter 1, downloaded the Google Toolbar — available at `toolbar.google.com` — to your computer. If you don't have the toolbar, don't worry; I explain a non-toolbar method in a moment.

2. **Select Cached Snapshot of Page from the drop-down list that appears.**

   If you're lucky, Google loads a page showing you what it has in its cache, so you know Google has indexed the page. (See Figure 2-1.) If you're unlucky, Google tells you that it has nothing in the cache for that page. That doesn't necessarily mean Google hasn't indexed the page, though.

   A *cache* is a temporary storage area in which a copy of something is placed. In the context of the Web, a cache stores a Web page.

If you don't have the Google Toolbar, you can instead go to Google (`www.google.com`) and type the following into the Google search box:

```
cache:http://yourdomain.com/
```

Replace *yourdomain.com* with your actual domain name. When you click Search, Google checks to see if it has the page in its cache.

What if Google doesn't have the page? Does that mean your page is not in Google? No, not necessarily. Google may not have gotten around to caching it. Sometimes Google grabs a little information from a page but not the entire page.

Now try this little trick. Search Google for the following:

```
site:yourdomain.com
```

This tells Google to find all the pages on the *yourdomain.com* site. You might also search for `site:yourdomain.com -pppppp`, which might give you a slightly different result (perhaps higher); this syntax tells Google to find all the pages that do not have the text *pppppp*. The dash (-) before the text tells Google to omit pages with this text. Of course, you can replace *pppppp* with any text that you're sure doesn't appear on your site.

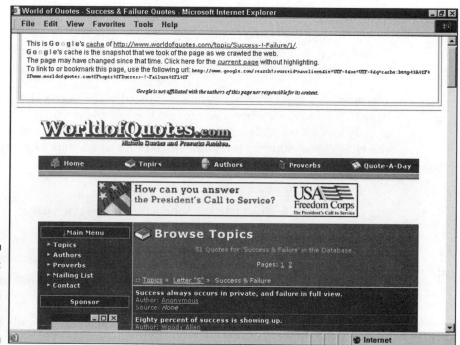

Figure 2-1:
A page
stored in
the Google
cache.

Google should show you all the pages on your site that it knows about. (For some reason, though, if you change the garbage text, Google will provide a different result; site:*yourdomain.com* -ppppp is not the same as site: *yourdomain.com* -oiuiyiy.) Look at the blue bar at the top of the search results. It says something like *Results 1 - 10 of about 254,000.* If your site has 30 pages, and it says *of about 30,* you're in good shape; Google has found them all. If it says *of about 3,* you have a problem — most of your pages are not indexed by Google.

What if Google doesn't return *any* search results? Try removing or adding the www. bit; that is, if you searched for site:*yourdomain.com*, try site:*www.yourdomain.com*, or vice versa. Sometimes Google returns results one way but not the other. Also, make sure that you didn't mistype the search string; try again to be sure. If nothing works, then Google doesn't know about your Web site.

TIP

You can search for a Web site at Google another way, too. Simply type the domain name into the Google search box and click Search. Google returns just the home page of that site. If you want to use the search box on the Google Toolbar to do this, type the domain name and then click the binoculars button. (If you type the domain name and press Enter, Google simply redirects your browser to the specified domain name.)

Yahoo!

To find out if your site is listed in Yahoo!, you can use the same search syntax used at Google: search for `site:yourdomainname.com`.

You must also check whether your site is listed in the Yahoo! Directory. You have to pay to get a commercial site into the Yahoo! Directory, so you may already know if you're listed there. If someone else may have registered the site with Yahoo!, you may not know whether it's there. Here's how to find out:

1. **Point your browser to** `dir.yahoo.com`.

   This takes you directly to the Yahoo! Directory search page.

2. **Type your site's domain name into the Search text box.**

   All you need is `yourdomain.com`, not `http://www.` or anything else.

3. **Make sure that the Directory option button is selected and then click Search.**

   If your site is in the Yahoo! Directory, Yahoo! displays that site's information on the results page.

The others

To find out if your site is listed with the other search systems, simply go to the search site, type the domain name, and click the Search button. In the case of all the major systems (see Chapter 1 for more about search systems), the results page will contain an entry for the specified domain if it's in the index. Other results may be placed on the page, too, but the first entry is the specified Web site if the information is available.

What if you're not listed?

First, if your site is not in Yahoo! or the Open Directory Project, you have to go to those systems and register your site. See Chapter 10 for information. What if you search for your site in the search engines and can't find it? That depends. If the site is not in Google, you have a huge problem. If it's not in the smaller search engines, that's less of a problem, of course, and quite common.

Here are two possible reasons why your site is not being indexed in the search engines:

- ✔ The search engines haven't found your site yet. The solution is relatively easy, though you won't get it done in an hour.

- ✔ The search engines, whether or not they have found your site, can't index it. This is a much bigger problem!

To find out how to make your pages search-engine-friendly, check out the section "Examining Your Pages," later in this chapter. For the lowdown on getting your pages indexed in the search engines, see the section "Getting Your Site Indexed," later in this chapter.

How to tell if your site is invisible

Some Web sites are virtually invisible. A search engine might be able to find the site, by following a link, for instance. But when it gets to the site, it can't read it or, perhaps, can read only parts of it. One of my clients built a Web site that had only three visible pages; all the other pages, including all the pages with product information, were invisible.

How does a Web site become invisible? I talk about this subject in more detail in Chapter 6, but here's a brief explanation. In most cases, the problem is that the site is *dynamic* — that is, a page is created on the fly when a browser requests it. The data is pulled out of a database, pasted into a Web page template, and sent to the user's browser. Search engines often won't read such pages, for a variety of reasons explained in detail in Chapter 6.

How can you tell if this is a problem? Take a look at the URL in the browser's location bar. Suppose that you see something like this:

```
http://www.yourdomain.edu/rodent-racing-scores/march/
                index.php
```

This address is okay. It's a simple URL path made up of a domain name, two directory names, and a filename. Now look at this one:

```
http://www.yourdomain.edu/rodent-racing/scores.php?prg=1
```

The filename ends with ?prg=1. This *parameter* is being sent to the server to let it know what information is needed for the Web page. If you have URLs like this, with just a single parameter, they're probably okay, especially for Google; however, a few search engines may not like them. Here's another example:

```
http://yourdomain.com/products/index.html?&DID=18&CATID=
            13&ObjectGroup_ID=79
```

This one's a real problem, even for Google, which does a good job of indexing dynamic pages. This URL has too much weird stuff after the filename: ?&DID= 18&CATID=13&ObjectGroup_ID=79. That's three parameters — DID=18, CATID=13, and ObjectGroup_ID=79 — which is too many. This URL is similar to a URL from one of my clients' sites (I changed the domain name, of course). Google *cannot* or *will not* index this page.

Another problem is caused by *session IDs* — URLs that are different every time the page is displayed. Look at this example:

```
http://yourdomain.com/buyAHome.do;jsessionid=
            07D3CCD4D9A6A9F3CF9CAD4F9A728F44
```

Each time someone visits this site, the server assigns a special ID number to the visitor. That means the URL is never the same, so Google won't index it.

Google probably can get to databased pages, but chooses not to. If Google sees links to a page that appears to be dynamic, it doesn't know whether the URL will change between sessions or whether many different URLs point to the same page. Google doesn't want to overload the site's server and also doesn't want garbage in its index.

If you have a clean URL with no parameters, the search engines should be able to get to it. If you have a single parameter in the URL, it may or may not be okay. Two parameters also may or may not be a problem, although they're more likely to be a problem than a single parameter. Three parameters are almost certainly a problem. If you think you have a problem, I suggest that you read Chapter 6.

Picking Good Keywords

Getting search engines to recognize and index your Web site can be a problem, as the first part of this chapter makes clear. Another huge problem — one that has little or nothing to do with the technological limitations of search engines — is that many companies have no idea what keywords (the words people are using to search for Web sites at the search engines) they should be using. They try to guess the appropriate keywords, without knowing what people are really using in the search engines.

In Chapter 4, I explain keywords in detail, but here's how to do a quick keyword analysis:

1. **Point your browser to** www.overture.com.

   You see the home page for Overture, a company that sells PPC (pay-per-click) ads in the search engines. (See Chapter 15 for more about PPC.)

2. **Click the Advertiser Center link at the top right of the page.**

3. **In the new page that appears, click the Tools button (it's a small tab near the top of the page).**

4. **In the new page that appears, click the Term Suggestion Tool link.**

   A small window opens with a search box.

5. **In the search box, type a keyword that you think people may be using to search for the sorts of products or services your site provides and then press Enter.**

   The tool returns a list of keywords, showing you how often that term and related terms are used on the Overture advertising network (see Figure 2-2).

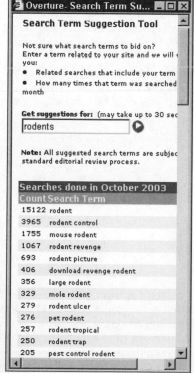

Figure 2-2: The Overture Search Term Suggestion Tool provides a quick way to check keywords.

You may find that the keyword you guessed is perfect. Or you may discover better words or, even if your guess was good, find several other great keywords. A detailed keyword analysis almost always turns up keywords or keyword phrases you need to know about.

Don't spend a lot of time on this task. See if you can come up with some useful keywords in a few minutes and then move on.

Examining Your Pages

Making your Web pages "search-engine-friendly" was probably not uppermost in your mind when you sat down to design your Web site. That means your Web pages — and the Web pages of millions of others — probably have a few problems in the search-engine-friendly category. Fortunately, such problems are pretty easy to spot; you can fix some of them quickly, but others are more troublesome.

Are you using frames?

In order to examine your pages for problems, you need to be able to read the pages' source code; remember, I told you you'd need to be able to understand HTML! In order to see the source code, choose View⇨Source in your browser.

When you first peek at the source code for your site, you may discover that your site is using frames. (Of course, if you built the site yourself, you already know whether it uses frames. However, you may be examining a site built by someone else.) You may see something like this in the page:

```
<HTML>
<HEAD>
</HEAD>
    <FRAMESET ROWS="20%,80%">
        <FRAME SRC="navbar.html">
        <FRAME SRC="content.html">
    </FRAMESET>
<BODY>
</BODY>
</HTML>
```

When you choose View⇨Source in Internet Explorer, you're viewing the source of the frame-definition document, which is the document that tells the browser how to set up the frames. In the preceding example, the browser creates two frame rows, one taking up the top 20 percent of the browser and the other taking up the bottom 80 percent. In the top frame, the browser places content taken from the navbar.html file; content from content.html goes into the bottom frame.

Framed sites don't do search engines much good. Search engines generally won't index the pages that are going to be placed into the frames, though they will index the frame-definition document . . . which rarely has keyword-rich indexable content. I discuss frames in more detail in Chapter 6, but here are a few quick fixes:

- ✔ Add TITLE and DESCRIPTION tags between the <HEAD> and </HEAD> tags. (To see what these tags are and how they can help with your frame issues, check out the next two sections.)

- ✔ Add <NOFRAMES> and </NOFRAMES> tags between the <BODY> and </BODY> tags, and place 200 to 300 words of keyword-rich content between the tags. The NOFRAMES text is designed to be displayed by browsers that can't work with frames, and search engines will read this text, although they won't rate it as high as normal text (because many designers have used NOFRAMES tags as a trick to get more keywords into a Web site).

- ✔ Include a number of links, in the text between the NOFRAMES tags, to other pages in your site to help the search engines find their way through.

Look at the *TITLE* tags

TITLE tags tell a browser what text to display in the browser's title bar, and they're very important to search engines. Quite reasonably, search engines figure that the TITLE tags may indicate the page's title — and therefore its subject.

Open your site's home page and then choose View⇨Source (in Internet Explorer) to view the page source. A text editor opens, showing you what the page's HTML looks like. Here's what you should see at the top of the page:

```
<HTML>
<HEAD>
<TITLE>Your title text is here</TITLE>
```

Here are a few problems you may have with your TITLE tags:

- ✔ **They're not there!** Many pages simply don't have TITLE tags. If these tags aren't there, you're not giving the search engines one of the most important pieces of information about the page's subject matter.

- ✔ **They're in the wrong position.** Sometimes you find the TITLE tags, but they're way down in the page. If they're too low in the page, search engines may not find them.

- ✔ **They're there, but they're poor.** The TITLE tags don't have the proper keywords in them.

Your TITLE tags should be immediately below the <HEAD> tag and should contain useful keywords. Have around 40 to 60 characters between the <TITLE> and </TITLE> tags (including spaces) and, perhaps, repeat the primary keywords once. If you're working on your Rodent Racing Web site, for example, you might have something like this (you can find out more about keywords in Chapter 4):

```
<TITLE>Rodent Racing Info. Rats, Mice, Gerbils, Stoats, all
        kinds of Rodent Racing</TITLE>
```

Examine the DESCRIPTION tag

The DESCRIPTION tag is important because search engines often index it (under the reasonable assumption that the description describes the contents of the page) and, in some cases, may use the DESCRIPTION tag to provide the site description on the search-results page.

Google usually doesn't use the DESCRIPTION tag to provide the description in the search results. Instead, it finds the search words in the page, grabs a snippet of information from around the words, and uses that as the description. However, if Google can't find the keywords in the page (if it finds the page based on its TITLE tag, for example, or links pointing at the page rather than page content), it may use the DESCRIPTION tag.

Assuming you have the HTML of your home page laid bare for all to see (you can do this by choosing View➪Source from the main menu of your browser when your home page is on-screen), you can take a quick look at the DESCRIPTION tag. It should look something like this:

```
<META NAME="description" CONTENT="your description goes
        here">
```

Sites often have the same problems with DESCRIPTION tags as they do with TITLE tags. The tags aren't there, or they're hidden away deep down in the page, or they simply aren't very good.

Place the DESCRIPTION tag immediately below the TITLE tags (see Figure 2-3) and create a keyworded description of up to 250 characters (again, including spaces). Here's an example:

```
<META NAME="description" CONTENT="Rodent Racing - Scores,
        Schedules, everything Rodent Racing. Whether
        you're into mouse racing, stoat racing, rats, or
        gerbils, our site provides everything you'll ever
        need to know about Rodent Racing and caring for
        your racers.">
```

Figure 2-3:
A clean
start to your
Web page,
showing the
TITLE tags
and the
DESCRIP-
TION tag.

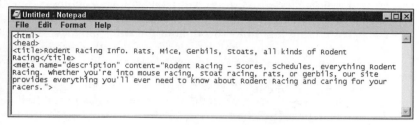

Sometimes Web developers switch the attributes in the tag, putting the CONTENT= first and then the NAME=, like this:

```
<META CONTENT="your description goes here"
        NAME="description">
```

Make sure that your tags do *not* do this. I don't know if the order of the attributes causes a problem for Google or the other big search engines, but I do know it confuses some smaller systems. There's no reason to do it, so don't.

Can the search engines get through?

Many sites have perfectly readable pages, with the exception that the search-bots can't negotiate the site navigation. The searchbots can reach the home page, index it, and read it, but they can't go any further. If, when you search Google for your pages, you find only the home page, this is likely the problem.

Why can't the searchbots find their way through? The navigation system may have been created using JavaScript, and because search engines ignore Java-Script, they don't find the links in the script. Look at this example:

```
<SCRIPT TYPE="javascript" SRC="/menu/menu.js"></SCRIPT>
```

In one of my clients' sites, this was how the navigation bar was being placed into each page: the page called an external JavaScript, held in menu.js in the menu subdirectory. The search engines won't read menu.js, so they'll never read the links in the script.

Here are a few simple ways you can help search engines find their way around your site, whether or not your navigation structure is hidden:

✔ **Create more text links throughout the site.** Many Web sites have a main navigation structure and then duplicate the structure by using simple text links at the bottom of the page. You should do the same.

✔ **Add a sitemap page to your site.** This page contains links to most or all of the pages on your Web site. Of course, you also want to link to the sitemap page from those little links at the bottom of the page.

Do the pages have anything for search engines to read?

You don't necessarily have to pick through the HTML code for your Web page to evaluate how search-engine-friendly it is. You can find out a lot just by looking at the Web page in the browser. Determine whether you have any text on the page. Page *content* — text that the search engines can read — is essential, but many Web sites don't have any page content on the front page and often have little or any on interior pages. Here are some potential problems:

✔ Having a (usually pointless) Flash intro on your site

✔ Embedding much of the text on your site into images, rather than relying on readable text

✔ Banking on flashy visuals to hide the fact that your site is actually light on content

✔ Using the wrong keywords in the text that you have (Chapter 4 explains how to pick keywords)

If you have these types of problems, they can often be time-consuming to fix. (Sorry, you may run over the one-hour timetable by several weeks.) The next several sections detail ways you might overcome the problems in the preceding list.

Eliminate Flash

Huh? What's Flash? You've seen those silly animations when you arrive at a Web site, with a little *Skip Intro* link hidden away in the page. Words and pictures appear and disappear, scroll across the pages, and so on. You create these animations with a product called Macromedia Flash. (You can find a wonderful parody of these annoying little items at www.skip-intro.com.)

I suggest that you kill the Flash intro on your site. I have very rarely seen a Flash intro that actually served any purpose. In most cases, they are nothing but an irritation to site visitors. (The majority of Flash intros are created because the Web designer likes playing with Flash.)

Replace images with real text

If you have an image-heavy Web site, in which all or most of the text is embedded onto images, you need to get rid of the images and replace them with real text. If the search engine can't read the text, it can't index it.

It may not be immediately clear whether text on the page is real text or images. You can quickly figure it out a couple of ways:

- ✔ Try to select the text in the browser with your mouse. If it's real text, you can select it character by character. If it's not real text, you simply can't select it — you'll probably end up selecting an image.

- ✔ Use your browser's View⇨Source command to look at the HTML for the page and then see if you can find the actual words in the text.

Use more keywords

The light-content issue can be a real problem. Some sites are designed to be light on content, and sometimes this approach is perfectly valid in terms of design and usability. However, search engines have a bias for content, for text they can read. (I discuss this issue in more depth in Chapter 5.) In general, the more text with keywords, the better.

Use the right keywords in the right places

Suppose that you do have text, and plenty of it. But does the text have the right keywords in it? The ones you uncovered at Overture a few minutes ago? It should.

If the reference to Overture doesn't ring a bell, check out the "Picking Good Keywords" section, earlier in this chapter.

Where keywords are placed and what they look like are also important. Search engines use position and format as clues to importance. Here are a few simple techniques you can use (but don't overdo it!):

- ✔ Use particularly important keywords — those that people are using to search for your types of products and services (see Chapter 4) — near the top of the page.

- ✔ Place keywords into <H> (heading) tags.

- ✔ Use bold and italic keywords (search engines take note of this).

✔ Put keywords into bulleted lists (search engines also take note of this).

✔ Use keywords multiple times on a page, but don't use a keyword or keyword phrase too often. If a word makes up more than, say, 5 to 10 percent of all the words on the page, it may be too much.

Make sure that the links between pages within your site contain keywords. Think about all the sites you've visited recently. How many use links with *no* keywords in them? They use buttons, graphic navigation bars, short little links that you have to guess at, *click here* links, and so on. Big mistakes.

I don't object to using the words *click here* in links. Some writers have suggested that you should never use *click here* because it sounds silly and because people know they're supposed to click. I disagree, and research shows that using the words can sometimes increase the number of clicks on a link. The bottom line is that you should rarely, if ever, use a link with only the words *click here* in the link text; you should include keywords in the link.

When you create links, include keywords in the links wherever possible. If on your rodent-racing site you're pointing to the scores page, don't create a link that says *To find the most recent rodent racing scores, click here* or, perhaps, *To find the most recent racing scores, go to the scores page.* Instead, get a few more keywords into the links, like this: *To find the most recent racing scores, go to the racing scores page.*

Getting Your Site Indexed

So your pages are ready, but you still have the indexing problem. Your pages are, to put in bluntly, just *not in the search engine!* How do you fix that problem?

For Yahoo! and the Open Directory Project, you have to go to those sites and register directly, but before doing that, you should read Chapter 10. With Google and the other major search engines, the process is a little more time-consuming and complicated.

The best way to get into the search engines is to have them *find* the pages by following links pointing to the site. In some cases, you can ask or pay the search engines to come to your site and pick up your pages, but you face two main problems with this:

✔ If you ask search engines to index your site, they probably won't do it. And if they do come and index your site, it may take weeks or months. Asking them to come to your site is unreliable.

✔ If you pay search engines to index your site, you have to pay for every URL you submit. The problem with paying, of course, is that you have to pay.

If you want to submit your site to the search engines for indexing, read Chapter 9, where I provide all the details.

So how do you get indexed? The good news is that you can often get indexed by some of the search engines *very* quickly. I'm not talking about a full-blown link campaign here, with all the advantages I describe in Chapters 12 and 13. You simply want to get search engines — particularly Google — to pick up the site and index it.

Find another Web site to link to it, right away. Call several friends, colleagues, and relatives who own or control a Web site, and ask them to link to your site. Of course, you want sites that are already indexed by the search engines. The searchbots have to follow the links to your site.

When you ask friends, colleagues, and relatives to link to you, specify what you want the links to say. No *click here* or company name links for you. You want to place keywords into the link text. Something like *Visit this site for all your rodent racing needs - mice, rats, stoats, gerbils, and all other kinds of rodent racing.* Keywords in links are a powerful way to tell a search engine what your site is about.

After the sites have links pointing to yours, it can take from a few days to a few weeks to get into the search engines. With Google, if you place the links right before Googlebot indexes one of the sites, you may be in the index in a few days. I once placed some pages on a client's Web site on a Tuesday and found them in Google on Friday. But Google can also take several weeks to index a site. The best way to increase your chances of getting into the search engines quickly is to get as many links as you can on as many sites as possible.

Google has an enormous index, currently around 3.3 *billion* pages. (To find the latest page count, go to Google and look at the copyright notice at the bottom of the page; next to the notice I can see, today, *Searching 3,307,998,701 Web pages*.)

Most other indexes are much smaller, so getting your pages indexed with them is more difficult. Fewer pages in the index mean fewer pages to channel searchbots from those search engines to your site. And there's less room in the index to hold your pages. A small index, by definition, doesn't hold many pages.

Chapter 3

Making Your Site Useful and Telling People about It

In This Chapter
▶ Understanding the basic rule of Web success
▶ Why search engines like content
▶ Making your site work for visitors and search engines

*O*bviously, it's important to create Web pages that search engines will read and index, pages that, you hope, will rank well in the search results for the keywords that are important to you. But if you're going to build a Web site, you need to step back and start at an even earlier stage — you need to figure out what purpose the site should serve and how it can accomplish that purpose.

Creating a *useful* site is the key. Even if your sole aim is to sell a product online, the more useful the site is to visitors, the more successful it's likely to be. Take Amazon.com, for instance. It certainly wasn't the first online retailer of books and music, or any of the other products it offers. But one of Amazon's real strengths is that it doesn't just sell products; it's a really *useful* site, in many ways:

✔ It provides tons of information about the products it sells, useful information even if you don't buy from Amazon.

✔ You can save information for later. If you find a book you're interested in but you can't afford to buy it right now or simply don't have time to read it, you can save a link to the book and come back next month, or next year, or five years from now.

✔ Other site owners can become partners and make money by promoting Amazon.

✔ Other businesses can easily sell their products through Amazon.

✔ You can read sample chapters from books, look at the tables of contents, listen to snippets of music from CDs, and so on.

✔ You can read product reviews from both professional reviewers and consumers.

Would Amazon be so successful if it just provided lists of the products it sells, rather than offering visitors a veritable bouquet of useful stuff? Absolutely not.

Consider this: The more useful your site is, the greater the chance of success. The more that people talk about your site, the more likely it is that journalists write about it, the more likely it is to be mentioned on radio or TV, the more people will link to it from their Web sites. Search engine marketing and non-search engine marketing are both important because either form of Web site promotion can lead to more links pointing to your site. And, as you find out in Chapters 12 and 13, links to your site are critical to search engine success.

With that in mind, this chapter focuses on the basics about what you need to do to create a successful Web site.

The Secret but Essential Rule of Web Success

Here's a simple rule to success on the Web:

Make your site useful and then tell people about it.

That's not so complicated, really. Figure out how your site can be useful to people and then find as many ways as possible to let people know about it. You'll use the search engines, of course, but you should be using other methods, too. Remember, the search engines are not the only way to get people to your site. In fact, many Web sites have succeeded without using the search engines as their primary method of attracting visitors to the site.

It's unlikely that search engines were a large factor in Amazon's success — Amazon grew rapidly mainly because of the enormous press attention it received, beginning in 1994. Today, I'd bet that relatively few people arrive at Amazon.com through the search engines. Rather, they already know the Amazon brand and go straight to the site, or they go through the hundreds of thousands of Amazon affiliate sites. Many successful companies have done little or nothing to promote themselves through the search engines, yet they still turn up at the top when you search for their products or services. Why? Because their other promotions have also helped to push them higher in the search engines, by creating thousands, even tens or hundreds of thousands, of links to them around the Internet.

The evolving "secret"

Over the last decade, a number of popular ideas about what makes a successful Web site have been bandied around, and all were wrong to some degree. Here are some of those secrets to successful Web sites:

- ✔ **Links:** When the Web began booming in 1994, it was all about *links*. You would hear in the press that the secret to a successful Web site was linking to other sites.

- ✔ **Cool:** Then people started saying that the secret of success was to make your site *cool*. Cool sites were more entertaining and more likely to attract repeat visitors.

- ✔ **Community:** Then people started talking about *community;* yeah, that's right, that's the secret! The secret to a successful Web site was creating a *community* where people could meet and chat with each other.

- ✔ **Content:** Then, around 2000, people discovered that the secret was *content*. By putting more stuff, particularly textual information, on your site, you could be more successful.

Specific one-size-fits-all secrets to success never make sense. The most harmful of the preceding ideas was that your site had to be cool. This silly idea led to the expenditure of billions of dollars on useless but pretty Web sites, most of which (thankfully!) have since disappeared. Unfortunately, some of the *it's-all-about-cool* crowd is still in the Web business and still convincing businesses to spend money on ridiculous, wasteful things such as Flash intros for their Web sites.

The real secret is . . .

. . . your Web site has to be *useful*. The problem with the secrets I just mentioned is that they're too specific, leading people to build sites that were in many cases inappropriate. Sure, links are important to Yahoo!, but they're much less so to the vast majority of Web sites. If you own an entertainment site, you may want to make it cool and entertaining. Certainly community can be an effective tool, but not every site has to have it. Content is very important, too — especially from a search engine perspective — but many successful Web sites don't have much content. (I talk in more detail about content in the next section because it's a special case.)

I've been saying this since 1997: *Forget cool, think useful.*

When you're planning your Web site, think about what kinds of folks you want to attract to the site. Then try to come up with ideas about what features and information might be *useful* to them. Your site may end up with a lot of link pages, providing a directory of sorts for people in your industry. Or maybe you really need a cool and entertaining site. Or perhaps you decide to use discussion groups and chat rooms as a way to build community and pull the crowds into your site; that's fine. Or maybe you decide to create a huge repository of information to attract a particular type of customer to your site. That's okay, too. Maybe you do *all* these things. But the important first step is to think about what you can do to make your site more useful.

A bias for content

Content is a special case. The Web's search engines are biased toward ranking content-heavy Web sites well for a couple of reasons:

✔ Search engines were originally academic research tools designed to find *text information*. Search engines mostly index text . . . that is, content.

✔ Search engines need something to base their judgments on. When you type a search term into a search engine, the search engine looks for the *words* you provided. So a Web site built with few words is at a disadvantage right from the start.

As you discover elsewhere in this book — such as in the discussion of Page-Rank in Chapter 12 — search engines do have other criteria for deciding if a Web site matches a particular search, most notably the number and type of links pointing to the site. But search engines do have a huge bias toward textual content.

Unfortunately, this bias, though little discussed, is often a real problem. The real world simply doesn't work in the manner in which the search engines see it. Here's an example.

Suppose that your business rents very expensive, specialized photographic equipment. Your business has the best prices and the best service of anyone renting this equipment. Your local customers love you, and few other companies match your prices and service or range of products. So you decide to build a Web site to reach customers elsewhere, and ship rentals by UPS and FedEx.

The search engines base your rank, to a great degree, on the number and type of keywords they find in your pages. To rank well, a competitor has added a bunch of pages about photography and photographic equipment to its site. To compete, you have to do the same.

Do your customers care? No, they just want to find a particular piece of equipment that fills their need, rent it, and move on quickly. All the additional information, the content that you've added, is irrelevant to them. It's simply clutter.

This is a common scenario. I recently discussed the content issue with a client who was setting up a Web site at which people could quickly get a moving-service quote. The client wanted to build a clean, sparse site, one that would allow customers to get the quote within a couple of minutes. "But we don't want all that stuff, that extra text, and nor do our clients!" he told me, and he had a good point.

You can't ignore the fact that search engines like content. However, you can compete other ways. One of the most important ways is getting links from other sites, as you discover in Chapter 12. Search engines like to see links on other sites pointing to your site. Sites that have hundreds, even thousands, of other sites linking to them often rank well. But they still need at least *some* content for the search engines to index. And the best situation is lots of useful content with lots of incoming links.

Making Your Site Work Well

I've been writing about site design for almost seven years, and I'm happy to say that many of the rules of good site design just happen to match what search engines like. And many of the cool tricks that designers love cause problems with the search engines. So I want to quickly review a few tips for good site design that will help both your site visitors and the search engines work with your site.

Limit the use of multimedia

Most multimedia used on the Web is pointless because it rarely serves a useful purpose to the visitor. It's there because Web designers enjoy working with it and because many people are still stuck in the old "you've got to be cool" mindset.

Look at the world's most successful Web sites, and you'll find that they rarely use multimedia — Flash animations and video, for example — for purely decorative purposes. Look at Amazon: Its design is simple, clean, black text on white background, with lots of text and very little in the way of animations, video, or sound (except, for instance, where it provides music samples in the site's CD area). Look at Yahoo! and Google, too, or CNN.com or eBay — they're not cool; they just get the job done.

You can employ multimedia on a Web site in some useful ways. I think it makes a lot of sense to use Flash, for instance, to create demos and presentations. However, Flash intros are almost *always* pointless, and search engines don't like them because Flash intros don't provide indexable content. Dump the Flash intro and put some real text on your home page instead. And any time you get the feeling that it would be nice to have an animation of some kind, or when your Web designer tells you that you should have some animation, slap yourself twice on the face and then ask yourself this: Who is going to benefit, the designer or the site visitor? If that doesn't dissuade you, have someone else slap you.

Use text, not graphics

A surprising number of Web sites use graphics to place text onto pages. Take a look at the Web site shown in Figure 3-1. Although this page appears to have a lot of text, absolutely *none* of the text you see is actually text. Every word is in an image file. Web designers often employ this technique so that all browsers can view their carefully chosen fonts. But search engines don't read the text in the images they run across, so this page provides *no* text that can be indexed by the search engines. Although this page may contain lots of useful keywords (you find out all about keywords in Chapter 4), the search engines read *nothing*. From a usability perspective, the design is bad, too, because all those images take much longer to download than the equivalent text would take.

Figure 3-1: This looks like text, but it's actually images, slowing down the page load and providing nothing for the search engines to read.

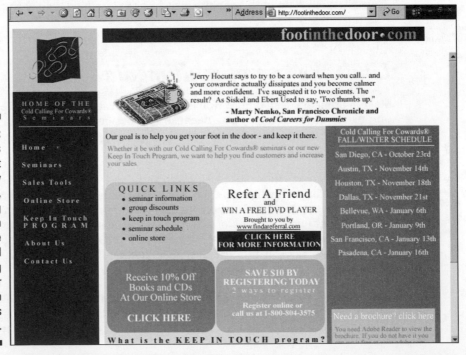

Use ALT text

When you place images in a Web page, it's a good idea to include `ALT` attribute text. The `ALT` attribute in an `IMG` tag was originally intended to provide a description of an image for people using text-based browsers, or browsers that are capable of displaying images but have the image display turned off. Few people browse without images turned on these days. However, `ALT` text can also be used by browsers designed for the blind, which read the text (including `ALT` text) out loud.

Search engines sometimes use the `ALT` text as one more clue about the page's subject matter. It's not as important as it used to be, but it can't hurt. Remember to put keywords in the `ALT` attribute, like this:

```
<IMG SRC="rodent.gif" WIDTH="500" HEIGHT="100" ALT="Rodent
              Racing Scores">
```

Don't be too clever

For several years, I've been advising people to stay one step behind in Web technology and try not to be too clever. From a usability standpoint, the problem is that not all browser types work the same; they have different bugs and handle technical tricks differently. If you're always working with the very latest Web-development technology, more of your visitors are likely to run into problems.

Cool technology often confuses the search engines, too. As my technical editor, Micah Baldwin, likes to say, "Google likes black text on a white background." In other words, Google, and other search engines, like *simple*. The more complicated your Web pages are, the harder it is for search engines to read and categorize them. You must strike a compromise between employing all the latest Web-design technology and tools and ensuring the search engines can read your pages. From a search engine perspective, in fact, one step behind probably isn't enough!

Don't be cute

Some sites do everything they can to be cute. The Coca-Cola site was a classic example of this a few years ago, though it finally got the message and changed. The site had icons labeled *Tour de Jour, Mind Candy, Curvy Canvas, Netalogue,* and so on. What do these things mean? Who knows? Certainly not the site visitor.

This sort of deranged Web design is far less common now than it used to be, but you still see it occasionally — particularly in sites designed by hip Web design firms. One incredibly irritating technique is the hidden navigation structure. The main page contains a large image with hotspots on it. But it's unclear where the hotspots are, or what they link to, until you point at the image and move the mouse around. This strikes me as the Web-design equivalent of removing the numbers from the front of the homes in a neighborhood. You can still figure out where people live; you just have to knock on doors and ask.

Sweet and sickly cuteness doesn't help your site visitors find their way around and almost certainly hurts you with the search engines.

Avoid frames

Framed Web sites were very popular a few years ago; fortunately, they've fallen out of favor to a great degree. From a usability standpoint, there's nothing wrong with frames. But here are a few reasons why they're less prevalent today:

- Many designers misused frames, making their sites hard to navigate. Often designers put too many frames into a browser window because they designed on large screens with high resolutions and forgot about the average Joe working with a small screen and low resolution. (Also, some browsers simply don't handle frames well, although that's much less of a problem now than it used to be.)

- Search engines don't handle frames well, for a whole list of reasons explained in Chapter 6.

I can think of few situations in which you can't use some other mechanism rather than frames, so I advise you to stay away from them.

Make it easy to move around

Web design is constantly getting better, but it still surprises me that designers sometimes make it difficult for visitors to move around a Web site. Think carefully about how your site is structured:

- Does it make sense from a visitor's standpoint?

- Can visitors find what they need quickly?

- Do you have *dangling* pages — pages where a visitor can't find a link to get back into your main site?

    Search engines don't like dangling pages, and consider what happens if someone on another site links directly to the page — visitors can get to the page but not to the rest of your site.

Step into your target visitors' shoes and think about what they would want on arriving at your site. Can your visitors get where they're going quickly and easily? If they can't, you're probably also making it hard for search engines to find their way around.

Provide different ways to find things

People think differently, so you need to provide them with numerous avenues for finding their way around your site. And by doing so, you're also giving more information to search engines and ensuring that search engines can navigate your site easily.

Here are some different navigational systems you can add to your site:

- **Sitemap.** This is a page with links to the different areas of your site, or even, in the case of small sites, to every page in the site.
- **Table of Contents or Index page.** You can sort the page thematically or alphabetically.
- **Navigation bars.**
- **Navigation text links.**

One technique that I like is to add simple text links near the *top,* rather than the bottom, of the page. Users with slow connections see these links quickly, and search engines are sure to find them. (Sometimes, on large and complex Web pages, search engines may miss links at the bottom of the page.)

Use long link text

It's a proven fact that Web users like long link text — links that are more than just a single word, but that actually describe where the link takes you if you click on it. Usability testing shows that long link text makes it much easier for visitors to find their way around a site. It's not surprising if you think about it; a long link provides more information to visitors about where a link will take them.

Unfortunately, many designers feel constrained by design considerations, forcing all navigation links, for instance, to conform to a size restriction. You often see buttons that have only enough room for ten or so characters, forcing the designer to think about how to say complicated things in one or two words.

Long links that explain what the referenced page is about are a great thing not only for visitors but also for search engines. By using keywords in the links, you're telling the search engines what the referenced pages are about.

You also have a problem if all the links on your site are on image buttons — search engines can't read images, so image buttons provide no information describing what the referenced page is *about*. You can't beat a well keyworded text link for passing information about the target page to the search engines.

Don't keep restructuring

Try to fix your site design before you get too far into the process. Sites that are constantly being restructured have numerous problems, including the following:

✔ Links from other Web sites into yours get broken, which is bad for potential visitors as well as for search engines . . . or, more precisely, bad for your position in the search engines because they won't be able to reach your site through the broken links.

✔ Anyone who may have bookmarked your page now has a broken bookmark.

It's a good idea to create a custom 404 error page, which is displayed in your browser if the server is unable to find a page you've requested. (Ask your Web server administrator how to do this; the process varies among servers.) Create a page with links to other areas of the site, perhaps even a sitemap, so that if visitors and searchbots can't find the right page, at least they'll be able to reach some page on your site. For all sorts of information about 404 errors and how to deal with them, see www.plinko.net/404.

Spell check and edit

Check your pages for spilling and editng errors. Not only do error-free pages make your site appear more professional to visitors, they also ensure that your valuable keywords are not wasted. If your potential site visitors are searching for *rodent racing,* for example, you don't want the term *rodint racing* in your Web pages.

Chapter 4

Picking Powerful Keywords

• •

In This Chapter

▶ Thinking up keyword phrases

▶ Using a free keyword tool to find more keywords

▶ Using Wordtracker for more detailed analyses

▶ Sifting through the list to pick the right keywords

• •

1 was talking with a client the other day who wanted to have his site rank well in the search engines. (I've changed the details of this story a tad to protect the client's privacy.) Let's say the client is a company with annual revenues in the millions of dollars (as indeed this client is), in the business of, oh, I dunno . . . staging rodent-racing events.

I did a little research and found that most people searching for rodent-racing events use the keywords *rodent racing*. (Big surprise, huh?) I took a look at the client's Web site and discovered that the words *rodent racing* didn't appear anywhere on the site's Web pages.

"You have a little problem," I said. "Your site doesn't use the words *rodent racing,* so it's unlikely that any search engine will find your site when people search for that."

"Oh, well," was the client's reply, "our marketing department objects to the term. We have a company policy to use the term *furry friend events.* The term rodent is too demeaning, and if we say we're racing them, the animal-rights people will get upset."

This is a true story, well, except for the bit about rodent racing and the furry friends thing. But in principle it happened. This company had a policy not to use the words that most of its potential clients were using to search for it.

You may be asking yourself how it's possible that a company can build a Web site only to discover later that the keywords its potential clients and visitors are using are not in the site. Well, I can think of a couple of reasons:

✔ Most sites are built without any regard for the search engines. The site designers simply don't think about the search engines or have little background knowledge about how search engines work.

✔ The site designers do think about the search engines, but they guess, often incorrectly, what keywords they should be using.

I can't tell you how the client and I resolved this problem because, well, we haven't yet resolved it. But I am going to tell you how to pick keywords that make sense for your site, as well as how to discover what keywords your potential site visitors are using to search for your products and services.

Understanding the Importance of Keywords

When you go to a search engine and try to find something, you type in a word, or several words, and click the Search button. The search engine then looks in its index for those words.

Suppose that you used the words *rodent racing*. Generally speaking, the search engine will look for various things:

✔ Pages that contain the exact phrase *rodent racing*

✔ Pages that don't have the phrase *rodent racing,* but do have the words *rodent* and *racing* in close proximity

✔ Pages that have the words *rodent* and *racing* somewhere, though not necessarily close together

✔ Pages with word stems; for instance, pages with the word *rodent* and the word *race* somewhere in the page

✔ Pages that have links pointing to them, in which the link text contains the phrase *rodent racing*

✔ Pages with links pointing to them with the link text containing the words *rodent* and *racing,* although not together

The process is actually a lot more complicated than this. The search engine doesn't necessarily show pages in the order I just listed — all the pages with the exact phrase, then all the pages with the words in close proximity, and so on. Rather, when considering the order in which to rank pages, the search engine takes into consideration other characteristics of the keyword or keyword phrase:

- ✔ Is the keyword phrase found in bold text?
- ✔ In italic text?
- ✔ In bulleted lists?
- ✔ In text larger than most of the other text on the page?
- ✔ In heading text (<H> tags)?
- ✔ . . . and hundreds of other criteria, all of which are secret!

Despite all the various complications, however, one fact is of paramount importance: If a search engine can't relate to your Web site the words that someone searches for, it has no reason to return your Web site as part of the search results.

Picking the right keywords is critical. As Woody Allen once said, "Eighty percent of success is showing up." If you don't play the game, you can't win. And if you don't choose the right keywords, you're not even showing up to play the game.

Understanding how to search helps you understand the role of keywords. Check out the Bonus Chapter to find out the different ways you can search using the search engines in general and Google in particular.

Thinking like Your Prey

It's an old concept: You should think like your prey. Companies often make mistakes with their keywords because they pick keywords based on how they — rather than their customers — think about their products or services. You have to stop thinking that you know what customers call your products. Do some research to find out what consumers really do call your products.

Do a little keyword analysis — check to see what people are actually searching for on the Web. You'll discover that words that you were positive people would use are rarely searched, and you'll find that you've missed a lot of common terms. Sure, you may get some of the keywords right, but if you're spending time and energy targeting particular keywords, you might as well get 'em all right!

The term *keyword analysis* can have several meanings:

- ✔ When I use it, I'm referring to what I'm discussing in this chapter: analyzing the use of keywords by people searching for products, services, and information.

- ✔ Some people use the term to mean *keyword-density* analysis, finding out how often a keyword appears in a page. Some of the keyword-analysis tools that you run across are actually keyword-density-analysis tools.

- ✔ The term also may be used to refer to the process of analyzing keywords in your Web site's access logs.

Starting Your Keyword Analysis

You have to do a keyword analysis — a check of what keywords people use to search on the Web — or you're wasting your time. Imagine spending hundreds of hours optimizing your site for a keyword you think is good, only to discover that another keyword or phrase gets two or three times the traffic. How would you feel? Sick? Stupid? Mad? Don't risk your mental health — do it right the first time.

Identifying the obvious keywords

Begin by typing the obvious keywords into a text editor or word processor — the ones you've already thought of, or, if you haven't started yet, the ones that immediately come to mind. Then study the list for a few minutes. What else can you add? What similar terms come to mind? Add them, too.

When you do your analysis, you'll find that some of the initial terms you think of aren't searched for very often, but that's okay. This list is just the start.

Looking at your Web site's access logs

Take a quick look at your Web site's access logs (often called *hit logs*), a subject I discuss in Chapter 18. You may not realize it, but most logs show you the keywords that people used when they clicked a link to your site at a search engine. (If your logs don't contain this information, you probably need another program!) Write down the terms that are bringing people to your site.

Examining competitors' keyword tags

You probably know who your competitors are (you should, anyway). Go to their sites and open the source code of a few pages at each site — just choose View⇨Source from the browser's menu bar to get a peek. Look for the `<META NAME="keywords">` tag and see if you find any useful keywords there. Often the keywords are garbage, or simply not there, but if you look at enough sites, you're likely to come up with some useful terms you hadn't thought of.

Brainstorming with colleagues

Talk to other friends and colleagues to see if they can come up with some possible keywords. Ask them something like, "If you were looking for a site at which you could find the latest scores for rodent races around the world, what terms would you search for?"

Give everyone a copy of your current keyword list and ask if they can think of anything to add to it. Usually, reading the terms will spark an idea or two, and you'll end up with a few more terms.

Looking closely at your list

After you've put together your initial list, go through it looking for more obvious additions. Don't spend too much time on this; all you're doing here is creating a preliminary list to run through a keyword tool, which will also figure out some of these things for you.

Obvious spelling mistakes

Scan through your list and see if you can think of any obvious spelling mistakes. Some spelling mistakes are incredibly important, with 10, 15, or 20 percent of all searches containing the word being misspelled, sometimes even more! For example, about one-fifth of all Britney Spears–related searches are misspelled, spread out over a dozen misspellings — which might allow me to take a cheap shot, but I have no intention of doing so.

The word *calendar* is also frequently misspelled. Look at the following list, an estimate of how often the single word *calendar* is searched for each day, in its various permutations:

> *calendar:* 10,605 times
> *calender:* 2,721
> *calander:* 1,549
> *calandar:* 256

Thirty percent of all searches on the word *calendar* are misspelled! (Where do I get these estimates, you're wondering? You find out later in this chapter, starting at "Using a keyword tool.")

TIP

If the traffic from a misspelling is significant, you may want to create a page on your site that uses that misspelling. Some sites contain what I call "Did You Mean" pages, such as the one shown in Figure 4-1. Some sites contain pages using misspellings in the TITLE tags, which can work very well. These don't have to be pages that many people see. After all, the only people who will see the misspelled titles in a search results page are those who misspelled the words in the first place!

One nice thing about misspellings is that often competitors have missed them, so you can grab the traffic without much trouble.

Synonyms

Sometimes similar words are easily missed. If your business is a home-related business, for instance, have you thought about the term *house?* Americans may easily overlook this word, using *home* instead, but other English-speaking countries use the word often. Still, add it to the list because you may find quite a few searches related to it.

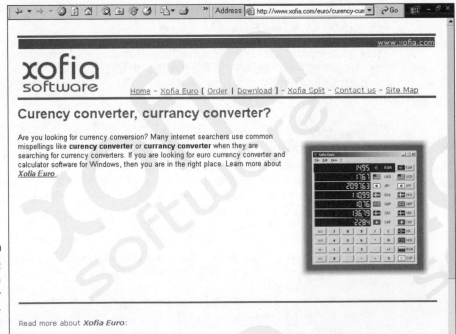

Figure 4-1:
A page designed for the spelling-challenged!

You might even use a thesaurus to find more synonyms. However, I show you some keyword tools that will run these kinds of searches for you — see "Using a keyword tool."

Split or merged words

You may find that although your product name is one word — RodentRacing, for instance — most people are searching for you using two words, rodent and racing. Remember to consider your customer's point of view.

Also, some words are employed in two ways. Some people, for instance, use the term *knowledgebase,* while others use *knowledge base.* Which is more important? Both should be on your list, but *knowledge base* is used around four to five times more often than *knowledgebase.* If you optimize your pages for *knowledgebase* (I discuss page optimization in Chapter 6), you're missing out on around 80 percent of the traffic!

Singulars and plurals

Go through your list and add singulars and plurals. Search engines treat singulars and plurals differently. For example, searching on rodent and rodents provides different results, so it's important to know which term is searched for most often. A great example is to do a search on book (1,635 searches per day, according to Wordtracker, which is discussed later in this chapter) and books (16,475 searches per day) in Google. A search on book returns Barnes and Noble as the number-one result, while books returns Amazon.com.

You don't need to worry about upper- versus lowercase. You can use rodent or Rodent or RODENT, for example. Most search engines aren't case sensitive. If you search for rodent (and probably almost 90 percent of all searches are in lowercase), virtually all search engines will find *Rodent* or *RODENT* — or *rODENT* or *ROdent,* for that matter.

Hyphenated words

Do you see any hyphenated words on your list that could be used without the hyphen, or vice versa? Some terms are commonly used both ways, so find out what your customers are using. Here are two examples:

- ✔ The terms *ecommerce* and *e-commerce* are fairly evenly split, with a little over 50 percent of searches using the latter term.
- ✔ The dash in *e-mail* is far less frequently used, with *email* being the most common term.

Find hyphenated words, add both forms to your list, and determine which is more common because search engines treat them as different searches.

Search engines generally treat a hyphen as a space. So searching for `rodent-racing` is the same as searching for `rodent racing`. However, there is a real difference between `e-commerce` and `ecommerce`, or `rodentracing` and `rodent-racing`.

Geo-specific terms

Is geography important to your business? Are you selling shoes in Seattle or rodents in Rochester? Don't forget to include terms that include your city, state, other nearby cities, and so on.

Your company name

If you have a well-known company name, add that to the list, in whatever permutations you can think of (Microsoft, MS, MSFT, and so on).

Other companies' names and product names

If people will likely be searching for companies and products similar to yours, add those companies and products to your list. That's not to say you should use these keywords in your pages — you can in some conditions, as I discuss in Chapter 6. But it's nice to know what people are looking for and how often they're looking.

Using a keyword tool

After you've put together a decent-size keyword list, the next step is to use a keyword tool. This tool will enable you to discover additional terms you haven't thought of and help you determine which terms are most important — which terms are used most often by people looking for your products and services.

Both free and paid versions of keyword tools are available. I discuss the freebies first, but I might as well cut to the chase and tell you that I recommend that you fork over the dough and use Wordtracker, the world's top search engine keyword tool. So you can skip to that section if you want, or read on.

The Overture Search Term Suggestion Tool

Overture is a pay-per-click service (you find out about these services in Chapter 15). As a service to its customers (and prospective customers), Overture provides a free tool that allows you to see how often a particular search term is used each month at Overture.

Here's how to find (and use) this tool:

1. **Point your browser to** www.overture.com.

   The Overture home page duly appears.

2. **Click the Advertiser Center link (usually somewhere near the top of the page).**

3. **On the new page that appears, click the Tools link, and then on the next page, click the Term Suggestion Tool link.**

   A secondary window pops up, with a text box in it.

4. **Type a search term and press Enter.**

   The tool tells you how often that term was searched for throughout the Overture network during the previous month. Figure 4-2 shows the results for the search term rodent.

Put your search term here and press Enter.   The number of times your search term was used in the Overture network in October.

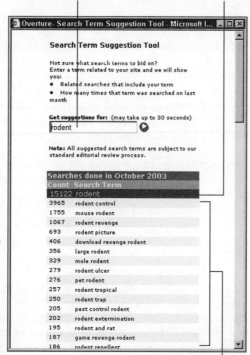

Figure 4-2:
The
Overture
Search Term
Suggestion
Tool.

Similar terms; click one to
see similar and related terms.

The number isn't terribly important; it's the relative levels that count. If one word was searched on 15,000 times last month, and another one 10,000, you can be pretty sure that, on the Overture network or not, the first term is the most important one.

Overture provides other search terms, too. It looks for similar and related terms, lists them, and also provides the number of times that those terms were searched for. You can click one of the additional terms, and Overture searches on that term, too, bringing up similar and related terms.

For each term in your list, use the Search Term Suggestion Tool to find out how many times the term is used each month and to find related terms. Add to your list any related terms that look like they may be appropriate for you (and note the number of times they're searched for).

This process takes what is referred to in the search-engine-optimization business as *a bloody long time*. (Well, the business in England, anyway.) This is why I suggest that you use Wordtracker, which I discuss shortly.

Other keyword tools

Several other keyword-analysis tools are available. Some of the other pay-per-click services provide tools, for instance, but, unlike Overture, you generally can't get to the tool until you have already set up an account or gone through some preliminary sign-up process.

FindWhat (www.findwhat.com) has a Keyword Center, which operates much like Overture's tool. Google has a pretty good tool, too, but you have to jump through some hoops to get to it if you haven't yet set up a pay-per-click account with Google AdWords (adwords.google.com).

To find some of the other software tools and Web-based services, do a search on keyword or keyword analysis. The top tool is Wordtracker, which is discussed in the next section.

Using Wordtracker

Wordtracker (www.wordtracker.com) is the tool that virtually all SEO professionals use. (SEO professionals also like to throw the term SEO around, rather than use the more unwieldy but clearer term *search engine optimization*.) I generally don't like endorsing a product in this manner; elsewhere in this book, I mention products and even state that they're good. But Wordtracker is a special case. I know of no other tool that matches it or that is anywhere near as popular. And it's cheap to use, so I recommend that you do so.

Wordtracker, owned by a company in London, England, has access to data from several very large *metacrawlers*. A metacrawler is a system that searches multiple search engines for you. For example, type a word into Dogpile's search box (`www.dogpile.com`), and the system searches at Google, Yahoo!, Ask Jeeves, AltaVista, and many others.

Wordtracker gets the information about what people are searching for from Metacrawler.com, Dogpile.com, and others, for a total of over 150 million searches each month. It stores two months of searches in its databases, somewhere around 310 million searches.

Wordtracker combines the data for the last 60 days and then allows its customers to search this database. Ask Wordtracker how often someone searched for the term `rodent`, and it will tell you that it had been searched for (at the time of writing) 77 times over the last 60 days but that the term `rodents` is far more popular, with 527 searches over the last 60 days.

Certain searches are seasonal — `pools` in the summer, `heaters` in the winter, and so on. Because Wordtracker has only the last 60 days of information, it may not be representative for a full year for some terms. And some searches may be influenced by the media. While searches for `paris hilton` were very high in November and December 2003, it's likely they'll be much lower by the time you read this. (We can hope, anyway.)

Here's what information Wordtracker can provide:

- ✔ The number of times in the last 60 days that the exact phrase you entered was searched for out of 310 million or so searches

- ✔ An estimate of how many times each day the phrase is used throughout all the Web's search engines

- ✔ Similar terms and synonyms, and the usage statistics about these terms

- ✔ Terms used in hundreds of competing sites' `KEYWORDS` meta tags, ranked according to frequency

- ✔ Common misspellings

- ✔ A comparison of how often a term is searched for with how many pages appear for that term — a nice way to find terms with relatively little competition

Do metacrawlers provide better results? Here's what Wordtracker claims:

✔ **Search results at the big search engines are skewed.** Many Web site owners use them to check their sites' rankings, sometimes several times a week. Thus, many searches are not true searches. Metacrawlers can't be used for this purpose, so they provide cleaner results.

✔ **Wordtracker analyzes searches to find what appear to be fake, automated searches.** Some companies carry out hundreds of searches an hour on particular keywords — company or product names, for instance — in an attempt to trick search engines into thinking these keywords generate a lot of interest.

Wordtracker is well worth the price. You can pay for access by the day (£4.20, around $7.25 currently), the week (£14/$24.15), the month (£28/$48.31), three months (£69/$119.04), or the year (£140/$241.53). Most professionals in the SEO business have a regular account with Wordtracker, but for individual sites, it may be worth just getting a day or two of access. One strategy is to build your list first, as described in this chapter, and then sign up for a day and run Wordtracker for that day. You may get enough done in a couple of hours; if not, you can always sign up for another day. (Of course these prices may change, so check the Wordtracker site.)

Anyone heavily involved in the Web and search engines can easily get addicted to this tool. Sometimes you've just got to know exactly how often people are searching for `paris hilton` (70,000 times a day), `paris hilton video` (46,000 times a day), `star wars kid` (8,000), or `craig the dog faced boy` (14).

Creating a Wordtracker project

Wordtracker lets you create projects so you can store different groups of terms — perhaps one for each Web site or, if you're a consultant, one for each client. The first thing you should do — after plunking down your money and setting up the standard username and password stuff — is create a project. Here's how:

1. **Click the Projects button on the main navigation page (which you see after you log in).**

   The Projects page appears, as shown in Figure 4-3.

2. **Give your project a name and then click the Change Project Name button to save the new name.**

Wordtracker allows you to have seven projects, storing different keyword lists. You can empty old projects and rename them as you move on to new Web projects. This may be an important feature if you're an SEO professional or a Web designer working on multiple Web sites.

3. **To load your existing list into the project, click the Import button, copy and paste the words from the list into the large text box (one entry per line, as shown in Figure 4-4), and click the Submit button.**

I recommend that you leave the Compressed Import option button selected. Doing so changes all the entries to lowercase, regardless of how you typed them. Remember that Google, and most other search systems, are not case sensitive anyway, so Rodent is the same as rodent.

After the list is imported, another page opens, which contains your list with a number in parentheses next to each keyword or keyword phrase; this is the count, the number of times the word or phrase appears in the database.

Type your new project name here.   Click here to set the new name.

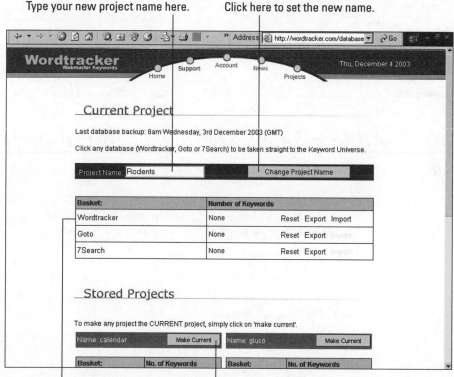

Figure 4-3:
Word-
tracker's
Projects
page.

Click here to view the words   Click here to load the selected project.
stored in the project.

Paste your keyword list here.

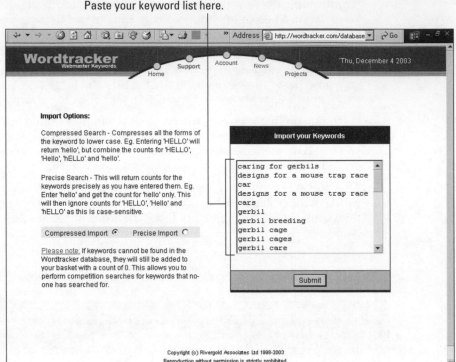

Figure 4-4:
The Import
page.

Adding keywords to your initial project list

To use Wordtracker to find more words that might be appropriate, follow these steps:

1. **Click the Home button in the navigation bar at the top of any Wordtracker page to go to the Wordtracker home page.**

2. **Click the Keyword Universe link.**

   You see the page shown in Figure 4-5.

3. **Type the first keyword in your list into the box on the left and then click the Proceed button.**

   Both the Lateral and Thesaurus check boxes are selected by default. Here's the lowdown on these options:

   • **Lateral:** Wordtracker looks for 200 Web sites it thinks are related to the word you typed, and grabs keywords from their KEYWORDS meta tags. (You find out more about the KEYWORDS meta tags in Chapter 6.)

   • **Thesaurus:** Wordtracker looks up the word in a thesaurus.

After clicking the Proceed button, wait a few minutes while Wordtracker builds a list. Then scroll down the left frame to see the list.

4. **Click a word in the list in the left frame to load the corresponding table in the right frame.**

   The table shows you actual searches from the Wordtracker database containing the word you clicked, and other keyword phrases containing that word. So, for instance, if you click *rodent,* you see search terms such as *rodents, rodent control, rodents revenge, rodent, rodent repellent, rodent pictures,* and so on.

Next to each term in the table, you see two numbers:

✔ **Count:** The number of times Wordtracker found the search term in its database. The database contains searches for 60 days — more than 310 million of them. So the count is the number of times the term was used in the last two months in the search engines from which Wordtracker builds its database.

✔ **Predict:** An estimate of how many times this term is likely to be used each day, in all the Internet search engines combined.

Wordtracker simply extrapolates from the count number to arrive at the predict number. Wordtracker assumes that the search engines it's working with account for a certain percentage of all searches, so it simply takes the count number and multiplies accordingly.

I believe these numbers are too low. From what I've seen and heard, these terms may actually be searched for 50 to 100 percent more often than the predict number. However, what counts is the relative, rather than absolute, number. If one phrase has a predict value of 12,000 times a day, and another one 6,000 times a day, the actual numbers may be 24,000 and 12,000, but what really matters is that one is much more than the other.

Here's what you can do with the list of search terms in the right frame:

✔ Click the Click Here to Add All Keywords to Your Basket link to add all the keyword phrases to your project. (The number next to the basket in the bottom frame increases as you add phrases to the project.)

✔ Click a term to add just that term to the project.

✔ Click the shovel icon in the Dig column to see similar terms. Click the shovel in the *rodents revenge* row, for example, to see a smaller list containing *download rodents revenge, rodents revenge download, download rodents revenge game,* and so on.

Type a word here and click Proceed.

Type keywords here and click Go.

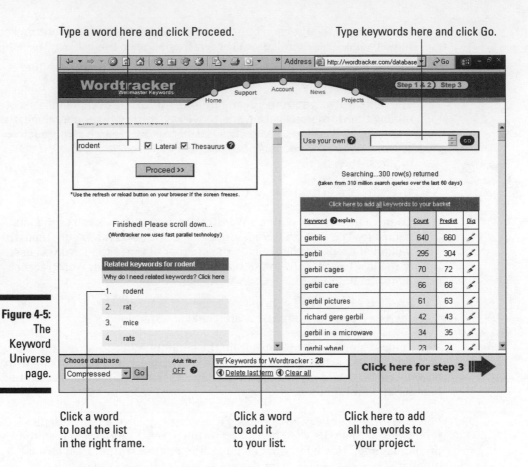

Figure 4-5:
The
Keyword
Universe
page.

Click a word
to load the list
in the right frame.

Click a word
to add it
to your list.

Click here to add
all the words to
your project.

Should you add all the words in the list at once, or one by one? That depends. If the list contains mostly words that seem to you to be relevant keywords, click the All link at the top to add them all — you can remove the few that are no good later. If most of the list seems to be garbage, scroll down the list and add only the useful words.

After you've finished tweaking the list, here are a couple of other things you can do:

✔ Click another keyword phrase in the left frame to load a new list in the right frame with search terms related to that phrase.

✔ Type another word from your original list into the box at the top of the left frame. Wordtracker then retrieves more terms related to it from the thesaurus and KEYWORDS meta tags.

✔ Type a term into the text box at the top of the right frame and click the Go button to create a list based on that term.

The left frame is handy because it runs your words through a thesaurus and grabs words from KEYWORDS meta tags. But I also like to use the text box at the top of the right frame: I grab a few keyword phrases from my list and copy them into the box (each one needs to be on a separate line). This is a quick way to find matching phrases for the terms already in your list. Typing a word into the text box at the top of the right frame is the same thing as clicking a word in the left frame — Wordtracker looks for real search phrases that include the word. Type (or paste) multiple words into that text box, and Wordtracker looks for matches for each of those words.

Cleaning up the list

After you've worked through your list, checking for relevant terms, click the Click Here for Step 3 link at the bottom of the page. On the Step 3 page, you see the first 100 words in your project, with the most common appearing first (see Figure 4-6).

Number of keywords in Rodents (28)   Wordtracker ▾ Go

Export Keywords   Email Keywords   Competition Search

◀ Keywords 1 - 20 ▾ of 28 ▶	Count	Delete
▶ gerbils	640	☐
▶ gerbil	295	☐
▶ rat race	90	☐
▶ gerbil cages	70	☐
▶ gerbil care	66	☐
▶ mouse trap race car	34	☐
▶ rodentia	27	☐
▶ gerbil breeding	18	☐
▶ mongolian gerbils	17	☐
▶ information on gerbils	17	☐
▶ mouse trap race cars	16	☐
▶ gerbils for sale	16	☐
▶ gerbil newscast	16	☐

Figure 4-6: Clean your keyword-phrase list here.

Scroll through this list carefully. Look for any keywords that really aren't appropriate. It's possible you'll find some, especially if you clicked the All link at the top of the previous page. To delete a term, select the check box to the right of the unwanted term and click the Delete button at the top. Then scroll to the bottom of the list and work your way up; if you delete 15 terms from the page, 15 more are pulled from the next page, so you need to check them as well. Use the right-pointing triangle at the top of the list to move to the next page.

Remove only those terms that are totally inappropriate. Don't worry too much right now about terms that are not used much or terms that may be too general. I get to that topic in a moment.

Exporting the list

When you're satisfied with your list, you can export it from Wordtracker. At the top of the Step 3 page, click the Export Keywords button to open a window that contains your compiled list. The window contains a list of keyword phrases — a simple list with no numbers. To display the list with the count and predict numbers, click the Click Here to Get a Tab Delimited List of Keywords link.

You can highlight this list and copy and paste it into a word processor or text editor. You can also click the Email Keywords button at the top of the Step 3 page to e-mail the list to yourself or a colleague.

Competitive analysis

By doing a competitive analysis, you can identify terms that are searched for frequently but yield few results. If you then use these keywords on your pages, your pages are more likely to rank high in the search engines because you face little competition from other sites.

To do a competitive analysis, click the Competition Search button at the top of the Step 3 page. On the next page that appears (as shown in Figure 4-7), you can check various search engines and directories, two at a time. Wordtracker tells you how often the term is searched for and how often the keyword phrase appears in Web pages in the indexes you selected.

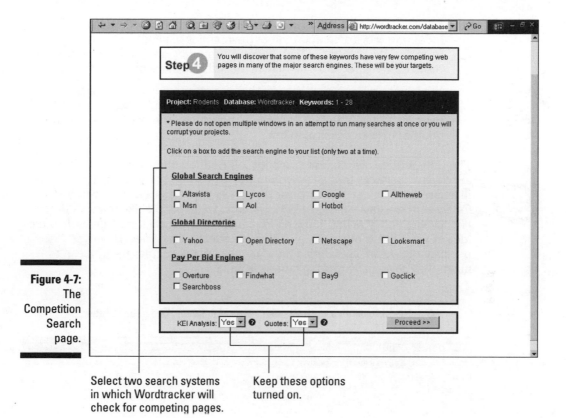

Figure 4-7:
The
Competition
Search
page.

Select two search systems
in which Wordtracker will
check for competing pages.

Keep these options
turned on.

At the bottom of the Competition Search page, you find the KEI Analysis and
Quotes drop-down list boxes. You generally want to keep these options
turned on:

✔ **Quotes:** Wordtracker encloses your search term in quotation marks
when entering it into the selected search engines. For instance, if your
phrase is *rodent racing,* Wordtracker searches for `"rodent racing"`.
The quotation marks tell the search engine that you want to find only
those pages that contain the exact term *rodent racing,* providing a better
idea of your true competition. If you search for the term without using
quotation marks, you get all the pages with the word *rodent* or *racing*
somewhere in the page (the terms don't necessarily appear together or
in order), which returns far more results. You want to leave the Quotes
option turned on because you're competing with sites that have the
exact term in their pages.

✔ **KEI Analysis:** Wordtracker calculates the KEI (Keyword Effectiveness Index), which is a comparison of the number of people searching for a term and the number of Web pages returned by a search engine for that term. (See Figure 4-8.) The higher the KEI, the more powerful the term.

KEI is not always useful. A term that has few competing pages and is searched upon infrequently can generate a high KEI. This term would have little benefit to you because although the competition is low, the number of searches is also low.

The Competition Search also provides information on pay-per-click (PPC) services — services that allow you to buy a position in the search results, as discussed in Chapter 15. Wordtracker shows you the prices that you'd pay for these terms in a variety of PPC systems. Some people like to run a PPC check even if they're not doing a PPC campaign because it may give them an idea of what terms other people think are effective for sales. However, just because others are spending a lot of money on a particular term doesn't mean they're actually making money from it!

The KEI indicates a phrase with a very high Count : Competition ratio.

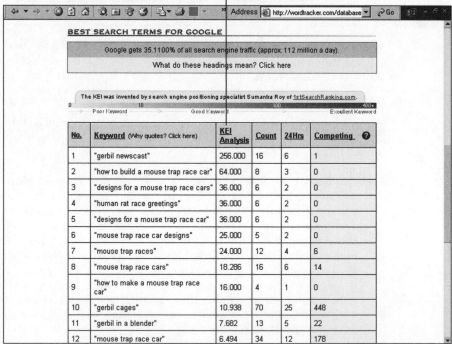

No.	Keyword (Why quotes? Click here)	KEI Analysis	Count	24Hrs	Competing
1	"gerbil newscast"	256.000	16	6	1
2	"how to build a mouse trap race car"	64.000	8	3	0
3	"designs for a mouse trap race cars"	36.000	6	2	0
4	"human rat race greetings"	36.000	6	2	0
5	"designs for a mouse trap race car"	36.000	6	2	0
6	"mouse trap race car designs"	25.000	5	2	0
7	"mouse trap races"	24.000	12	4	6
8	"mouse trap race cars"	18.286	16	6	14
9	"how to make a mouse trap race car"	16.000	4	1	0
10	"gerbil cages"	10.938	70	25	448
11	"gerbil in a blender"	7.682	13	5	22
12	"mouse trap race car"	6.494	34	12	178

Figure 4-8: The Competition Report.

Within the figure:
BEST SEARCH TERMS FOR GOOGLE

Google gets 35.1100% of all search engine traffic (approx. 112 million a day).

What do these headings mean? Click here

The KEI was invented by search engine positioning specialist Sumantra Roy of 1stSearchRanking.com.

0   10   100   400+

Poor Keyword   Good Keyword   Excellent Keyword

Address http://wordtracker.com/database   Go

More ways to find keywords

Wordtracker has a number of other search tools available (although I use mainly the ones I discuss earlier in the chapter):

- ✔ **Full Search:** Wordtracker returns similar terms in the same conceptual ballpark (a very large ballpark, though).

- ✔ **Simple Search:** You can dump a bunch of keyword phrases into a text box to find actual search terms that include those keywords. For example, `rat` turns up *rat terrier, pet rats, naked mole rat,* and so on.

- ✔ **Exact/Precise Search:** This is a mixture of several tools, including the Exact Search, the Compressed Exact Search, and the Precise Search.

- ✔ **Compressed Search:** This is useful for finding plurals and singulars of words from a single list.

- ✔ **Comprehensive Search:** You can dig out a few useful related terms mixed in with a large number of unrelated terms.

- ✔ **Misspelling Search:** This is a good way to find common misspellings of your keywords.

Choosing Your Keywords

When you've finished working with a keyword tool, look at the final list to determine how popular a keyword phrase actually is. You may find that many of your original terms are not worth bothering with. My clients often have terms on their preliminary lists — the lists they put together without the use of a keyword tool — that are virtually never used. You'll also find other terms near the top of the final list that you hadn't thought about. The next several sections help you clean up this list.

Removing ambiguous terms

Scan through your list for ambiguous terms, keyword phrases that probably won't do you any good for various reasons.

You missed the target

Take a look at your list to determine whether you have any words that may have different meanings to different people. Sometimes you can immediately spot such terms. One of my clients thought he should use the term *cam* on his site. To him, the term referred to *Complementary and Alternative Medicine*. But to the vast majority of searchers, *cam* means something different. Search Wordtracker on the term `cam`, and you come up with phrases such as *web cams, web cam, free web cams, live web cams, cam, cams, live cams, live web cams,* and so on. To most searchers, the term *cam* refers to Web cams, cameras used to place pictures and videos into Web sites. The phrases from this example generate a tremendous amount of competition, but few of them would be useful to my client.

Ambiguous terms

A client of mine wanted to promote a product designed for controlling fires. One common term he came up with was *fire control system*. However, he discovered that when he searched on that term, most sites that turned up don't promote products relating to stopping fires. Rather, they're sites related to *fire control* in the military sense: weapons-fire control.

This kind of ambiguity is something you really can't determine from a system such as Wordtracker, which tells you how often people search on a term. In fact, it's often hard to spot such terms even by searching to see what turns up when you use the phrase. If a particular type of Web site turns up when you search for the phrase, does that mean people using the phrase are looking for that type of site? You can't say for sure. A detailed analysis of your Web site's access logs may give you an idea; see Chapter 18 for the details.

Very broad terms

Look at your list for terms that are incredibly broad, too general to be of use. You may be tempted to go after high-ranking words, but make sure that people are really searching for your products when they type in the word.

Suppose that your site is promoting *degrees in information technology*. You discover that around 40 people search for this term each day, but approximately 1,500 people a day search on the term *information technology*. Do you think many people searching on the term *information technology* are really looking for a degree? Probably not. Although the term generates 40,000 to 50,000 searches a month, few of these will be your targets. Here are a few reasons why you should forgo this term:

✔ It's probably a very competitive term, which means ranking well on it would be difficult.

✔ You may be better off spending the time and effort focusing on another, more relevant term.

✔ It's difficult to optimize Web pages for a whole bunch of search terms (see Chapter 6), so if you optimize for one term, you won't be optimizing for another, perhaps more appropriate, term.

Picking keyword combinations

Sometimes it's a good idea to target terms lower down on your list, rather than the ones up top, because the lower terms *include* the higher terms. Suppose that you're selling an e-commerce system and you find the following list (the numbers are the *predict* numbers, the number of times that Wordtracker believes the term is used each day):

```
1828          e-commerce
1098          ecommerce
881           shopping cart
574           shopping cart software
428           shopping carts
260           ecommerce software
130           ecommerce solutions
109           e-commerce software
92            e-commerce solutions
58            shopping carts and accessories
26            ecommerce software solution
```

Notice the term *e-commerce.* This is probably not a great term to target because it's very general and has a lot of competition. But lower down on the list is the term *e-commerce solutions.* This term is a combination of two keyword phrases: *e-commerce* and *e-commerce solutions.* Thus, you can combine the predict numbers: 1,828 searches a day plus 130 a day. If you target *e-commerce solutions* and optimize your Web pages for that term, you're also optimizing for *e-commerce.*

Notice also the term *ecommerce* (which search engines regard as different from *e-commerce*) and the term a little lower on the list, *ecommerce software.* A term even lower down encompasses both of these terms: *ecommerce software solution.* Optimize your pages for *ecommerce software solution,* and you've just optimized for three terms at once.

Use the keyword-analysis procedure I've described in this chapter, and you'll have a much better picture of your keyword landscape. Unlike the majority of Web site owners, you'll have a good view of how people are searching for your products and services.

Part II
Building Search-Engine-Friendly Sites

The 5th Wave   By Rich Tennant

"Maybe your keyword search, 'legal secretary, love, fame, fortune', needs to be refined."

In this part . . .

Time for the details. In this part, you discover things that help your site rank well in the search engines . . . and things that almost guarantee that your site won't do well in the search engines. Understand the information in this part, and you're way ahead of most Web site owners, designers, and developers.

You find out what search engines like to find in your Web pages (the things that are likely to help your site rank well): simplicity, text content with the right keywords, keywords in heading tags and bold text, and so on. You also discover what things have the opposite effect, making search engines stumble when they reach your site or even leave the site without reading any pages. From frames to dynamically generated pages to session IDs, these things can be the kiss of death if you're not careful.

I also let you in on a few secrets that the search engines hate, techniques that people often use to "trick" the search engines but that can also be dangerous. Many folks in the search-engine-optimization business shy away from these techniques, for fear of having their pages penalized or entire sites banned from the search engines.

Finally, this part shows you ways to quickly build the content on your site. Content is king as far as the search engines are concerned, but the problem is where to find enough text to satisfy them.

Chapter 5

Creating Pages That Search Engines Love

*I*n this chapter, you find out how to create Web pages that search engines *really* like, pages that can be read and indexed and that put your best foot forward. Before you begin creating pages, I recommend that you read not only this chapter but also Chapter 6 to find out how to avoid things that search engines hate. There are a lot of ways to make a Web site work, and ways to break it, too, so before you get started creating your pages, you should be aware of the problems you may face and what you can do to avoid them.

I'm assuming that you or your Web designer understands HTML and can create Web pages. I focus on the most important search-engine-related things you need to know while creating your pages. It's beyond the scope of this book to cover basic HTML and Cascading Style Sheets.

Preparing Your Site

When creating a Web site, the first thing to consider is *where* to put your site. By that, I mean the Web server and the domain name.

Finding a hosting company

Although many large companies place their Web sites on their own Web servers, most companies don't do this — shouldn't do this, in fact, because there's simply no way you can do it anywhere near as cheaply and reliably as a good hosting company can do it. Rather, they place their sites on servers owned by a hosting company. Although you have to take in consideration many different factors when selecting a hosting company, I focus on the factors that are related to search engine optimization. When looking for a hosting company, make sure that it offers the following features:

- ✔ **Allows you to upload Web pages that you've created all by your lonesome.** Some services provide simple tools you can use to create Web pages; it's fine if they provide these tools as long as you also have the ability to create pages yourself. You must have control over the HTML in your pages.

- ✔ **Provides an access-log-analysis tool or, if you plan to use your own analysis tool, a way to get to the raw access logs.** A log-analysis tool shows you how many people visit your site and how they get there. See Chapter 18 for more information.

- ✔ **Allows you to use your own domain name.** Don't get an account in which you have a subdirectory of the hosting company's domain name.

You need to consider many issues when selecting a hosting company, most of which are not directly related to the search engine issue. If you want to find out more about what to look for in a hosting company, I've posted an article about selecting a host on my Web site, at www.SearchEngineBulletin.com.

Picking a domain name

Google actually reads URLs, looking for keywords in them. For instance, if you have a Web site with the domain name rodent-racing.com and someone searches at Google for rodent racing, Google sees rodent-racing.com as a match. Because a dash appears between the two words, Google recognizes the words in the domain name. (Google also interprets periods and slashes as word separators.) If, however, you use an underscore or some other character, or if you run the words together (rodent_racing_events.com or rodent racingevents.com), Google doesn't see the words in the URL.

To see this concept in action, use the allinurl: search syntax at Google. Type allinurl:rodent, for example, and Google finds URLs that contain the word *rodent* (including the directory names and filenames).

So putting keywords into the domain name and separating keywords with dashes do provide a small benefit. Another advantage to adding dashes between words is that it's relatively easy to come up with a domain name that's not already taken. Although it may seem like most of the good names were taken long ago, you can pretty easily come up with some kind of keyword phrase, separated with dashes, that is still available.

Furthermore, the search engines don't care what first-level domain you use; you can have a `.com`, `.net`, `.biz`, `.tv`, or whatever; it doesn't matter. Now, having said all that, let me tell you my philosophy regarding domain names. In the search engine optimization field, it has become popular to use dashes and keywords in domain names, but the lift provided by keywords in domain names is very small, and you should take into consideration other, more important factors when choosing a domain name:

> ✔ **A domain name should be short, easy to spell, and easy to remember.** And it should pass the "radio" test. Imagine you're being interviewed on the radio and want to tell listeners your URL. You want something that you can say that is instantly understandable, without having to spell it. You don't want to have to say "rodent dash racing dash events dot com"; it's better to be able to say "rodent racing events dot com."

> ✔ **In almost all cases, you should get the `.com` version of a domain name.** If the `.com` version is taken, do *not* try to use the `.net` or `.org` version for branding purposes! People remember `.com`, even if you say `.org` or `.net` or whatever, so if you're planning to promote your Web site in print, on the radio, on TV, on billboards, and so on, you need the `.com` version.

Several years ago, I recommended to the folks at a nonprofit client of mine that they register the `.com` version of their domain name (they'd been using `.org` for years). During the few hours that the `.com` domain was not yet pointing to their site, but was pointing to the domain registrar's site, the company received several calls from people trying to get to its Web site. These people wanted to let the company know that something was wrong with its server because its domain name was pointing to the wrong place. For years, the company printed all its materials using `.org`; they had never printed anything with `.com` because they didn't own it; however, people were still trying to get to `.com`.

Another classic example is Rent.com and Rent.net. These were two different Web sites, owned by two different companies. Rent.net spent millions of dollars on advertising; every time I saw a Rent.net ad on a bus, I had to wonder how much of the traffic generated by these ads actually went to Rent.com! (Rent.net is now out of business — Rent.com isn't. I don't know if that's a coincidence!)

Are keyworded domain names worth the trouble? Because the lift provided by keywords in the domain name is rather small — and, in fact, putting too many keywords into a name can actually hurt your placement — it's probably better to focus on a single, brandable domain name (a .com version).

Don't use a domain-forwarding service for Web sites you want to turn up in the search engines. Many registrars now allow you to simply forward browsers to a particular site: A user types www.domain1.com, and the registrar forwards the browser to www.domain2.com, for instance. Such forwarding systems often use frames (discussed in Chapter 6), which means the search engines won't index the site properly. Your site should be properly configured by using the name-server settings, not a simple forward.

Understanding What a Search Engine Sees

What a search engine sees when it loads one of your pages is not the same as what your browser sees. To understand why, you need to understand how a Web page is created. Here's a quick explanation (see Figure 5-1):

1. A user types a URL into his browser, or clicks a link, causing the browser to send a message to the Web server asking for a particular page.

2. The Web server grabs the page and quickly reads it to see if it needs to do anything to the page before sending it.

3. The Web server compiles the page, if necessary.

   In some cases, the Web server may have to run ASP or PHP scripts, for instance, or it may have to find an *SSI (server side include),* an instruction telling it to grab something from another page and insert it into the one it's about to send.

4. After the server has completed any instructions, it sends the page to the browser.

5. When the browser receives the page, it reads through the page looking for instructions and, if necessary, further compiles the page.

6. When it's finished, the browser displays the page for the user to read.

   Here are a few examples of instructions the browser may receive:

   • It may find a <SCRIPT> tag, telling it to load a JavaScript from another file — it must then request this file from the server.

- It may find JavaScripts embedded into the file, in which case it runs those scripts.

- It may find references to images or other forms of media, and have to pull those into the page and read CSS (Cascading Style Sheets) instructions to see how the text should be formatted.

So, that's what happens normally when Web pages are created. But the search-bots, used by the search engines to index pages, work differently. When they request a page, the server does what it normally does, constructing the page according to instructions, and sends it to the searchbot. But the searchbot doesn't follow all the instructions in the page — it just reads the page. So, for example, it doesn't run scripts in the page.

ASP and PHP scripts are little programs that are written into Web pages. The scripts are read by a program working in association with the Web server when a page is requested. The searchbots see the results of the scripts because the scripts have been run by the time the Web server sends the page. Server side includes (SSIs) are simple statements placed into the HTML pages that name another file and, in effect, say to the Web server, "Grab the information in this file and drop it into the Web page here." Again, the searchbots see the information in the SSI because the Web server inserts the information before sending the Web page.

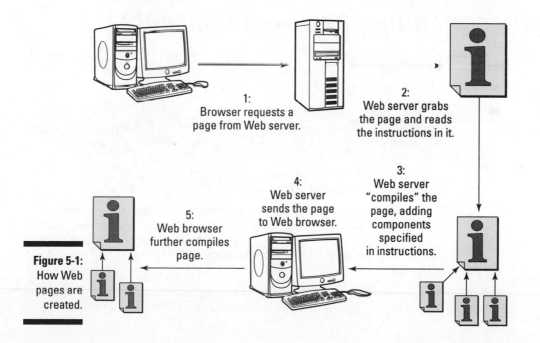

1: Browser requests a page from Web server.

2: Web server grabs the page and reads the instructions in it.

3: Web server "compiles" the page, adding components specified in instructions.

4: Web server sends the page to Web browser.

5: Web browser further compiles page.

Figure 5-1: How Web pages are created.

You can add instructions that build the page in two ways:

- ✔ **Browser-side (or *client-side,* but that strikes me as a very geeky term) instructions:** Browser-side instructions are generally ignored by search-bots. For instance, if you create a page with a navigation system that is built with JavaScript, the search engines won't see it. Some people can even use browser-side instructions to *intentionally* hide things from the search engines.

- ✔ **Server-side instructions:** If you use an SSI to place navigation into the site, the searchbots *will* see it because the Web server uses the SSI before sending the information to the searchbots.

Of course, it's possible for an SSI to place browser-side instructions into a page. In this case, the searchbot sees the instructions — because the server has placed them there — but will ignore them.

This is a very important concept. Remember:

- ✔ Server-side = visible to searchbots

- ✔ Browser-side = not visible to searchbots

Understanding Keyword Concepts

Here's the basic concept: You're putting keywords into your Web pages in such a manner that the search engines can get to them, can read them, and will regard them as significant.

Your keyword list is probably very long, perhaps hundreds of keywords, so you need to pick a few to work with. (If you haven't yet developed a keyword list, page back to Chapter 4 for details.) The keywords you pick should be either

- ✔ Words near the top of the list that have many searches.

- ✔ Words lower down on the list that you feel may be worth targeting because you have relatively few competitors. That is, when someone searches for the keyword phrase using an exact search ("`rodent racing`" rather than `rodent racing`), the search engine finds relatively few pages.

Pick one or two phrases per page

You're going to optimize each page for one or two keyword phrases. By *optimize,* I mean create the page in such a manner that it has a good chance of ranking well for the chosen keyword phrase or phrases, when someone actually uses them in a search engine.

You can't optimize a page well for more than one keyword phrase at a time. The TITLE tag is one of the most important components on a Web page, and the best position for a keyword is right at the beginning of that tag. And only one phrase can be placed at the beginning of the tag, right? (However, sometimes, as you find out in Chapter 4, you can combine keyword phrases — optimizing for *rodent racing scores* also, in effect, optimizes for *rodent racing.*)

Have a primary and a secondary keyword phrase in mind for each page you're creating, but also consider all the keywords you're interested in working into the pages. For instance, you might create a page that you plan to optimize for the phrase *rodent racing.* But you also have several other keywords you want to have scattered around your site: *rodent racing scores, handicap, gerbil, rodentia, furry friend events,* and so on. Typically, you pick one main phrase for each page, but try to incorporate the other keyword phrases throughout the page, where appropriate.

Check for keyword prominence

The term *prominence* refers to where the keyword appears — how prominent it is within a page component (the body text, the TITLE tag, and so on). A word near the top of the page is more prominent than one near the bottom; a word at the beginning of a TITLE tag is more prominent than one at the end; a word at the beginning of the DESCRIPTION meta tag is more prominent than one at the end; and so on.

Prominence is good. If you're creating a page with a particular keyword or keyword phrase in mind, make that term prominent — in the body text, in the TITLE tag, in the DESCRIPTION meta tag, and elsewhere — to convey to the search engines that the keyword phrase is important in this particular page. Consider this title tag:

```
<TITLE>Everything about Rodents - Looking after Them, Feeding
     Them, Rodent Racing, and more.</TITLE>
```

When you read this, you can see that *Rodent Racing* is just one of several terms the page is related to. The search engine comes to the same conclusion because the term is at the end of the title, meaning it's probably not the predominant term. But what about the following tag?

```
<TITLE>Rodent Racing - Looking after Your Rodents, Feeding
        them, Everything You Need to Know</TITLE>
```

Placing *Rodent Racing* at the beginning of the tag places the stress on that concept more; the search engines are likely to conclude that the page is mainly about Rodent Racing.

Watch your keyword density

Another important concept is *keyword density*. When a user searches for a keyword phrase, the search engine looks at all the pages that contain the phrase and checks the *density* — the ratio of the search phrase to the total number of words in the page.

For instance, suppose that you search for `rodent racing` and the search engine finds a page that contains 400 words, with the phrase *rodent racing* appearing 10 times — that's a total of 20 words. Because 20 is 5 percent of 400, the keyword density is 5 percent.

Keyword density is important, but you can overdo it. If the search engine finds that the search phrase makes up 50 percent of the words in the page, it may decide that the page was created purely to grab the search engine's attention for that phrase and then ignore it. On the other hand, if the density is too low, you risk having the search engines regard other pages as more relevant for the search.

Place keywords throughout your site

Suppose that someone searches for `rodent racing`, and the search engine finds two sites that use the term. One site has a single page in which the term occurs, and the other site has dozens of pages containing the term. Which site will the search engine think is most relevant? The one that has many pages related to the subject, of course.

Some search engines — such as Google — often provide two results from a site, one indented below the other. So if your site has only one page related to the subject, this can't happen.

To see how this works in the real world of search engines, refer to Figure 5-2, which appears a little later in the chapter. You'll notice that Google provides two pages from the Britney Spears Guide to Semiconductor Physics. (The site's owner has done a great job of getting his site ranked high in the search engines. After all, Britney Spears's lectures — on semiconductor physics, radiative and non-radiative transitions, edge emitting lasers, and VCSELs — are not what she is best known for and probably of little interest to most of her fans. Yet this site appears in positions 2 and 3 when people search for britney spears.)

In most cases, you're not likely to grab a top position simply by creating a single page optimized for the keyword phrase. You may need dozens, perhaps hundreds, of pages to grab the search engines' attention.

Creating Your Web Pages

When you're creating your Web pages, you need to focus on two essential elements: the underlying structure of the pages and the text you plunk down on the pages. The next sections fill you in on what you need to look out for.

Filenames

Search engines do get clues about the nature of a site from the site's domain name as well as from the site's directory structure. The added "lift" is probably not large, but every little bit counts, right? You might as well name directories, Web pages, and images by using keywords.

So, for example, rather than creating a file named gb123.jpg, you can use a more descriptive name, such as rodent-racing-scores.jpg. Don't have too many dashes in the filenames, though — don't use more than a couple — because the search engine is likely to ignore the name, if not penalize the page (that is, omit the page from the index).

You can separate keywords in a name with dashes or periods, but not underscores. Search engines also see the / symbol in a URL as a separator.

Directory structure

It may be a good idea to keep a flat directory structure in your Web site — keep your pages as close to the root domain as possible, rather than have a complicated multilevel directory tree. Create a directory for each navigation tab and keep all the files in that directory. Most search engine spiders have difficulty finding pages that are two directory levels or deeper within your site, and many observers believe that search engines downgrade pages that are lower down in the directory structure. This effect is probably relatively small, but in general, you're better off using a structure with two or three sub-levels, rather than five or ten. For instance, the first page that follows would be weighted more highly than the second page:

```
http://www.domainname.com/dir1/page.html
http://www.domainname.com/dir1/dir2/dir3/dir4/page.html
```

The TITLE tags

Most search engines use the site's TITLE tag as the link and main title of the site's listing on the search results page, as shown in Figure 5-2.

Figure 5-2:
Search results from Google, showing where components come from.

This is the URL of the page.   This text comes from between the page's TITLE tags.

If the Web site is in the Open Directory Project's directory, Google provides the category.

TITLE tags not only tell a browser what text to display in the browser's title bar, but they're also very important for search engines. Searchbots read the page titles and use the information to determine what the pages are about. If you have a keyword between your TITLE tags that competing pages don't have, you have a good chance of getting at or near the top of the search results.

The TITLE is one of the most important components as far as search engines are concerned. However, these tags are usually wasted because few sites bother placing useful keywords in them.

I searched at Google for intitle:welcome to find out how many pages have the word *welcome* in their TITLE tags. The result? Around 80 million! Around 7 million have *welcome to* in the title (allintitle:"welcome to"). Having *Welcome to* as the first words in your title is a waste of space, only slightly more wasteful than your company name! Give the search engines a really strong clue about your site's content by using a keyword phrase in the TITLE tags. Here's how:

1. **Place your TITLE tags below the <HEAD> tag.**

2. **Place 40 to 60 characters between the <TITLE> and </TITLE> tags (that includes spaces).**

3. **Put the keyword phrase you want to focus on for this page at the very beginning of the TITLE.**

   If you want, you can repeat the primary keywords once.

   Limit the number of two-letter words and very common words (known as *stop words*), such as *as, the,* and *a,* because the search engines ignore them.

Here is an example TITLE:

```
<TITLE>Rodent Racing Info. Rats, Mice, Gerbils, Stoats, all
            kinds of Rodent Racing</TITLE>
```

The TITLE and often the DESCRIPTION (explained in the next section) appear on the search results page. So your TITLE and DESCRIPTION should encourage people to visit your site.

The DESCRIPTION meta tag

Meta tags are special HTML tags that can be used to carry information, which can then be read by browsers or other programs. When search engines began, Webmasters included meta tags in their pages to make it easy for search engines to determine what the pages were about. Search engines also used these meta tags when deciding how to rank the page for different keywords.

The DESCRIPTION meta tag describes the Web page to the search engines. The search engines use this meta tag two ways:

✔ They read and index the text in the tag.

✔ In many cases, they use the text verbatim in the search results page. That is, if your Web page is returned in the search results page, the search engine grabs the text from the DESCRIPTION tag and places it under the text from the TITLE tag so the searcher can read your description.

In most cases, Google *doesn't* use the text from the DESCRIPTION meta tag in its search results page. Rather, Google grabs a block of text near where it found the search keywords on the page, and then uses that text in the results page.

Using the DESCRIPTION meta tag is important for the following reasons:

✔ Sometimes Google *does* use the DESCRIPTION you provide. If it can't find the keywords in the page (perhaps it found the page based on its TITLE tag or links pointing at the page rather than page content, for instance), it uses the DESCRIPTION.

✔ Google, and other search engines, do index the DESCRIPTION.

✔ Other search engines use the DESCRIPTION tag.

The DESCRIPTION meta tag is pretty important, so you should use it. Place the DESCRIPTION tag immediately below the TITLE tags and then create a nice keyworded description of up to 250 characters (again, including spaces). Here's an example:

```
<META NAME="description" CONTENT="Rodent Racing - Scores,
          Schedules, everything Rodent Racing. Whether
          you're into mouse racing, stoat racing, rats, or
          gerbils, our site provides everything you'll ever
          need to know about Rodent Racing and caring for
          your racers.">
```

It's okay to duplicate your most important keywords once, but don't overdo it, or you'll upset the search engines. Don't, for instance, do this:

```
<META NAME="description" CONTENT="Rodent Racing, Rodent
          Racing, Rodent Racing, Rodent Racing, Rodent
          Racing, Rodent Racing, Rodent Racing, Rodent
          Racing, Rodent Racing, Rodent Racing">
```

Overloading your DESCRIPTION (or any other page component) with the same keyword or keyword phrase is known as *spamming* (a term I hate, but hey, I don't make the rules), and trying such tricks may get your page penalized; rather than *help* your page's search engine position, it may actually cause search engines to omit it from their indexes.

Sometimes Web developers switch the attributes in the tag: `<META CONTENT= "your description goes here" NAME="description">` for instance, rather than `<META NAME="description" CONTENT="your description goes here">`. Make sure that your tags don't do the former because some search engines choke on such tags.

The KEYWORDS meta tag

The KEYWORDS meta tag was originally created as an indexing tool; a way for the page author to tell search engines what the page is about by listing, yep, keywords. Although quite important in the past, this meta tag isn't as important these days. Some search engines do use it, but many don't, and the most important search engine, Google, doesn't. Still, you might as well include the KEYWORDS meta tag. You do have a list of keywords, after all.

Don't worry too much about the tag — it's not worth spending a lot of time over. Here are a few points to consider:

- **Limit the tag to 10 to 12 words.** Originally, the KEYWORDS tag could be very large, up to 1,000 characters. These days many search engine observers are wary of appearing to be "spamming" the search engines by stuffing keywords into any page component, and so recommend that you use short KEYWORDS tags.

- **You can separate each keyword with a comma and a space.** However, you don't have to use both — you can have a comma and no space, or a space and no comma.

- **Make sure that most of the keywords in the tag are also in the body text.** Some search engines say that keywords in the tag should also appear in the Web page itself but as no major search system gives this tag significant weight, it's not critical anyway. Many people also use the KEYWORDS tag as a good place to stuff spelling mistakes that are commonly searched.

- **Don't use a lot of repetition.** You shouldn't do this, for instance: *Rodent Racing, Rodent Racing, Rodent Racing, Rodent Racing, Rodent Racing, Rodent Racing,* or even *Rodent Racing, Rodent Racing Scores, Rodent Racing, Gerbils, Rodent Racing Scores, Rodent Racing.* . . .

- **Some search engines are case sensitive, so it's probably a good idea to lowercase your keywords.** Some people say you should make the first letter of each word uppercase; others say it doesn't make any difference. (However, I'm really talking about "every *tiny* bit" counts here. Some of these KEYWORD issues are not going to make a huge amount of difference!)

- **Don't use the same** KEYWORD **tag in all your pages.** You could create a primary tag to use in your first page and then copy it to other pages and move terms around in the tag.

Here's an example of a well-constructed KEYWORD tag:

```
<META NAME="keywords" CONTENT="rodent racing, racing rodents,
             gerbils, mice, mose, raceing, mouse, rodent races,
             rat races, mouse races, stoat, stoat racing">
```

Other meta tags

What about other meta tags? Sometimes if you look at the source of a page, you see all sorts of meta tags, as shown in Figure 5-3. Meta tags are useful for various reasons, but from a search engine perspective, you can forget almost all of them. (And most meta tags really aren't of much use for any purpose.)

You've heard about DESCRIPTION and KEYWORDS meta tags, but also of relevance to search engine optimization are the REVISIT-AFTER and ROBOTS meta tags:

- ✔ REVISIT-AFTER is intended to tell search engines how often to reindex the page. Save the electrons; don't expect search engines to follow your instructions. Search engines reindex pages on their own schedules.

- ✔ ROBOTS is used to block search engines from indexing pages. (I discuss this topic in detail later in this chapter.) But many Web authors use it to *tell* search engines to index a page. Here's an example:

  ```
  <META NAME="robots" CONTENT="ALL">
  ```

  This tag is a waste of time. If a search engine finds your page and wants to index it, and hasn't been blocked from doing so, it will. And if it doesn't want to index a page, it won't. Telling the search engine to do so doesn't make a difference.

Here's a special Google meta tag that you can use a couple of ways. Here's one example:

```
<META NAME="googlebot" CONTENT="nosnippet">
```

This meta tag tells Google not to use the description *snippet,* the piece of information it grabs from within a Web page to use as the description; instead it will use the DESCRIPTION meta tag. Here's another example:

```
<META NAME="googlebot" CONTENT="noarchive">
```

This meta tag tells Google not to place a copy of the page into the cache. If you have an average corporate attorney on staff who doesn't like the idea of Google storing a copy of your company's information on its servers, you could tell Google not to. (By the way, it seems likely that Google's automatic caching feature breaks copyright law, though this is an issue that hasn't been tested yet.)

```
<meta name="resource-type" content="document">
<meta http-equiv="pragma" content="no-cache">
<meta name="revisit-after" content="1">
<meta name="classification" content="Arts and Crafts">
<meta name="description"
content="New York Alive! Photographs is an online gallery containing dozens of signed, original, custom-
printed black and white photographs of New York City, its landmarks, buildings, neighborhoods, people,
and places.  Buy original images for home or office direct from the photographers.">
<meta name="keywords"
content=" New York City, New York, New York NY, NYC, skyline, landmarks, buildings, Manhattan,
Brooklyn, neighborhood, neighbourhood, neighborhoods, neighbourhoods, photography, fine, fine art, art,
artist, artists, artistic, arts, photo, photographic, photographs, photograph, photographer, photographers,
pictures, black, black and white, white, images, imagery, image, gallery, galleries, virtual, online, on-line,
exhibits, exibits, exhibition, exhibitions, exhibit, contemporary, Central Park, Greenwich Village, Soho,
Wall Street, Statue of Liberty, Harlem, Washington Heights, Lower East Side, Ethnic, Empire State
Building, Flatiron, Flat Iron, Building, Chrysler, Brooklyn Bridge, Wall Street, New York Stock Exchange,
Chinatown, Little Italy, Yankees, people">
<meta name="robots" content="ALL">
<meta name="distribution" content="Global">
<meta name="rating" content="General">
<meta name="copyright" content="(c) Naomi Diamant, 2000. All rights reserved.">
<meta name="author" content="Abacus Consultants">
<meta http-equiv="reply-to" content="abacusconsultants@yahoo.com">
<meta name="language" content="English">
<meta name="doc-type" content="Public" ">
<meta name="doc-class" content="Completed">
<meta name="doc-rights" content="Copywritten Work">
```

Figure 5-3:
An example
of all sorts
of meta
tags you
generally
don't need.
I've bolded
the names
to make
them easier
to see.

These Google meta tags may work, but a number of users report that sometimes they don't.

Image ALT Text

You use the <IMG> tag to insert images into Web pages. This tag can include the ALT= attribute, which means *alternative* text. (For a page to comply with HTML 4.01 standards, you must include this attribute.) ALT text was originally text that was displayed if the browser viewing the page could not display images. These days, the ALT text is also used by programs that speak the page (for blind people), and in many browsers, the ALT text also appears in a little pop-up box when you hold your mouse over an image for a few moments.

ALT tags are also read by search engines. Why? Because these tags offer another clue about the content of the Web page. How much do ALT tags help? Almost not at all these days, because some Web designers have abused the technique by stuffing ALT attributes with tons of keywords. But using ALT tags can't hurt (assuming you *don't* stuff them with tons of keywords, but simply drop a few in here and there) and may even help push your page up a little in the search engine rankings.

You can place keywords in your ALT attributes like this:

```
<IMG SRC="rodent-racing-1.jpg" ALT="Rodent Racing - Ratty
         winners of our latest Rodent Racing event">
```

Flush the Flash animation

Using Flash animations sometimes makes sense, but usually it doesn't. Many Web designers place fancy Flash animations on their home pages just to make them look cool. But rarely do these animations serve any purpose beyond making site visitors wait a little longer to get into the site. Some search engines can now read and index Flash stuff (albeit not well), but generally Flash animations don't contain any useful text for indexing. So if you include Flash on your home page, the most important page on your site, the page is worthless from a search engine perspective.

Even if a page with Flash animation *does* appear in the search results — perhaps because you used the perfect TITLE tag — the search engine won't have much to work with. For example, in Figure 5-4, the search engine may grab the following text:

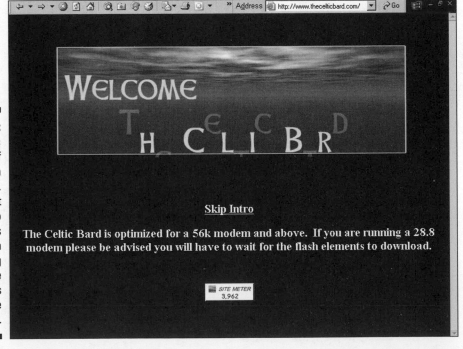

Figure 5-4: A classic example of a Flash animation. At least this site designer is honest in explaining that some site visitors will have to wait.

Skip Intro. The Celtic Bard is optimized for a 56k modem and above. If you are running a 28.8 modem please be advised you will have to wait for the Flash elements to download.

This text is probably not what you want the search engine to index.

Most Flash animations automatically forward the browser to the next page — the *real* home page — after they've finished running. If you do decide to include Flash, make sure that you include a clearly visible Skip Intro link somewhere on the page.

Don't embed text in images

Many sites use images heavily. The overuse of images is often the sign of an inexperienced Web designer, in particular one who is very familiar with graphic-design tools — perhaps a graphic artist who has accidentally run into some Web business. Such designers often create their entire pages in a graphic-design program, including the text, and then save images and insert them into the Web page.

The advantage of this approach is that it gives the designer much more control over the appearance of the page — and is often much faster — than using HTML to lay out a few images and real text. But this approach has significant drawbacks. Such pages transfer across the Internet much more slowly, and because the pages contain no real text, the search engines don't have anything to index. For example, the text in Figure 5-5 isn't real text; the text is part of one large image. This may be the perfect text to get you ranked highly for your most important keyword phrase, but because it's a picture and not real text, it won't do you any good.

Adding body text

You need text in your page. How much? More than a little, but not too much. Maybe 100 to 250 words are good. Don't get too hung up on these numbers, though. If you put an article in a page, and the article is 1,000 words, that's fine. But in general, something in the 100–250 word range is good.

That amount of content allows you to really define what the page is about and will help the search engine understand what the page is about.

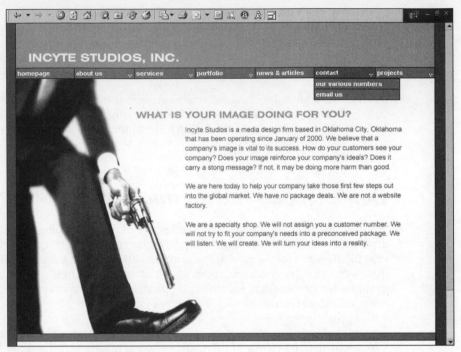

INCYTE STUDIOS, INC.

homepage | about us | services | portfolio | news & articles | contact | projects

our various numbers

email us

WHAT IS YOUR IMAGE DOING FOR YOU?

Incyte Studios is a media design firm based in Oklahoma City, Oklahoma that has been operating since January of 2000. We believe that a company's image is vital to its success. How do your customers see your company? Does your image reinforce your company's ideals? Does it carry a stong message? If not, it may be doing more harm than good.

We are here today to help your company take those first few steps out into the global market. We have no package deals. We are not a website factory.

We are a specialty shop. We will not assign you a customer number. We will not try to fit your company's needs into a preconceived package. We will listen. We will create. We will turn your ideas into a reality.

Figure 5-5:
This entire page is invisible to the search engines. It's made up of one large image and a JavaScript navigation tool.

Keep in mind that a Web site needs content in order to be noticed by the search engines. (For more on this topic, see Chapter 2.) If the site doesn't have much content for the search engine to read, the search engine will have trouble determining what the page is about and may not properly rank it. In effect, the page loses points in the contest for search engine ranking. Certainly keywords in content are not all there is to being ranked in the search engines; as you find out in Chapters 12 and 13, for instance, linking to the pages is also very important. But keywords in content are very significant, so the search engines have a natural bias toward Web sites with a large amount of content.

This bias toward content could be considered to be very unfair. After all, your site may be the perfect fit for a particular keyword search, even if you don't have much content in your site. In fact, inappropriate sites often appear in searches simply because they have a lot of pages, some of which have the right keywords.

Suppose that your Rodent Racing Web site is the only site in the world at which you can buy tickets for rodent-racing events. Your site doesn't provide a lot of content because rodent-racing fans simply want to be able to buy the tickets. However, because your site has less content than other sites, it is at a disadvantage to sites that have lots of content related to rodent racing, even if these other sites are not directly related to the subject.

You really can't do much to confront this problem, except to add more content! (Try to get into a habit of adding one page of quality content per day to your site.) You can find some ideas on where to get content in Chapter 8.

Creating headers: CSS vs. <H> tags

Back when the Web began, Web browsers defined what Web pages looked like. A designer could say, "I want body text here, and a heading there, and an address over there," but the designer had no way to define what the page actually looked like. The browser decided. The browser defined what a header looked like, what body text looked like, and so on. The page might appear one way in one browser program, and another way in a different program.

These days, designers have a great new tool available to them: Cascading Style Sheets (CSS). With CSS, designers can define exactly what each element should look like on a page.

Now, here's the problem. HTML has several tags that define headers: <H1>, <H2>, <H3>, and so on. These headers are useful in search engine optimization, because when you put keywords into a heading, you're saying to a search engine, "These keywords are so important that they appear in my heading text." Search engines pay more attention to them, weighing them more heavily than keywords in body text.

But many designers have given up on using the <H> tags and rely solely on CSS to make headers look the way they want them to. The plain <H> tags are often rather ugly when displayed in browsers, so designers don't like to use them. <H> tags also cause spacing issues; for example, an <H1> tag always includes a space above and below the text contained in the tag.

However, there's no reason why you can't use both <H> tags *and* Cascading Style Sheets. You can use style sheets two basic ways:

- ✔ Create a style class and then assign that class to the text you want to format.
- ✔ Define the style for a particular HTML tag.

Many designers do the former; they create a style class in the style sheet, like in the following example:

```
.headtext { font-family: Verdana, Arial, Helvetica, sans-
          serif; font-size: 16px; font-weight: bold; color:
          #3D3D3D }
```

Then they assign the style class to a piece of text like this:

```
<DIV CLASS="headtext">Rodent Racing for the New
           Millennium!</div>
```

In this example, the `headtext` class makes the text appear the way that the designer wants the headings to appear. But as far as the search engines are concerned, this is just normal body text.

A better way is to define the `<H>` tags in the style sheets, as in the following example:

```
H1 {
font-family: Verdana, Arial, Helvetica, sans-serif;
font-size: 16px;
font-weight: bold;
color: #3D3D3D
}
```

Now, whenever you add an `<H1>` tag to your pages, the browser reads the style sheet and knows exactly what font family, size, weight, and color you want. It's the best of both worlds — you get the appearance you want, and the search engines know it's an `<H1>` tag.

Text formatting

You can also tell the search engines that a particular word might be significant several other ways. If the text is in some way different from most of the other text in the page, the search engines may assume that it's been set off for some reason, that the Web designer has treated it differently because it *is* in some way different and more significant than the other words.

Here are a few things you can do to set your keywords apart from the other words on the page:

- ✔ Make the text **bold.**
- ✔ Make the text *italic.*
- ✔ Use title case for the phrase — that is, the first letter in each word is uppercase, and the other letters are lowercase.
- ✔ Put the keywords in bullet lists.

For each page, you have a particular keyword phrase in mind; this is the phrase for which you use the preceding techniques.

Another way to emphasize the text is to make a piece of text larger than the surrounding text (just make sure that you do this in a way that doesn't look tacky). For example, you can use <H> tags for headers, but also use slightly larger text at the beginning of a paragraph or for subheaders.

Creating links

Links in your pages serve several purposes for the searchbots:

- ✔ They help searchbots find other pages in your site.
- ✔ Keywords in links tell search engines about the pages that the links are pointing at.
- ✔ Keywords in links also tell the search engines about the page containing the links.

You need links into — and out of — your pages. You don't want *dangling* pages — pages with links into them but no links out. All your pages should be part of the navigation structure. But it's also a good idea to have links within the body text, too.

Search engines read link text not only for clues about the page being referred to, but also for hints about the page containing the link. I've seen situations in which links convinced a search engine that the page the links pointed to were relevant for the keywords used in the links, even though the page didn't contain those words. The classic example was an intentional manipulation of Google, late in 2003, to get it to display George Bush's bio (www.whitehouse. gov/president/gwbbio.html) when people searched for the term *miserable failure*. This was done by a small group of people using links in blog pages. Despite the fact that this page contains neither the word *miserable,* nor the word *failure,* and certainly not the term *miserable failure,* a few dozen links with the words *miserable failure* in the link text were enough to trick Google.

So when you're creating pages, create links on the page to other pages, and make sure that other pages within your site link back to the page you're creating, using the keywords that you have placed in your TITLE.

Don't create simple Click Here links or You'll Find More Information Here links. These words don't help you. Instead, create links like these:

> For more information, see our rodent-racing scores page.

> Our rodent-racing background page will provide you the information you're looking for.

> Visit our rat events and mouse events pages for more info.

Links are critical. Web developers have played all sorts of tricks with keywords — overloading TITLE tags, DESCRIPTION tags, ALT attributes, and so on — and all these tricks are well known to the search engines and don't do much anymore. The search engines constantly look for new ways to analyze and index pages, and link text is a good way for them to do that. In the same way that it's hard for a Web designer to manipulate a TITLE tag — because search engines can easily spot overloading — it's also difficult to manipulate link text.

In Chapters 12 and 13, you find out about another aspect of links, getting links from other sites to point back to yours.

Using other company and product names

Here's a common scenario. Many of your prospective visitors and customers are searching online for other companies' names, or the names of products produced or sold by other companies. Can you use these names in your pages?

Yes, but be careful how you use them. Many large companies are aware of this practice, and a number of lawsuits have been filed that relate to the use of keywords by companies other than the trademark owners. Here are a few examples:

- A law firm that deals with Internet domain disputes sued Web-design and Web-hosting firms for using its name, Oppedahl & Larson, in their KEYWORDS meta tags. These firms thought that merely having the words in the tags could bring traffic to their sites. The law firm won. Duh! (Didn't anyone ever tell you not to upset large law firms?)

- Playboy Enterprises sued Web sites that were using the terms *playboy* and *playmates* throughout their pages, site names, domain names, and meta tags to successfully boost their positions. Not surprisingly, Playboy won.

- Insituform Technologies Inc. sued National Envirotech Group after discovering that Envirotech was using its name in its meta tags. Envirotech lost. The judge felt that using the name in the meta tag without having any relevant information in the body of the pages was clearly a strategy for misdirecting people to the Envirotech site.

So, yes, you can get sued. But then again, you can get sued for anything. In some instances, the plaintiff loses. Playboy won against a number of sites, but lost against former playmate Terri Welles. Playboy didn't want her to use the terms *playboy* and *playmate* on her Web site, but she believed she had the right to, as a former Playboy Playmate. A judge agreed with her, possibly after being swayed by her charms during a visit to www.terriwelles.com.

The real point of this Terri Welles case is that nobody owns a word, a product name, or a company name. They merely own the right to use it in certain contexts. Thus, Playboy doesn't own the word *playboy* — you can say *playboy,* and you can use it in print. But Playboy does own the right to use it in certain contexts and to stop other people from using it in those same contexts.

If you use product and company names to mislead or misrepresent, you could be in trouble. But you can use the terms in a valid, non-fraudulent manner. For instance, you can have a product page in which you compare your products to another, named competitor. That's perfectly legal. No, I'm not a lawyer, but I'm perfectly willing to play one on TV given the opportunity. And I would bet that you won't be seeing the courts banning product comparisons on Web sites.

If you have information about competing products and companies on your pages, used in a valid manner, you can also include the keywords in the TITLE, DESCRIPTION, and KEYWORDS, as Terri Welles has done:

```
<META NAME="keywords" CONTENT="terri, welles, playmate,
        playboy, model, models, semi-nudity, naked,
        censored by editors, censored by editors, censored
        by editors, censored by editors, censored by
        editors, censored by editors, censored by editors,
        censored by editors">
```

And there's nuthin' Playboy can do about it.

To some degree, all this is a moot point, anyway. Just stuffing a competitor's name into the KEYWORDS tag won't do much for your search engine ranking, although some companies drop competitor's names into the body text in a totally irrelevant way. The bigger debate is the question of whether companies should be allowed to buy keywords related to competing products and companies. (See Chapter 15 for information on buying keywords.)

Preparing for local search

Some search engines are adding local search capabilities, and such tools will become much more important in the future. For instance, go to Google and search on the word pizza along with your zip code — pizza 80203, for instance (see Figure 5-6). Google searches for the word *pizza* in pages that also include that zip code.

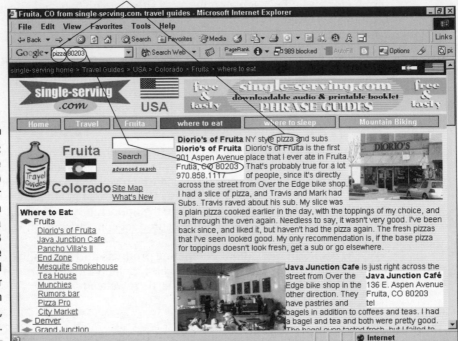

Figure 5-6:
This page
was the top
result for
the search
pizza
80203
because the
word and
number
appear in
the page,
near the top.

Such a search often brings up pages from Yellow Page sites and directories of various kinds, but if you have, for instance, a retail brick-and-mortar business, you should try to optimize your pages to give them a chance to appear in such searches. Here are a few ways to do that:

✔ Include your full address in your Web pages (street, city, state, and zip code). Although you could put the address in the footer, it's better to put it near the top of the page somewhere. (Remember the discussion of *prominence?* No? Then reread the "Check for keyword prominence" section, earlier in this chapter.)

✔ Find other reasons to mention the city and zip code in the body of your text and, if possible, in `<H>` tags; use bold font on some of the references, too.

✔ Include the full address in your `TITLE` and `DESCRIPTION` meta tags.

Creating navigation structures that search engines can read

Your navigation structure needs to be visible to the search engines. As I explain earlier in this chapter, some page components are simply invisible to search engines. For instance, a navigation structure created with JavaScript won't work for the search engines. If the only way to navigate your Web site is with the JavaScript navigation, you have a problem. The only pages the search engines will find are the ones with links pointing to them from other Web sites; the search engines won't be able to find their way around your site.

Here are a few tips for search-engine-friendly navigation:

✔ If you use JavaScript navigation, or some other technique that is invisible (which is covered in more detail in Chapter 6), make sure that you have a plain HTML navigation system, too, such as basic text links at the bottom of your pages.

✔ Even if your navigation structure is visible to search engines, you may want to have these bottom-of-page links as well. They're convenient for site visitors and provide another chance for the search engines to find your other pages.

Yet another reason for bottom-of-page, basic text navigation: If you have some kind of image-button navigation, you don't have any keywords in the navigation for the search engines to read.

✔ Add a site map page and link to it from your main navigation. It provides another way for search engines to find all your pages.

✔ Whenever possible, provide keywords in text links as part of the navigation structure.

Blocking searchbots

You may want to block particular pages, or even entire areas of your Web site, from being indexed. Here are a few examples of pages or areas you may want to block:

✔ Pages that are under construction.

✔ Pages with information that is mainly for internal use. (You should probably password-protect that area of the site, too.)

✔ Directories in which you store scripts and CSS style sheets.

Using the ROBOTS meta tag or the robots.txt file, you can tell the search engines to stay away. The meta tag looks like this:

```
<META NAME="robots" CONTENT="noindex, nofollow">
```

This tag does two things: noindex means don't index this page, and nofollow means don't follow the links from this page.

To block entire directories on your Web site, create a text file called robots. txt and place it in your site's root directory — which is the same directory as your home page. When a search engine comes to a site, it generally requests the robots.txt file first; it requests http://www.domainname. com/robots.txt.

The robots.txt file allows you to block specific search engines and allow others, although this is rarely done. In the file, you specify which search engine (user agent) you want to block and from which directories or files. Here's how:

```
User-agent: *
Disallow: /includes/
Disallow: /scripts/
Disallow: /info/scripts/
Disallow: /staff.html
```

Because this User-agent is set to *, all searchbots are blocked (if you know the name of a particular searchbot you want to block, replace the asterisk with that name) from www.domainname.com/includes/, www.domainname.com/ scripts/, www.domainname.com/info/scripts/ directories, and the www.domainname.com/staff.html file.

Be careful with your robots.txt file. If you make incomplete changes and end up with this:

```
User-agent: *
Disallow: /
```

then you've just blocked all the search engines from your entire site.

Chapter 6

Avoiding Things That Search Engines Hate

In This Chapter

▶ Working with frames and iframes

▶ Creating a readable navigation system

▶ Reducing page clutter

▶ Dealing with dynamic Web pages

*I*t is possible to look at your Web site in terms of its *search engine friendliness*. (Chapter 5 of this book does just that.) It is equally possible, however, to look at the flip side of the coin — things people often do that hurt their Web site's chances with search engines, in some cases even making their Web sites invisible to the search engines.

This tendency on the part of Web site owners to shoot themselves in the foot is very common. In fact, as you read through this chapter, you are quite likely to find things that you're doing that are hurting you. Paradoxically, serious problems are especially likely for sites created by mid- to large-size companies using sophisticated Web technologies.

Steering you clear of the major design potholes is what this chapter is all about. Guided by the principle First Do No Harm, the following sections show you the major things to avoid when setting up your Web site.

Dealing with Frames

Frames were very popular a few years ago, but they are much less so these days, I'm glad to say. A framed site is one in which the browser window is broken into two or more frames, each of which holds a Web page (as shown in Figure 6-1).

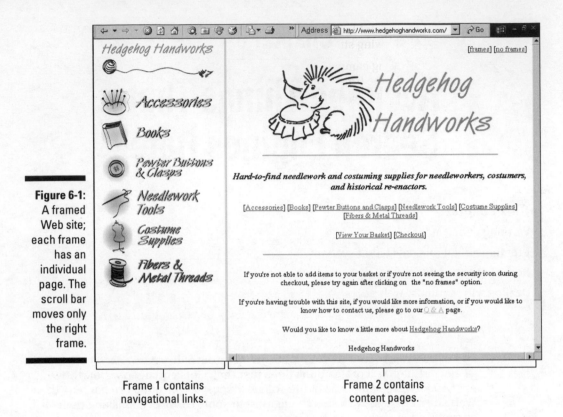

Figure 6-1:
A framed
Web site;
each frame
has an
individual
page. The
scroll bar
moves only
the right
frame.

Frame 1 contains
navigational links.

Frame 2 contains
content pages.

Frames cause a number of problems. Some browsers don't handle them well —
in fact, the first frame-enabled browsers weren't that enabled and often crashed
when loading frames. In addition, many designers created framed sites without
properly testing them. They built the sites on large, high-resolution screens, so
they didn't realize that they were creating sites that would be almost unusable
on small, low-resolution screens.

From a search engine perspective, frames create the following problems:

✔ Some search engines have trouble getting through the frame-definition
or frameset page to the actual Web pages.

✔ If the search engine gets through, it indexes individual pages, not frame-
sets. Each page is indexed separately, so pages that make sense only as
part of the frameset end up in the search engines as independent pages.
(Jump ahead to Figure 6-2 to see an example of a page, indexed by Google,
that belongs inside a frameset.)

✔ You can't point to a particular page in your site. This may be a problem in the following situations:

- Linking campaigns (see Chapters 12 and 13). Other sites can link to only the front of your site; they can't link to specific pages during link campaigns.

- Pay-per-click campaigns (see Chapter 15). If you're running a pay-per-click campaign, you can't link directly to a page related to a particular product.

- Placing your products in shopping directories (see Chapter 14). In this case, you need to be able to link to a particular product page.

Search engines index URLs — single pages, in other words. By definition, a framed site is a collection of URLs, and as such, search engines don't know how to properly index the pages. In fact, here's what the top search engine had to say when my technical editor, Micah Baldwin of Current Wisdom, asked about frames:

> "Google does support frames to the extent that it can. Frames can cause problems for search engines because frames don't correspond to the conceptual model of the Web. In this model, one page displays only one URL. Pages that use frames display several URLs (one for each frame) within a single page. If Google determines that a user's query matches the page as a whole, it will return the entire frameset. However, if the user's query matches an individual frame within the larger frameset, Google returns only the relevant frame. In this case, the entire frameset of the page will not appear."

Google often does just that, returning a page pulled out of its frame.

The HTML Nitty-Gritty of Frames

Here's an example of a frame-definition, or frameset, document:

```
<HTML>
<HEAD>
</HEAD>
<FRAMESET ROWS="110,*">
<FRAME SRC="navbar.htm">
<FRAME SRC="main.htm">
</FRAMESET>
</HTML>
```

This document describes how the frames should be created. It tells the browser to create two rows, one 110 pixels high and the other * high — that is, whatever room is left over. It also tells the browser to grab the `navbar.htm` document and place it in the first frame — the top row — and place `main.htm` into the bottom frame.

Most of the bigger search engines can find their way through the frameset to the `navbar.htm` and `main.htm` documents, so Google, for instance, indexes those documents. Some older systems may not, however, effectively making the site invisible to them.

But suppose the pages *are* indexed. Pages that were intended for use inside a frameset are individually indexed in the search engine. In Figure 6-2, you can see a page that I reached from Google — first (on the left) in the condition that I found it and then in the frameset it was designed for.

I found this page indexed in Google . . .   . . . it really belongs in this frame.

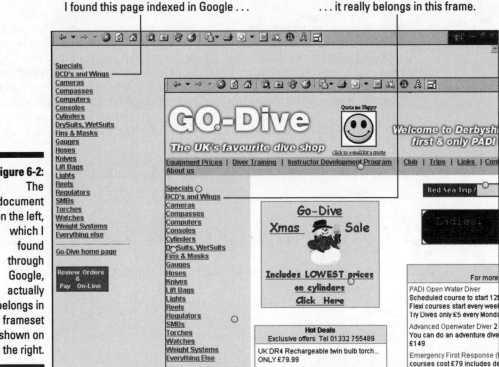

Figure 6-2:
The document on the left, which I found through Google, actually belongs in the frameset shown on the right.

This is not a pretty sight — or site, as it were. But you can work around this mess by doing the following:

- Provide information in the frame-definition document to help search engines index it.
- Ensure that all search engines can find their way through this page into the main site.
- Make sure that pages are open in the correct frameset (perhaps).

The next sections give you the details for following these strategies.

Providing search engines with the necessary information

The first thing you can do is to provide information in the frame-definition document for the search engines to index. First, add a TITLE and your meta tags, like this:

```
<HTML>
<HEAD>
<TITLE>Rodent Racing - Scores, Mouse Events, Rat Events,
         Gerbil Events - Everything about Rodent
         Racing</TITLE>
<meta name="description" content="Rodent Racing - Scores,
         Schedules, everything Rodent Racing. Whether
         you're into mouse racing, stoat racing, rats, or
         gerbils, our site provides everything you'll ever
         need to know about Rodent Racing and caring for
         your racers.">
<META NAME="keywords" CONTENT="Rodent Racing, Racing Rodents,
         Gerbils, Mice, Mouse, Rodent Races, Rat Races,
         Mouse Races, Stoat, Stoat Racing, Rats, Gerbils">
</HEAD>
<FRAMESET ROWS="110,*">
<FRAME SRC="navbar.htm">
<FRAME SRC="main.htm">
</FRAMESET>
</HTML>
```

Then, at the bottom of the FRAMESET, add <NOFRAMES> tags — <NOFRAMES> tags were originally designed to enclose text that would be displayed by a browser that couldn't handle frames — with <BODY> tags and information inside, like this:

```
<FRAMESET ROWS="110,*">
<FRAME SRC="navbar.htm">
<FRAME SRC="main.htm">
```

```
<NOFRAMES>
<BODY>
<H1>Rodent Racing - Everything You Ever Wanted to Know about
          Rodent Racing Events and the Rodent Racing
          Lifestyle</H1>
<P>[This site uses frames, so if you are reading this, your
          browser doesn't handle frames]</P>
<P>This is the world's top rodent-racing Web site. You won't
          find more information about the world's top
          rodent-racing events anywhere else ...[more info]
</BODY>
</NOFRAMES>
</FRAMESET>
</HTML>
```

The `<NOFRAMES></NOFRAMES>` tags were originally intended to display text for browsers that don't handle frames. Although few people still use such browsers, you can use the `NOFRAMES` tags to provide information to the search engines that they can index. For example, you can take the information from `main.htm` and place it into the `NOFRAMES` area. Provide 200 to 400 words of keyword-rich text to give the search engines something to work with. Make sure that the content between the `<NOFRAMES>` tags is about your site, and is descriptive and useful to visitors.

Google suggests that the `<NOFRAMES>` area should be for alternate content (though as every good editor knows, it probably means alternative), and says that . . .

"If you use wording such as 'This site requires the use of frames,' or 'Upgrade your browser,' instead of providing alternate content on your site, then you will exclude both search engines and people who have disabled frames on their browsers. For example, audio Web browsers, such as those used in automobiles and by the visually impaired, typically do not deal with such frames. You read more about the `<NOFRAMES>` tag in the HTML standard here at the following URL: `www.w3.org/TR/REC-html40/present/frames.html#h-16.4....`"

Unfortunately, many Web designers use the `NOFRAMES` tags as a convenient place to add keywords, even if the page is not a frame-definition document. For this reason, search engines may treat the text within the tags in one of three ways: ignore it if it's not within `FRAMESET` tags; downgrade it, awarding fewer points to text in a `FRAMESET`; or ignore it altogether.

Providing a navigation path

You can easily provide a navigation path in the `NOFRAMES` area. Simply add links in your text to other pages in the site. Include a simple text-link navigation system on the page and remember to link to your sitemap.

Remember also to do the following:

- Give *all* your pages unique <TITLE> and meta tags, as shown in Figure 6-3. Many designers don't bother to do this for pages in frames because browsers read only the TITLE in the frame-definition document. But search engines index these pages individually, not as part of a frameset, so they should all have this information.

- Give *all* your pages simple text navigation systems so that a search engine can find its way through your site.

You'll run into one problem using these links inside the pages. The links will work fine for people who arrive at the page directly through the search engines, and any link that simply points at another page will work fine in that situation or for someone who arrives at your home page and sees the pages in the frames. But any link that points at a frame-definition document rather than another page won't work properly (unless you use the fix I'm about to describe) if someone is viewing the page in a frame.

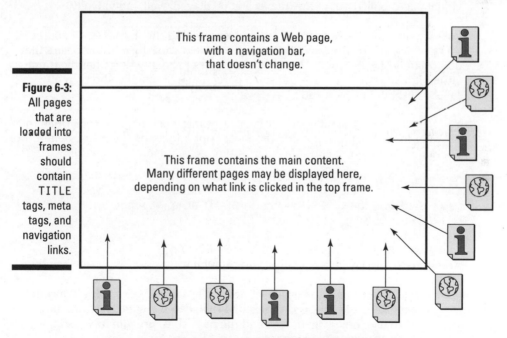

Figure 6-3: All pages that are loaded into frames should contain TITLE tags, meta tags, and navigation links.

This frame contains a Web page, with a navigation bar, that doesn't change.

This frame contains the main content. Many different pages may be displayed here, depending on what link is clicked in the top frame.

Pages loaded into frames should contain TITLEs, meta tags, and simple text navigation links to help the search engines index the pages and travel through the site.

Suppose that you have a link back to the frame-definition document for your home page. If someone is viewing one of your pages inside a frame, as you intended it to be viewed, and clicks the link, the frame definition loads the new frameset into the existing frameset. Now, rather than seeing, say, two frames, the visitor sees three frames — the two new frames are loaded into the current frame. To get around this problem, use the _top target, like this:

```
<a href="index.html" TARGET = "_top">Home</a>
```

This "breaks" the frames, opening the index.html document alone in the browser window.

Opening pages in a frameset

Given the way search engines work, pages in a Web site will be indexed individually. (Refer to Figure 6-3.) If you've created a site using frames (hey, it takes all kinds!), presumably you want the site displayed in frames. You don't want individual pages pulled out of the frames and displayed, well, individually.

You can use JavaScript to force the browser to load the frameset. Of course, this won't work for the small percentage of users working with browsers that don't handle JavaScript . . . but those browsers probably don't handle frames, either. It also won't work for the small percentage of people who turn off JavaScript; but hey, you can't have everything.

You have to place a small piece of JavaScript into each page so that when the browser loads the page, it reads the JavaScript and loads the frame-definition document. It's a simple little JavaScript that goes something like this:

```
<script language="javascript">
<!--
if (top == self) self.location.href = "index.html";
// -->
</script>
```

Admittedly, this JavaScript causes two problems:

- ✔ The browser loads the frameset defined in index.html, which may not include the page that was indexed in the search engine. Visitors may have to use the navigation to find the page that, presumably, had the content they were looking for.
- ✔ The Back button doesn't work correctly, because each time the browser sees the JavaScript, it loads the index.html file again.

Another option is to have a programmer create a customized script that loads the frame-definition document and drops the specific page into the correct frame. If you work for a company with a Web-development department, this is a real possibility.

The only really good fix is to not use frames in the first place! I've spent a lot of time on frames, for one purpose really: so that you can quickly fix a site that is using frames. But you shouldn't be building Web sites with frames. You may need to fix what someone else did or what you did in earlier, less knowledgeable, days. In general, though, frames are used far less today than they were five years ago — for good reason: They are an unnecessary nuisance. Sure, frames may be appropriate in a few instances, but the general rule is this: If you think it would be a good idea to build a Web site using frames, you're almost certainly wrong!

Handling iframes

The *iframe* is a special type of frame. This is an Internet Explorer feature and not something that is as common as normal frames. An iframe is an inline floating frame. It allows you to grab content from one page and drop it into another, in the same way you can grab an image and drop it into the page. The tag looks like this:

```
<iframe src ="page.html">
          </iframe>
```

It has similar problems to regular frames. In particular, some search engines don't see the content in the iframe, and the ones that do index it separately.

You can add a link within the <IFRAME> tag so that older searchbots will find the document, like this:

```
<iframe src="page.html"><a href="page.html" target="_blank">
          Click here for more Rodent Racing information if
          your browser doesn't display content in this
          internal frame.</a></iframe>
```

You can also use the JavaScript discussed in the preceding section to load your home page and to provide a link at the bottom of the iframe content that people can use to load your home page.

Fixing Invisible Navigation Systems

Navigation systems that never show up on search engines' radar screens are a common problem, probably even more common than the frames problem I cover in the previous section. Fortunately, you can deal with a navigation system problem very easily.

Many Web sites use navigation systems that are invisible to search engines. In Chapter 5, I explain the difference between *browser-side* and *server-side* processes, and this issue is related. A Web page is compiled in two places — on the server and in the browser. If the navigation system is created in the browser, it's probably not visible to a search engine.

Examples of such systems include those created using

✔ Java applets

✔ JavaScripts

✔ Macromedia Flash

How can you tell if your navigation has this problem? If you created the pages yourself, you probably know how you built the navigation, although you may be using an authoring tool that did it all for you. So if that's the case, or if you're examining a site that was built by someone else, here are a few ways to figure out how the navigation is built:

✔ If navigation is created with a Java applet, when the page loads you probably see a gray box where the navigation sits for a moment or two, with a message such as *Loading Java Applet*.

✔ Look in the page's source code and see how its navigation is created.

✔ Turn off the display of JavaScript and other active scripting and then reload the page to see if the navigation is still there. I explain how to do this under "Turning off scripting and Java," a little later in this chapter.

Looking at the source code

Take a look at the source code of the document to see how it's created. Open the raw HTML file or choose View⇨Source from the browser's main menu, and then dig through the file looking for the navigation.

If the page is large and complex, or if your HTML skills are correspondingly small and simple, you may want to try the technique under "Turning off scripting and Java."

Here's an example. Suppose that you find the following code where the navigation should be:

```
<applet code="MenuApplet" width="160" height="400"
        archive="http://www.yourdomain.com/menu.jar">
```

This is a navigation system created with a Java applet. Search engines don't read applet files, so they won't see the navigation. Here's another example:

```
<script type="javascript" src="/menu/menu.js"></script>
```

This one is a navigation tool created with JavaScript. Search engines have difficulty reading JavaScript, so they won't see this navigation system either.

Here's an example of a Flash-based navigation system (links in Flash navigation systems can't be read by many search engines):

```
<embed src="flash/rcbank_nav02.swf" quality=high pluginspage=
       "http://www.macromedia.com/shockwave/download/inde
       x.cgi?P1_Prod_Version=ShockwaveFlash" type=
       "application/x-shockwave-flash" width="750"
       height="84"></embed>
```

The preceding examples are pretty easy to identify. The script calls a Java applet or JavaScript, and you know that the searchbots don't read these, so they won't see the navigation. Here's another form that can create a problem:

```
<a href="javascript:void(0)" onclick="Javascript:window.open
         ('http://yourdomain.com/rat-race/','Rat Race','
         width=550,height=600,left=20,top=20,screenX=0,
         screenY=100,resizable=yes,scrollbars=yes')"
         onMouseOut="MM_swapImgRestore()"onMouseOver="MM_sw
         apImage('rat_race','','images/rat_race2.gif',1)">
         <img src="images/rat_race1.gif" alt="Living and
         Shopping" name="rat_race"></a>
```

This link uses JavaScript *event handlers* to do several things when triggered by particular events:

- ✔ onclick: Runs when someone (guess!) clicks the link. This opens a new window and places the referenced document in that window.

- ✔ onMouseOver: Runs when someone points at the link. In this case, it runs the MM_swapImage function, which changes the image file used for this navigation button.

- ✔ onMouseOut: Runs when the mouse is moved away from the link. In this case, it runs the MM_swapImgRestore function, presumably to display the original image.

This is a real link, but it won't work if JavaScript is turned off because the URL normally goes in the href= attribute of the anchor tag (the <A> tag); href= is disabled in this link because it uses JavaScript to do all the work. Search engines won't follow a link like this.

Turning off scripting and Java

You can also turn off scripting and Java in the browser, and then look at the pages. If the navigation has simply disappeared, or if it's there but doesn't work anymore, you've got a problem.

Here's how to disable the settings in Internet Explorer (other browsers are similar):

1. **Choose Tools⇨Internet Options from the main menu.**

   The Internet Options dialog box appears.

2. **Click the Security tab.**

   The Security options appear, as shown in Figure 6-4.

3. **Click the Custom Level button to open the Security Settings dialog box.**

4. **Select the Microsoft VM⇨Java Permissions⇨Disable Java option button.**

   This stops Java applets from running.

5. **Select the Active Scripting⇨Disable option button, as shown in Figure 6-5.**

   This disables JavaScripts and other similar scripts.

6. **Click the OK button, answer Yes in the message box, and click the OK button again in the Internet Options dialog box.**

Now reload the page that you want to check — use the Reload or Refresh button — and see if the navigation is still there. If it is, try to use it. Does it still work? If the navigation has gone or if it's broken, this is something that the search engines will have a problem with. (Figures 6-6 and 6-7 show you how effective this little trick can be. Navigation bar? Now you see it, now you don't.)

When you reload the page, you may notice that other page components disappear, if they're created with scripts. You may find that other things important for the search engines have gone, too.

Disabling scripting and Java doesn't stop Flash from working, and unfortunately there is no simple, quick, and temporary way to stop Flash from working in Internet Explorer. Some other browsers do have such a tool, though. Your best option for Internet Explorer is to install some other kind of blocking software, such as PopUpCop (www.popupcop.com) or jTFlashManager (www.jtedley.com/jtflashmanager).

Fixing the problem

If you want, you can continue to use these invisible menus and navigation tools. They can be attractive and effective. The search engines won't see them, but that's okay because you can add a secondary form of navigation, one that duplicates the top navigation.

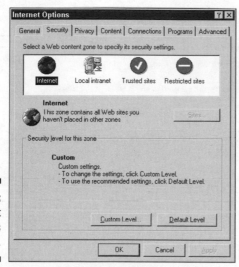

Figure 6-4:
The Internet
Options
dialog box.

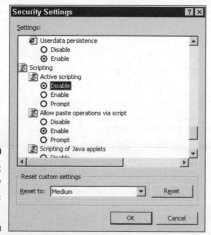

Figure 6-5:
The Security
Settings
dialog box.

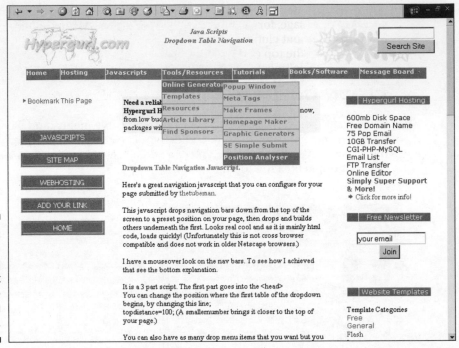

Figure 6-6:
This page
has a
JavaScript
naviga-
tion menu
bar. . . .

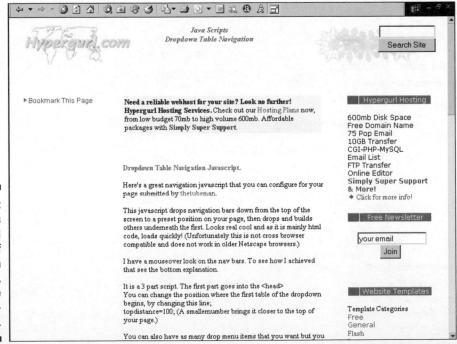

Figure 6-7:
. . . oops, it's
gone. I
turned off
scripting in
the browser,
and the
menu dis-
appeared.

You can duplicate the navigation structure by using simple text links at the bottom of the page, for instance. If you have long pages or extremely cluttered HTML (I talk about clutter in the next section), you may want to place small text links near the top of the page to make sure search engines get to them, perhaps in the leftmost table column. (Table columns on the right are lower down on the page as far as the HTML is concerned, and search engines read the text in the HTML instead of viewing the page as people do.)

Reducing the Clutter in Your Web Pages

Simple is good; cluttered is bad. The more cluttered your pages, the more work it is for search engines to dig through them. What do I mean by clutter? I'm referring to everything in a Web page that is used to create the page but that is not actual page content.

For instance, one of my clients had a very cluttered site. The HTML source document for the home page had 21,414 characters, of which 19,418 were characters other than spaces. However, the home page did not contain a lot of text: 1,196 characters, not including the spaces between the words.

So if 1,196 characters were used to create the words on the page, what were the other 18,222 characters used for? Things like this:

- JavaScripts: 4,251 characters
- JavaScript event handlers on links: 1,822 characters
- The top navigation bar: 6,018 characters
- Text used to embed a Flash animation near the top of the page: 808 characters

The rest is the normal clutter that you always have in HTML: tags used to format text, create tables, and so on. The problem with this page was that a search engine had to read 17,127 characters (18,701 including spaces) *before it ever reached the page content.* Of course, the page did not have much content, and what was there was hidden away below all that HTML.

This clutter above the page content means that some search engines may not reach it. Fortunately, you can use some simple methods to unclutter this and other pages. (There were some very obvious ways to remove around 11,000 text characters without much effort — so obvious that I'll soon have you doing it after you've read the next few sections.)

Use external JavaScripts

You don't need to put JavaScripts inside a page. JavaScripts generally should be placed in an *external file* — a tag in the Web page "calls" a script that is pulled from another file on the Web server — for various reasons:

- ✔ **They're actually safer outside the HTML file.** By that, I mean they're less likely to be damaged while making changes to the HTML.

- ✔ **They're easier to manage externally.** Why not have a nice library of all the scripts in your site in one directory?

- ✔ **The download time is slightly less.** If you use the same script in multiple pages, the browser downloads the script once and caches it.

- ✔ **They're easier to reuse.** You don't need to copy scripts from one page to another and fix all the pages when you have to make a change to the script. Just store the script externally and change the external file to automatically change the script in any number of pages.

- ✔ **Doing so removes clutter from your pages!**

Creating external JavaScript files is easy. Simply take the text between the <SCRIPT></SCRIPT> tags, save it in a text editor, and save that file on your Web server (as a .js file — mouseover_script.js, for instance).

Then add an src= attribute to your <SCRIPT> tag to refer to the external file, like this:

```
<script language="JavaScript" type="text/javascript"
        src="/scripts/mouseover_script.js"></script>
```

In this example, placing scripts in external files would have removed over 20 percent of the text characters from the file.

Use document.write to remove problem code

If you have a complicated top navigation bar — one with text colors in the main bar that change when you point at a menu and/or drop-down lists, also with changing colors — you can easily get code character counts peaking at 5,000 to 6,000 characters. That's a lot of characters! Add some Flash animation, and you're probably up to 7,000 characters, which can easily end up being a significant portion of the overall code for the page. You can easily remove all this clutter by using JavaScript to write the text into the page. Here's how:

1. **In an external text file, type this text:**

```
<!--
document.write("")
//-->
```

2. **Grab the entire code you want to remove from the HTML page and then paste it between the following quotation marks:**

```
document.write("place code here")
```

3. **Save this file and place it on your Web server.**

4. **Call the file from the HTML page by adding an** `src=` **attribute to your** `<SCRIPT>` **tag to refer to the external file, like this:**

```
<script language="JavaScript" src="/scripts/navbar.js"
        type="text/javascript"></script>
```

Of course, if you remove the navigation — remember, the searchbots won't read these JavaScripts, so they won't see the navigation — from the page, you won't have navigation that the search engines can follow. So remember to add simple text navigation somewhere else on the page (maybe at the bottom, now that the page is much smaller). Simple text navigation takes up much less room than a complex navigation bar.

Use external CSS files

If you can stick JavaScript stuff into an external file, it shouldn't surprise you that you can do the same thing — drop stuff into a file that is then referred to in the HTML file proper — with Cascading Style Sheets (CSS) information. For reasons that are unclear to me, many designers place CSS information directly into the page, despite the fact that the ideal use of a style sheet is *external.* Just think about it — one of the basic ideas behind style sheets is to allow you to make formatting changes to an entire site very quickly. If you want to change the size of the body text or the color of the heading text, you make one small change in the CSS file, and it affects the whole site immediately. If you have your CSS information in each page, though, you have to change each and every page. Rather defeats the object of Cascading Style Sheets, doesn't it?

Here's how to remove CSS information from the main block of HTML code. Simply place the targeted text in an external file — everything between and including the `<STYLE></STYLE>` tags — and then *call* the file in your HTML pages by using the `<LINK>` tag, like this:

```
<link rel="stylesheet" href="site.css" type="text/css">
```

Move image maps to the bottom of the page

Image maps (described in detail later in the chapter) are images that contain multiple links. One way to clean up clutter in a page is to move the code that defines the links to the bottom of the Web page, right before the </BODY> tag. Doing so doesn't remove the clutter from the page, but moves the clutter to the end of the page where it won't get between the top of the page and the page content, making it more likely that the search engines will reach the content.

Don't copy and paste from MS Word

That's right, don't copy text directly from Microsoft Word and drop it into a Web page. You'll end up with *all sorts* of formatting clutter in your page!

Here's one way to get around this problem:

1. **Save the file as an HTML file.**

   Word provides various options to do this, but you want to use the simplest: Web Page (Filtered).

2. **In your HTML-authoring program, look for a Word-cleaning tool!**

   Word has such a bad reputation that HTML programs are now starting to add tools to help you clean the text before you use it. Dreamweaver has such a thing, and even Microsoft's own HTML-authoring tool, FrontPage, has one (it's in the Optimize HTML dialog box, on the Options menu).

Managing Dynamic Web Pages

Chapter 5 explains how your standard, meat-and-potatoes Web page gets assembled in your browser so that you, the surfer, can actually see it. But you can assemble a Web page more than one way. For example, the process can go like this:

1. The Web browser requests a Web page.

2. The Web server sends a message to a database program requesting the page.

3. The database program reads the URL to see exactly what is requested, compiles the page, and sends it to the server.

4. The server reads any instructions inside the page.

5. The server compiles the page, adding information specified in SSIs (server side includes) or scripts.

6. The server sends the file to the browser.

Pages pulled from databases are known as *dynamic pages,* as opposed to the normal *static pages* that don't come from the database. They're dynamic because they're created *on the fly,* when requested. The page doesn't exist until a browser requests it, at which point the data is grabbed from a database and put together with a CGI, an ASP, or a PHP program, for instance, or one of the many content-management systems (such as BroadVision, Ektron CMS, or ATG Dynamo).

Unfortunately, dynamic pages can create problems. Even the best search engines sometimes don't read them. Of course, a Web page is a Web page, whether created on the fly or days (or months) beforehand. After the searchbot receives the page, the page is already complete. So why don't search engines always read dynamic pages? Because search engines don't want to read them (or their programmers don't want them to, that is). Of course, they *can* read dynamic pages. Again, a page is a page.

The search engine programmers have learned that dynamic pages are often problem pages. Here are a few of the problems searchbots can run into reading dynamic pages:

✔ Dynamic pages often have only minor changes in them. A searchbot reading these pages may end up with hundreds of pages that are almost exactly the same, with nothing more than minor differences to distinguish one from the other.

✔ The search engines are concerned that databased pages might change frequently, making search results inaccurate.

✔ Searchbots sometimes get stuck in the dynamic system, going from page to page to page among tens of thousands of pages. On occasion, this happens when a Web programmer hasn't properly written the link code, and the database continually feeds data to the search engine, even crashing your server.

✔ Hitting a database for thousands of pages can slow down the server, so searchbots often avoid getting into situations in which that is likely to happen.

✔ Sometimes URLs can change (I talk about *session IDs* in a moment), so even if the search engine does index the page, the next time someone tries to get there, it'll be gone; and search engines don't want to index dead links.

Finding out if your dynamic site is scaring off search engines

You can often tell if search engines are likely to omit your pages just by looking at the URL. Go deep into the site; if it's a product catalog, for instance, go to the furthest subcategory you can find. Then look at the URL. Suppose that you have a URL like this:

```
http://www.yourdomain.edu/rodent-racing-scores/march/
           index.php
```

This is a normal URL that should have few problems. It's a static page — or at least looks like a static page, which is what counts. Compare this URL with the next one:

```
http://www.yourdomain.edu/rodent-racing/scores.php?prg=1
```

This filename ends with ?prg=1. This is almost certainly a databased dynamic page; ?prg=1 is a *parameter* that is being sent to the server to let it know what information is needed for the Web page. This URL is probably okay, especially for Google, although a few search engines may not like it. Now look at the following URL:

```
http://yourdomain.com/products/index.html?&DID=18&CATID=
           13&ObjectGroup_ID=79
```

This URL is worse. It contains three parameters: DID=18, CATID=13, and ObjectGroup_ID=79. Three parameters are too much, and Google probably won't index this page. This is a real URL from one of my clients' sites (I changed the domain name, of course), and Google does not index this page.

If you have a *clean* URL with no parameters, the search engines should be able to get to it. If you have a single parameter, it's probably okay for the major search engines, though not necessarily for older systems. If you have two parameters, it may be a problem, or it may not, although two parameters are more likely to be a problem than a single parameter. Three parameters are almost certainly a problem.

You can also find out if a page in your site is indexed by using the following techniques:

✔ If you have the Google Toolbar, open the page you want to check and then click the i button and select Cached Snapshot of Page. Or go to Google and type cache: *YourURL*, where *YourURL* is the URL of the site you're interested in. If Google displays a cached page, it's there, of course. If Google doesn't display it, move to the next technique. (For more on the Google Toolbar — including where to download it from — see Chapter 1.)

✔ Go to Google and type the URL of the page into the text box and click Search. If the page is in the index, Google displays some information about it.

✔ Use similar techniques with other search engines if you want to check them for your page. Take a look at their help pages for more information.

Fixing your dynamic Web page problem

So, how do you get search engines to take a look at your state-of-the-art dynamic Web site? Here are a few ideas:

✔ **Find out if the database program has a built-in way to create static HTML.** Some e-commerce systems, for instance, will spit out a static copy of their catalog pages, which is intended for search engines. When visitors click a Buy button, they're taken back into the dynamic system.

✔ **Modify URLs so they don't look like they're pointing to dynamic pages.** You can often help fix the problem by removing characters such as ?, #, !, *, %, and & and reducing the number of parameters to one. Talk with the programmer who is responsible for the database system for the specifics.

✔ **Use a URL rewrite trick — a technique for changing the way URLs look.** Different servers have different tools available; mod_rewrite, for instance, is a tool used by the Apache Web server (a very popular system). *Rewriting* is a system whereby the server can convert fake URLs into real URLs. The server might see, for instance, a request for a page at

```
http://yourdomain.com/showprod/20121.html
```

The server knows that this page doesn't exist and that it really refers to the following URL:

```
http://yourdomain.com/ showprod.cfm?&DID=7&User_ID=
        2382175&st=6642&st2=45931500&st3=
        -43564544&topcat_id=20018&catid=
        20071&objectgroup_id=20121.
```

In other words, this technique allows you to use what appear to be static URLs, yet still grab pages from a database. This is complicated stuff, so if your server administrator doesn't understand it, it may take him or her a few days to figure it all out.

✔ **Find out if the programmer can create static pages from the database.** Rather than creating a single Web page each time it's requested, the database could "spit out" the entire site periodically — each night for instance, or when the database is updated — creating static pages with normal URLs.

✔ **You can get your information into some search engines by using an XML feed (often known as a *trusted feed*).** However, note that if you use a trusted feed, you'll be charged for every click to your site — and even then, it wouldn't get you anywhere with Google, the world's most popular search engine, because Google does not have this service. See Chapter 15 for more information.

✔ **You can get pages into search engines by using a paid-inclusion program.** (See Chapter 15.) Paid inclusion can be expensive (around $150 per page for several of the top search engines), and Google, the most important search engine, doesn't offer this service.

Want to find out more about URL rewriting? Here are a couple of places to look:

✔ www.asp101.com/articles/wayne/extendingnames

✔ httpd.apache.org/docs/mod/mod_rewrite.html

Using Session IDs in URLs

Just as dynamic Web pages can throw a monkey wrench into the search engine machinery, session IDs can make search engine life equally interesting. A *session ID* identifies a particular person visiting the site at a particular time, which enables the server to track what pages the visitor looks at and what actions the visitor takes during the session. If you request a page from a Web site — by clicking a link on a Web page, for instance — the Web server that has the page sends it to your browser. Then if you request another page, the server sends that page, too, but the server doesn't know that you are the same person. If the server needs to know who you are, it needs a way to identify you each time you request a page. It does that by using session IDs.

Session IDs are used for a variety of reasons, but the main purpose is to allow Web developers to create various types of interactive sites. For instance, if the developers have created a secure environment, they may want to force visitors to go through the home page first. Or the developers may want a way to pick up a session where it left off. By setting cookies on the visitor's computer containing the session ID, the developers can see where the visitor was in the site at the end of the visitor's last session. (A *cookie* is a text file containing information that can be read only by the server that set the cookie.)

Session IDs are common when running a software application that has any kind of security (such as requiring a login), or needs to store variables, or wants to defeat the browser cache — that is, ensure that the browser always displays information from the server, never from its own cache. Shopping cart systems typically use session IDs — that's how the system can allow you to place an item in the shopping cart and then go away and continue shopping. It *recognizes* you based on your session ID.

Session IDs can be created in two ways:

- ✔ They can be stored in cookies.
- ✔ They can be displayed in the URL itself.

Some systems are set up to store the session ID in a cookie but then use a URL session ID if the user's browser is set to not accept cookies. (Relatively few browsers, perhaps a percent or two, don't accept cookies.) Here's an example of a URL containing a session ID:

```
http://yourdomain.com/index.jsp;jsessionid=
          07D3CCD4D9A6A9F3CF9CAD4F9A728F44
```

The `07D3CCD4D9A6A9F3CF9CAD4F9A728F44` piece of the URL is the unique identifier assigned to the session.

If a search engine recognizes a URL as including a session ID, it probably won't read the referenced page because the server can handle a session ID two different ways when the searchbot returns. Each time the searchbot returns to your site, the session ID will have expired, so the server could do either of the following:

- ✔ **Display an error page, rather than the indexed page, or perhaps the site's default page (generally the home page).** In other words, the search engine has indexed a page that won't be there if someone clicks the link in the search results page. This is admittedly less common than the next server behavior.

- ✔ **Assign a new session ID.** The URL that the searchbot originally used has expired, so the server replaces the ID with another one, changing the URL. So the spider could be fed multiple URLs for the same page.

Even if the searchbot does read the referenced page (and sometimes they do), it probably won't index it or won't index much of your site. Webmasters sometimes complain that a search engine entered their site, requested the same page over and over, and left without indexing most of the site. The searchbot simply got confused and left. Or sometimes the search engine doesn't recognize a session ID in a URL — one of my clients has hundreds of URLs indexed by Google, but because they are all long-expired session IDs, they all point to the site's main page.

Dealing with session IDs is like a magic trick. Sites that were invisible to search engines suddenly become visible! One site owner in a search engine discussion group described how his site had never had more than six pages indexed by Google, yet within a week of removing session IDs, Google had indexed over 600 pages.

When sites are run through URLs with session IDs, you can do various things, as described in the following list:

- ✔ **Instead of using session IDs in the URL, store session information in a cookie on the user's computer.** Each time a page is requested, the server can check the cookie to see if session information is stored there. (Few people change their browser settings to block cookies.) However, the server shouldn't *require* cookies, or you could run into further problems (as you find out in a moment).

- ✔ **Get your programmer to omit session IDs if the device requesting a Web page from the server is a searchbot.** The server will deliver the same page to the searchbot but won't assign a session ID, so the searchbot can travel throughout the site without using session IDs. (Every device requesting a page from a Web server identifies itself, so it's possible for a programmer to send different pages according to the requestor — something I talk more about in Chapter 7.) This is known as *User-Agent delivery* (User-Agent refers to the device — browser, searchbot, or some other kind program — that is requesting a page).

The above User-Agent method does have one potential problem. It's a technique sometimes known as *cloaking* — where a server sends one page to the search engines and another to real site visitors. Search engines generally don't like cloaking because Web designers often try to trick the search engines by providing different content from what the site visitor sees. Of course, in the context of using the technique to avoid the session-ID problem, that is not the intent; it's a way to show the *same* content that the site visitor sees, so it isn't true cloaking. However, the (slight) danger is that the search engines may view it as cloaking if they discover what is happening. For more on cloaking, see Chapter 7.

Examining Cookie-Based Navigation

Cookies — the small text files that a Web server can store on a site visitor's hard drive — can often prove as indigestible to search engines as dynamic Web pages and session IDs. Imagine this scenario: You visit a site that is using cookies, and at some point, the server decides to store a cookie. It sends the information to your browser, and the browser duly creates a text file, which it then stores on your computer's hard drive. This text file might contain a session ID (as discussed in the preceding section) or something else. Systems that remember who you are so you don't have to log in each time you visit the site are using cookies to do this.

Cookies are sometimes used for navigation purposes. For instance, you may have seen *crumb trails,* a series of links showing where you have been as you travel through the site. Crumb trails look something like this:

```
Home->Rodents->Rats->Racing
```

This is generally information being stored in a cookie and is read each time you load a new page. Or the server may read the cookie to determine how many times you've visited the site or what you did the last time you were on the site, and direct you to a particular page based on that information.

If you're using Internet Explorer on Microsoft Windows, follow these steps to see what these cookie files look like:

1. **Choose Tools⇨Internet Options from the main menu.**

   The Internet Options dialog box appears.

2. **In the Internet Options dialog box, make sure that the General tab is selected.**

3. **Click the Settings button in the Temporary Internet Files area.**

   The Settings dialog box appears.

4. **In the Settings dialog box, click the View Files button.**

   A Windows Explorer window opens, displaying the directory containing your temporary files, including cookies. The files are named `Cookies:` *username@domainname*`.com`. For instance, when I visited the nokiausa. com Web site, the server created a cookie called `Cookie:peter kent@ nokiausa.com`.

5. **Double-click any of these cookie files to view the file's contents; a warning message appears, but ignore it and click Yes.**

   The cookie opens in Notepad.

Here are the contents of the cookie that was set by nokiausa.com; this cookie contains a session ID:

```
session_idA_da6Bj6pwoLg=_nokiausa.com/_1536_1240627200_
          30394925_36557520_29597255_*
```

There's nothing wrong with using cookies, *unless* they're *required* in order to navigate through your site. A server can be set up to simply refuse to send a Web page to a site visitor if the visitor's browser doesn't accept cookies. That's a problem for several reasons:

- ✔ A few browsers simply don't accept cookies.

- ✔ A small number of people have changed their browser settings to refuse to accept cookies.

- ✔ Searchbots can't accept cookies.

If your Web site *demands* the use of cookies, you won't get indexed. That's all there is to it! The searchbot will request a page, your server will try to set a cookie, and the searchbot won't be able to accept it. The server won't send the page, so the searchbot won't index it.

How can you check to see if your site has this problem? Change your browser's cookies setting and see if you can travel through the Web site. Here's how (for Internet Explorer):

1. **Choose Tools⇨Internet Options from the main menu.**

   The Internet Options dialog box appears.

2. **In the Internet Options dialog box, click the Privacy tab.**

3. **On the Privacy tab, click the Advanced button.**

   The Advanced Privacy Settings dialog box appears, as shown in Figure 6-8.

4. **Select the Override Automatic Cookie Handling check box — if it's not already selected.**

5. **Select both of the Prompt option buttons.**

   You want to get prompts from both first-party cookies and third-party cookies. I recommend that you select Prompt rather than Block to make it easier to test your site. Now each time a server tries to set a cookie, you see a warning box, and you can accept or block the cookie at will.

6. **Click OK to close the Advanced Privacy Settings dialog box.**

7. **In the Internet Options dialog box, click the General tab.**

8. **On the General tab, click the Delete Cookies button. Note that some sites won't recognize you when you revisit them, until you log in again and they reset their cookies.**

9. **Click the OK button in the confirmation-message box.**

10. **Click the OK button to close the dialog box.**

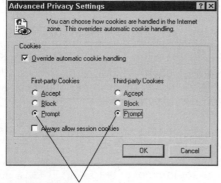

Figure 6-8:
The
Advanced
Privacy
Settings
dialog box.

Select these two option buttons.

Now go to your Web site and see what happens. Each time the site tries to set a cookie, you see a message box, as shown in Figure 6-9. Block the cookie and then see if you can still travel around the site. If you can't, the searchbots can't navigate it either.

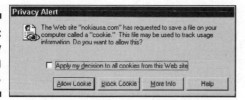

Figure 6-9:
The Privacy
Alert dialog
box.

How do you fix this problem?

✔ **Don't require cookies.** Ask your site programmers to find some other way to handle what you're doing with cookies, or do without the fancy navigation trick.

✔ **As with session IDs, you can use a User-Agent script that treats search-bots differently.** If the server sees a normal visitor, it requires cookies; if it's a searchbot, it doesn't.

Fixing Bits and Pieces

Forwarded pages, image maps, and special characters can also cause problems for search engines. The next few sections take a quick look.

Forwarded pages

Search engines don't want to index pages that automatically forward to other pages. You've undoubtedly seen pages telling you that something has moved to another location and that you can click a link or wait a few seconds for the page to automatically forward the browser to another page. This is often done with a REFRESH meta tag, like this:

```
<meta http-equiv="refresh" content="0;
          url=http://yourdomain.com">
```

This meta tag forwards the browser immediately to yourdomain.com. Quite reasonably, search engines don't like these pages. Why index a page that doesn't contain information but forwards visitors to the page *with* the information? Why not index the target page? That's just what search engines do. If you use the REFRESH meta tag, you can expect search engines to ignore the page (unless it's a very slow refresh rate, over ten seconds, which is specified by the number immediately after content=).

Image maps

An image map is an image that has multiple links. You might create the image like this:

```
<img name="main" src="images/main.gif" usemap="#m_main">
```

The usemap= parameter refers to the map instructions. You can create the information defining the hotspots on the image — the individual links — by using a <MAP> tag, like this:

```
<map name="m_main">
<area shape="rect" coords="238,159,350,183"
          href="page1.html">
<area shape="rect" coords="204,189,387,214" href="
          page2.html">
<area shape="rect" coords="207,245,387,343" href="
          page3.html">
<area shape="rect" coords="41,331,155,345" href="
          page4.html">
<area shape="rect" coords="40,190,115,202" href="
          page5.html">
<area shape="rect" coords="42,174,148,186" href="
          page6.html">
<area shape="rect" coords="40,154,172,169" href="
          page7.html">
```

```
<area shape="rect" coords="43,137,142,148" href="
          page8.html">
<area shape="rect" coords="45,122,165,131" href="
          page9.html">
<area shape="rect" coords="4,481,389,493" href="
          page10.html">
<area shape="rect" coords="408,329,588,342" href="
          page11.html">
     <area shape="rect" coords="410,354,584,391" href="
          page12.html">
     </map>
```

Will search engines follow these links? Many search engines don't read image maps — although the problem is not as serious as it was a few years ago. The solution is simple: Use additional simple text links in the document.

Special characters

Don't use special characters, such as accents, in your text. To use unusual characters, you have to use special codes in HTML, and the search engines generally don't like these codes. If you want to write the word *rôle,* for example, you can do it three ways:

```
R&ocirc;le
R&#244;le
rôle
```

Note that the third method displays okay in Internet Explorer but not in a number of other browsers. But you probably shouldn't use any of these forms because the search engines don't like them, and therefore won't index these words. Stick to basic characters.

Chapter 7

Dirty Deeds — Facing the Consequences

- -

In This Chapter

▶ Examining the principles of tricking the search engines

▶ Exploring the basic techniques

▶ Doorway pages, redirects, cloaking, and more

▶ Understanding how you may be penalized

- -

*E*veryone wants to fool the search engines. And the search engines know it. That's why search engine optimization is such a strange business, a hybrid of technology and, oh, I dunno . . . industrial espionage, perhaps? The search engines don't want you to know exactly how they rank pages because if you did, you would know exactly how to trick them into giving you top positions.

Now for a bit of history. When this whole search engine business started out, the search engines just wanted people to follow some basic guidelines — make the Web site readable, provide a TITLE tag, provide a few keywords related to the page's subject matter, and so on — and then the search engines would take it from there.

What happened, though, is that Web sites started jostling for position. For example, although the KEYWORDS meta tag seemed like a great idea, so many people misused it (by repeating words and using words that *weren't* related to the subject matter) that it eventually became irrelevant to the search engines. Eventually, the major search engines stopped giving much weight to the tag or just ignored it altogether.

The search engines try to hide their methods as much as they can, but it sometimes becomes apparent what the search engines want, and at that point, people start trying to give it to them, in a manner that the search engines regard as manipulative. That's what this chapter is about. This chapter discusses what things you should avoid doing because you risk upsetting the search engines and getting penalized — potentially even getting booted from a search engine for life! You should also be careful about working with search engine marketers that tout these methods, because they can lead you into trouble.

Understanding the Basic Principles of Tricking the Search Engines

Before getting down to the nitty-gritty details about tricking the search engines, I focus on two topics: why you need to understand the dangers of using dirty tricks and what the overriding principles behind tricking the search engines are based on.

Should you or shouldn't you?

Should you use the tricks in this chapter, and if not, why not? You'll hear several reasons for not using tricks. The first I'm not going to belabor, because I'm not sure the argument behind this reason is very strong: ethics. You'll hear from many people that the tricks in this chapter are unethical, that those who use them are cheating and one step on the evolutionary ladder above pond scum (or one step below pond scum, depending on the commentator).

Self-righteousness is in ample supply on the Internet. Maybe they're right, maybe not. I do know that many people who try such tricks also have great reasons for doing so and are not the Internet's equivalent of Pol Pot or Attila the Hun. They're simply trying to put their best foot forward in a difficult technical environment.

Many people have tried search engine tricks because they've invested a lot of money in Web sites that turn out to be invisible to the search engines. These folks can't afford to abandon their sites and start again (see Chapter 6 for a discussion of why search engines sometimes can't read Web pages). You can, rightly so, point out that these folks can deal with the problem in other ways, but that just means the people involved are misinformed, not evil. The argument made by these tricksters might go something like this: Who gave the search engines the right to set the rules, anyway?

One could argue that doing pretty much anything beyond the basics is cheating. After all, smart Webmasters armed with a little knowledge can make the sorts of adjustments discussed elsewhere in this book, pushing their Web sites up in the ranks above sites that are more appropriate for a particular keyword phrase yet are owned by folks with less knowledge.

Ethics aside, the really good reason for avoiding egregious trickery is that it may have the opposite effect and *harm* your search engine position. And a corollary to that reason is that other, legitimate ways exist to get a good search engine ranking. (Unfortunately, these are often more complicated and time-consuming.)

How are tricks done?

The idea behind most search engine tricks is simple:

> To confuse the search engines into thinking your site is more appropriate for certain keyword phrases than they would otherwise believe, generally by showing the search engine something that the site visitor doesn't see.

The search engines want to see what the site visitors see, yet at the same time they know they can't. It will be a long, long time before search engines will be able to see and understand the images in a Web page. Right now, they can't even read text in the images, although that's something that could be possible soon. But to view and understand the images as a real person sees them, Michael Jackson could well be President of the United States before that happens.

The search engine designers have started with this basic principle:

> What we see — with the exception of certain things we're not interested in (images, JavaScript navigation systems, and so on) and of certain technical issues that are not important to the visitor (the DESCRIPTION meta tag, what <H> tag has been applied to a heading, and so on) — should be what the user sees.

For various reasons, the searchbots are not terribly sophisticated. They generally don't read JavaScript, Cascading Style Sheets, and so on, because of the complexity of doing so. In theory, they could read these things, but it would greatly increase the time and hardware required. So by necessity, they ignore certain components. Here's one other important principle:

> The text on the page should be there for the benefit of the site visitor, not the search engines.

Ideally, the search engine designers want Web designers to act as if the search engines don't exist. (Of course, this is *exactly* what many Web designers have done and the reason why so many sites rank poorly in the search engines!) The search engine designers want their programs to determine which pages are the most relevant for a particular search query. They want you — the Web designer — to focus on creating a site that serves your visitors' needs and let the search engines determine which site is most appropriate for which searcher.

What the search engines don't want is for you to show one version of a page to visitors and another version to the search engines because you feel that version is what the search engine will like most.

Do these tricks work?

For the moment, all the tricks in this chapter do work, at least in some circumstances for some search engines. This may be a little surprising, considering that some of these tricks are very crude and have been known to the search engines for a long time. You'll still find crudely keyword-stuffed pages and pages with hidden text sometimes ranking well in the search engines. Some of this search engine spam does filter through. But most major search engines are much better at recognizing the tricks and eliminating those pages.

Could you use every trick in the book and rank first for your keyword? Sure, but your rank may not last long, and the penalty it could incur will last for a long time. (Although in most cases the pages will simply drop in rank as the search engines apply an algorithm that recognizes the trick, in some cases a search engine could decide to remove all pages from a particular site from the index, permanently.)

As Micah Baldwin, my technical editor, likes to point out, "If your competitors are ranking higher than you, it's not because of the tricks they played, it's because of the good, solid search engine optimization work you didn't do." These tricks can be dangerous. You may get caught in one of several ways:

- ✔ A search engine algorithm may discover your trickery, and your page or your entire site could be dropped from the search engine.

- ✔ A competitor might discover what you're doing and report you to the search engines. Google has stated that it prefers to let its algorithms track down cheaters and uses reports of search engine spamming to tune these algorithms, but Google will take direct action in some cases.

- ✔ Your trick may work well for a while, until a major search engine changes its algorithm to discover the trickery . . . at which point your site's ranking will drop like a rock.

If you follow the advice from the rest of this book, you'll surpass 80 percent of your competitors.

Concrete Shoes, Cyanide, TNT — An Arsenal for Dirty Deeds

The next few sections take a look at some of the search engine tricks that are employed on the Web.

Keyword stacking and stuffing

You may run across pages that contain the same word or term, or maybe several words or terms, repeated over and over again, often in hidden areas of the page (such as the `<KEYWORD>` tag), though sometimes visible to visitors. This is one of the earliest and crudest forms of a dirty deed, one that the search engines have been aware of for years. You'd think keyword stacking wouldn't work, but the search engines aren't perfect, and sometimes keyword-stacked pages slip through.

Take a look at Figure 7-1. The Web designer has repeated the word *glucosamine* numerous times, each one in a hyperlink to give it a little extra oomph. I found this page in Google by searching for the term `glucosamine glucosamine glucosamine`, which shows that the page hasn't been kicked out of the index. It's possible it may have been penalized in some way — it doesn't turn up in the first 900 results at Google.

Look at this tactic from the search engine's perspective. Repeating the word glucosamine over and over isn't of any use to a site visitor, so it's understandable why search engine designers don't appreciate this kind of thing.

The terms *keyword stacking* and *keyword stuffing* are often used interchangeably, though some people regard keyword stuffing as something a little different — placing inappropriate keywords inside image `ALT` attributes and in hidden layers.

Hiding (and shrinking) keywords

Another old (and very crude) trick is to hide text. This trick is often combined with keyword stuffing, placing large amounts of text into a page and hiding it from view. For instance, take a look at Figure 7-2. I found this page in Google (also by searching for `glucosamine glucosamine glucosamine`). It has hidden text at the bottom of the page.

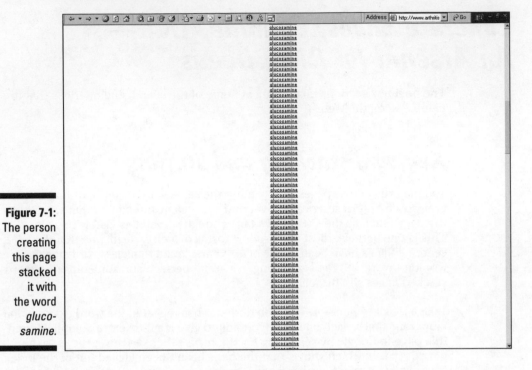

Figure 7-1:
The person
creating
this page
stacked
it with
the word
*gluco-
samine.*

There's a big space at the bottom of this page . . .

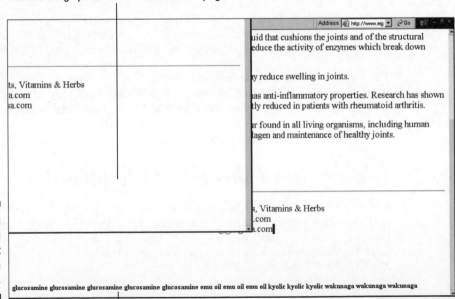

Figure 7-2:
This text is
hidden at
the bottom
of the page.

. . . but if you drag the cursor down from the end of the text, you'll see the hidden text.

If you suspect that someone has hidden text on a page, you can often make it visible by clicking inside text at the top of the page and dragging the mouse to the bottom of the page to highlight everything in between. You can also look in the page's source code.

How did this designer make the text disappear? Down at the bottom of the source code (choose View⇨Source), I found this:

```
<FONT SIZE=7 COLOR="#ffffff"><H6>glucosamine glucosamine
      glucosamine glucosamine glucosamine emu oil emu
      oil emu oil kyolic kyolic kyolic wakunaga wakunaga
      wakunaga</H6></FONT>
```

Notice the COLOR="#ffffff" piece; ffffff is hexadecimal for the color white. The page background is white, so, abracadabra, the text disappears.

Here are some other tricks used for hiding text:

✔ **Placing the text inside** <NOFRAMES> **tags.** Some designers do this even if the page isn't a frame-definition document.

✔ **Using hidden fields.** Sometimes designers hide words in a form's hidden field (<INPUT TYPE="HIDDEN">).

✔ **Using hidden layers.** Style sheets can be used to position a text layer underneath the visible layer or outside the browser.

Because hidden text takes up space, designers often use a very small font size. This is another trick that search engines may look for and penalize.

Here's another variation: Some Web designers make the text color just a little different from the background color to make it hard for the browser to catch. However, the text remains invisible, especially if it's at the bottom of the page preceded by several blank lines. Search engines can look for ranges of colors to determine if this trick is being employed.

Hiding links

A variation on the old hidden text trick is to hide links. As you discover in Chapters 12 and 13, links provide important clues to search engines about the site's purpose. Some Web designers create links specifically for the search engines to find, but not intended for site visitors. Links can be made to look exactly like all the other text on a page or may even be hidden on punctuation marks — visitors are unlikely to click a link on a period, so the link can be made invisible. Links may be placed in transparent images or invisible layers, in small images, or in <NOFRAMES> tags, or hidden in any of the ways discussed earlier for hiding ordinary text.

Using unrelated keywords

This is a crude and perhaps little-used technique: using keywords that you know are being searched upon frequently, yet which have little or nothing to do with the subject of your site. A few years ago, many Web designers thought it was clever to place the word *sex* in their KEYWORDS meta tag or hide it somewhere in the page. This technique is used less frequently these days because these words are so incredibly competitive, and anyway, it's better to focus on keywords that can actually attract the right kind of visitor.

Duplicating pages and sites

If content with keywords is good, then twice as much content is better, and three times as much is better still, right? Some site developers have duplicated pages and even entire sites, making virtual photocopies and adding the pages to the site or placing duplicated sites at different domain names.

Sometimes called *mirror pages* or *mirror sites,* these duplicate pages are intended to help a site gain more than one or two entries in the top positions. If you can create three or four Web sites that rank well, you can dominate the first page of the search results, with from four to eight entries out of the first ten. (Google, for instance, will display one or two pages from a site.)

Some people who use this trick try to modify each page just a little to make it harder for the search engines to recognize duplicates. The search engines, in particular Google, have designed tools to find duplication and will often drop a page from their indexes if they find it's a duplicate of another page at the same site. Duplicate pages found across different sites are generally okay, which is why content syndication (see Chapter 13) can work well, but entire duplicate sites are something the search engines frown on.

Page swapping and page jacking

Here are a couple of variations on the duplication theme:

   ✔ **Page swapping:** This is a little-used technique of placing one page at a site and then, after the page has attained a good position, removing it and replacing it with a less-optimized page. One serious problem with this technique is that some search engines now reindex pages very quickly, and it's impossible to know *when* the search engines will return.

> ✔ **Page jacking:** Some truly unethical search engine marketers have employed the technique of using other peoples' high-ranking Web pages, in effect stealing pages that perform well for a while. This is known as *page jacking*.

Doorway and Information Pages

A *doorway page* is created solely as an entrance from a search engine to your Web site. Doorway pages are sometimes known as *gateway pages* and *ghost pages*. The idea is to create overly optimized pages that are picked up and indexed by the search engines and, hopefully, will rank well and thus channel traffic to the site.

Search engines hate doorway pages because they break one of the cardinal rules: They're intended for search engines, not visitors. The sole purpose of a doorway page is to channel people from the search engines to the real Web site.

One man's doorway page is another man's *information page* — or what some people call *affiliate pages, advertising pages,* or *marketing pages.* The difference between a doorway page and an information page is that the information page is designed for use by the visitor in such a manner that the search engines will rank it well, whereas the doorway page is designed in such a manner that it's utterly useless to the visitor because it's intended purely for the search engine; in fact originally doorway pages were stuffed full of keywords, duplicated hundreds of times.

Doorway pages typically don't look like the rest of the site, having been created very quickly or even by some kind of program. Doorway pages are part of other strategies. The pages used in *redirects* and *cloaking* (discussed in the next section) are, in effect, doorway pages.

Where do you draw the line between a doorway page and an information page? That's a question I'm not going to answer; it's for you to ponder and remains a matter of debate in the search engine optimization field. If a client asks me to help him in the search engine race and I create pages designed to rank well in the search engines but in such a manner that they're still useful to the visitor, have I created information pages or doorway pages? Most people would say that I've created legitimate information pages.

Suppose, however, that I create lots of pages designed for use by the site visitor, pages that, until my client started thinking about search engine optimization, would have been deemed unnecessary. Surely these pages are, by *intent*, doorway pages, aren't they, even if one could argue that they're useful in some way?

Varying degrees of utility exist, and I know people in the business of creating "information" pages that are useful to the visitor in the author's opinion only! Also, a number of search engine optimization companies create doorway pages that they simply *call* information pages.

Still, an important distinction exists between the two types of pages, and creating information pages is a widely used strategy. The search engines don't know your *intent,* so if you create pages that appear to be useful, are not duplicated dozens or hundreds of times, and don't break any other rules, chances are they'll be fine.

Here's a good reality check. Be honest: Are the pages you just created really of use to your site visitors? If you submitted these pages to Yahoo! or The Open Directory Project for review by a human, would the site be accepted? If the answer is no, these are probably not information pages; they're just doorway pages.

Using Redirects and Cloaking

Redirects and *cloaking* are pretty much the same thing. The intention is to show one page to the search engines but a completely different page to the site visitor. Why do people want to do this? Here are a few reasons:

- ✔ If a site has been built in a manner that makes it invisible to search engines, cloaking allows the site owner to deliver indexable pages to the search engines while retaining the original site.

- ✔ The site may not have much textual content, making it a poor fit for the search engine algorithms. Although search engine designers might argue that this fact means the site isn't a good fit for a search, this argument clearly doesn't stand up to analysis and debate.

- ✔ Each search engine prefers something slightly different. As long as the search engines can't agree on what makes a good search match, why should they expect site owners and developers to accept good results in some search engines and bad results in others?

I've heard comments such as the following from site owners, and I can understand the frustration:

The search engines are defining how my site should work and what it should look like, and if the manner in which I want to design my site isn't what they like to see, that's not my fault! Who gave them the right to set the rules of commerce on the Internet?!

What might frustrate — and anger — site owners more is if they realized that several major search engines actually *do* accept cloaking, as long as you pay them. (See the information on trusted feeds in Chapter 9; a trusted feed is, in effect, a form of cloaking.) So cloaking is a crime, but several search engines say, pay us, and we'll help you do it. (Is that a fee, a bribe, or a protection-racket payment?)

Understanding redirects

A *redirect* is the automatic loading of a page without user intervention. You click a link to load a Web page into your browser, and within seconds, the page you loaded disappears, and a new one appears. Designers often create pages that are designed for the search engines — optimized, keyword-rich pages — that redirect visitors to the real Web site which is not so well optimized. The search engines read the page, but the visitors never really see it.

Redirects can be carried out in various ways:

✔ By using the REFRESH meta tag. But this is an old trick the search engines discovered long ago; most search engines won't index a page that has a REFRESH tag that bounces the visitor to another page in less than ten seconds or so.

✔ By using JavaScript to automatically grab the next page within a split second.

✔ By using JavaScript that is tripped by a user action that is almost certain to occur. In Figure 7-3 you can see an example of this at work. The large button on this page has a JavaScript mouseover event associated with it; when users move their mice over the image — as they're almost certain to do — the mouseover event triggers, loading the next page.

You're unlikely to get penalized for using a redirect. But a search engine may ignore the redirect page. That is, if the search engine discovers that a page is redirecting to another page — and, to be honest, the search engines often don't find these redirect pages unless they use a REFRESH meta tag — it simply ignores the redirect page and indexes the destination page. Search engines reasonably assume that redirect pages are merely a way station on the route to the real content.

Figure 7-3:
The mouse pointer triggers a JavaScript mouseover event on the image, loading another page.

Examining cloaking

Cloaking is a more sophisticated trick than a redirect, harder for the search engines to uncover than a basic REFRESH meta tag redirect. When browsers or searchbots request a Web page, they send information about themselves to the site hosting the page — for example, "I'm Version 6.1 of Internet Explorer," or "I'm Googlebot." The cloaking program quickly looks in its list of searchbots for the device requesting the page. If the device isn't listed, the cloaking program tells the Web server to send the regular Web page, the one intended for site visitors. But if the device name is listed in the searchbot list — as it would be for Googlebot, for instance — the cloaking program sends a *different* page, one that the designer feels is better optimized for that particular search engine. (The cloaking program may have a library of pages, each designed for a particular search engine or group of engines.)

Here's how the two page versions differ:

✔ **Pages provided to the search engine:** Often much simpler; created in a way to make them easy for the search engines to read; have lots of heavily keyword-laden text that would sound clumsy to a real person

✔ **Pages presented to visitors:** Often much more attractive, graphic-heavy pages, with less text and more complicated structures and navigation systems

The search engines don't like cloaking. Conservative search engine marketers steer well clear of this technique. Here's how Google defines cloaking:

> "The term 'cloaking' is used to describe a Web site that returns altered Web pages to search engines crawling the site."

Well, that's pretty clear; cloaking is cloaking is cloaking. But wait a minute. . . .

> "In other words, the Web server is programmed to return different content to Google than it returns to regular users, usually in an attempt to distort search engine rankings."

Hang on, that's not the same thing. . . .

> "This can mislead users about what they'll find when they click on a search result. To preserve the accuracy and quality of our search results, Google may permanently ban from our index any sites or site authors that engage in cloaking to distort their search rankings."

Notice a few important qualifications: *altered pages. . . usually in an attempt to distort search engine rankings . . . cloaking to distort their search engine rankings.*

This verbiage is a little ambiguous and seems to indicate that Google doesn't totally outlaw the technical use of cloaking; it just doesn't like you to use cloaking in order to cheat. Some would say that using cloaking to present to Google dynamic pages that are otherwise invisible, for instance (see Chapter 6), would be an acceptable practice. However, as I've pointed out, many in the business disagree and advise that you never use cloaking in any circumstance.

The Ultimate Penalty

Just how much trouble can you get into by breaking the rules? The most likely penalty isn't really a penalty. It's just that your pages won't work well with a search engine's algorithm, so they won't rank well. Remember the pages I mention earlier in the chapter, the one with the word glucosamine repeated over and over, and the page with the hidden text? These types of pages don't rank well in Google, although they may have when they were originally created; the algorithm is constantly changing.

It is possible to get the ultimate penalty, to have your entire site booted from the index. Here's what Google has to say about it:

> "We investigate each report of deceptive practices thoroughly and take appropriate action when abuse is uncovered. At minimum, we will use

the data from each spam report to improve our site ranking and filtering algorithms. The result of this should be visible over time as the quality of our searches gets even better."

Google is describing what I just explained — that it will tweak its algorithm to downgrade pages that use certain techniques. But . . .

"In especially egregious cases, we will remove spammers from our index immediately so they don't show up in search results at all. Other steps will be taken as necessary."

One of the dangers, then, of using tricks, is that someone might report you, and if the trick is bad enough, you'll get the boot. (Where will they report you? For Google, here's the address: www.google.com/contact/spamreport.html. Remember that people reporting spam are also investigated, so don't throw stones in a glass house.)

What do you do if you think you've been penalized? For example, suppose your site is dropped from Google. It may not be a penalty — perhaps your site was not available at the point at which Google tried to reach it. But if the site doesn't return to the index after a few weeks (Google will try again later and if it finds it reindex), then you may have been penalized.

Sometimes sites get penalized due to unintentional mistakes. Perhaps you hired a Web-development team that implemented various tricks without your knowing, or perhaps your company gave you a site to look after long after the tricks were used. Or maybe you purchased a domain name that was penalized due to dirty tricks in the past (just changing owners is not enough to automatically lift the penalty). Stuff happens: Be truthful and explain the situation to the folks at Google.

If you think your site has been banned, clean away any dirty tricks from your site and then e-mail help@google.com to explain that you fixed your site. Don't expect a rapid reply. Wait a couple of weeks and then try again. Still no reply? Try again after another couple of weeks, and if you still can't get a response, try calling 650-330-0100 and then pressing 0 to ask the operator who you can talk to about the problem. You may be given another e-mail address to try, along with a password to put in the Subject line. (The password is changed each day.)

Chapter 8

Bulking Up Your Site — Complete with Content

*C*ontent is often a very important factor in getting a high ranking in the search engines. (Not convinced? Check out Chapter 3, where I present my definitive argument for the primacy of content.) What do I mean by content? *Content,* in the broadest sense, is a geeky Web term that means "stuff on your Web site." A *content-rich* Web site is one that contains lots and lots of information for people to see, read, and use.

For search engines, content has a more narrow definition: words, and lots of 'em. So if you're interested in search engine optimization, you should concentrate on the *text* part of your Web site's content (the right text, of course, using the keywords you find out about in Chapter 4). You don't need to care about pictures, video, or sound — at least as far as the search engines are concerned — because those forms of content don't help you get higher rankings. You don't need Flash animations, either, because although some search engines are starting to index them, most do not. Moreover, Flash animations generally don't contain much indexable text.

What you should be concerned about is text, words that the search engines can read. Now, it's not *always* necessary to bulk up your site by adding textual content — in some cases, it's possible to get high search engine rankings with a small number of keyword-laden pages. If that's your situation, congratulations, sit back and enjoy the fruits of your rather minimal labors, and skip this chapter. But if you don't find yourself in this happy situation, this chapter helps you get there.

You may find that your competitors have Web sites stacked full of content. They have scores of pages, perhaps even hundreds of pages, full of text that is nicely laden with all the juicy keywords you're interested in. That's tough to compete with.

Content is not a subject covered in many books, newsletters, or Web sites related to search engine optimization and ranking. Most publications say, "You need content, so create some." But I believe this issue is critical, and that it's not a subject that should be glossed over with such trite comments, especially when several simple ways exist to *find* content. If you know the shortcuts, creating content doesn't have to be difficult. This chapter describes a slew of shortcuts to free and low-cost content, such as government materials, marketing and technical documents from manufacturers, and even something new called *copyleft*.

Three Methods for Creating Content

You can compete in the search engines several different ways. You can create well-optimized pages, get lots of links into your site, target keywords that competitors have missed, or put content on your site. (Chapter 1 has more on such "basic" strategies.) In some cases, when going up against a well-entrenched competitor, you may have no choice but to fight on several fronts. You may find that you *must* do something to stack your site with content.

You may be wondering at what point you should stop adding content. I recommend evaluating competing sites to help you make that determination. Compare your site to competitors that rank well in search engines. All major search engines now use some kind of link popularity to rate Web pages. If you're sure that your site has more well-optimized pages than those competing sites, it may be time to stop adding content. Instead, you may want to focus on getting links into your site and thereby raising your Google PageRank. (For more on Google PageRank, check out Chapter 15.)

I've got some bad news and some good news about creating content. The bad news is that the obvious way to create content — writing it yourself or getting someone else to write it for you — is a huge problem for many people. Most people find writing difficult, and even if they find it easy, the results are often less than appealing. Perhaps you know someone who can write well and you can convince this person to write a few paragraphs for you. But are your powers of persuasion sufficient to get you 10, 20, or 50 pages? You can always pay someone for content, but the problem with paying is that it costs money.

The good news is that you can use some shortcuts to create content, tricks of the trade that can help you quickly bulk up your Web site (even if your writing skills match those of a dyslexic gerbil and your funds make the Queen of

England's bikini budget look large in comparison). Note, though, that these tricks involve using *someone else's content*.

Here are the three different ways to get content for your site.

✔ Write your own content.

✔ Convince (force, bribe) someone else to create your content.

✔ Find existing content from somewhere else.

Writing Your Own Stuff

The obvious way to create content, for many small-site owners anyway, is to start writing articles. That's not a terrible idea in many cases. Thousands of sites rank well using content from the sites' owners. If you use the write-it-yourself approach, keep the following points in mind:

✔ **Writing content is time consuming, even for good writers.** You may want to evaluate whether you can devote the time to writing and maintaining your own content and then allocate time in your schedule to do so.

✔ **Many people are *not* good writers.** Not only is the writing process time-consuming, but the results are often rather pathetic (so I won't go into detail on this one).

✔ **If you *do* write your own stuff, pleeze spill chuck it.** Then have it edited by someone who has more than a third-grade education, and then spill chuck it again.

Do *not* rely on a word processor's grammar checker. This tool is worse than useless for most writers. Grammar checkers are of benefit only to *those what already has* a good grasp of grammar.

Summaries of online articles

Here's a quick way to get keywords onto your page:

1. **Use the search engines to track down articles related to your subject area.**

2. **Create a library area on your Web site, in which you link to these articles.**

3. **For each link, write a short, keyword-laden summary of what the article is all about.**

The advantage to this kind of writing is that it's fairly quick and easy.

You may want to include the first few sentences of the article. This comes under the gray area of copyright *fair use* (which you find out about in this book's appendix). What really counts is what the article's owner thinks. In most cases, if you contact the article's owner (and you really don't *have* to contact the owner), the owner is happy to have you summarize the article, excerpt a small portion of it, and link to his or her site. Most people recognize that *this is good for them!* However, occasionally you'll find someone who just doesn't get it and creates a fuss. Just remove the link and move on.

You may want to approach the owners of the sites you're linking to, to ask them to add a link back to your site. See Chapter 13 for more information.

Ideally, you don't want to link out of your site too much, though don't get paranoid about how much is too much. Just be aware that linking out of your site *leaks* PageRank out of the site. (Not sure what this leaking business is all about? Check out Chapter 12, which gives you all the messy details.)

Reviews of Web sites

Similar to the last tactic, you can link to useful Web sites and write short (yes, keyword laden) reviews of each one. Before you undertake such a program, read Chapter 13 to find out about gathering links from other sites.

Product reviews

Write short (um, keyword laden) reviews of products related to the subject matter covered by your site. An additional benefit of such a program is that eventually people may start sending you free stuff to review.

Convincing Someone Else to Write It

You may find that having articles written (by others) specifically for your site is rather appealing for two reasons. First, someone else does the work, not you. Second, if it doesn't turn out well, someone else (not you) gets blamed.

One approach, assuming you can't force someone to write for you, is to pay someone. Luckily (for you), writers are cheap. For some reason, people often have a bizarre idea of a glamorous writing life that's awaiting them. (It's been almost a decade since I wrote my first bestseller, and I'm still waiting for the groupies to turn up.) So you may be able to find someone to write for you for $10 or $12 an hour, depending on where you live and how well you lie. Or maybe you can find a high-school kid who can string a few coherent words together and is willing to work for less.

If you work for a large corporation, you may be able to convince a variety of people to write for you, people who may assume it's actually part of their job (again, depending on how well you lie). Spread the work throughout various departments — marketing, technical support, sales, and so on — and it may turn into a decent amount of content. Still, you can use quicker and easier ways to get content, as described in the next section.

If you pay someone to write for you, get a simple contract saying that the work is a *work for hire* and that you are buying all rights to it. Otherwise, you don't own it and can use it only for limited purposes that are either stated in the contract or are more or less obvious. If you ask someone to write an article for your Web site and don't get a contract giving you full rights, you can't later decide to syndicate the article on other sites or in newsletters. (Chapter 13 has more on this syndication stuff.) If an employee writes the material for you on company time, the work is generally considered a work for hire and the property of the company. However, if you have a very small company with an informal employment relationship and the writing is outside the scope of the employee's normal work, you should probably get the employee to sign a contract.

Using OPC — Other People's Content

Writing your own content (or hiring someone to do it) is the slow way to create content. Using someone else's content — now that's the quick way. See the following list of quick content sources for your site (I explain the details later in the chapter):

- ✔ **Product information:** Contact the manufacturer or distributor of the products you sell on your site for marketing and sales materials, technical documentation, and so on.

- ✔ **Web sites and e-mail newsletters:** Contact the owners of other sites and e-mail newsletters and ask them if you can use their work.

- ✔ **Government sources:** Check U.S. Government Web sites for free materials.

- ✔ **Content syndication sites:** A number of sites provide free content for the asking.

- ✔ **Traditional syndication services:** Numerous companies sell materials you can use on your site.

- ✔ **RSS syndication feeds:** This is a new, geeky technique for feeding syndicated content into Web sites.

- ✔ **Open content and copyleft:** This is an unusual new movement probably based on the old Internet maxim, *information wants to be free.*

- ✔ **Search pages:** You can search at a site to generate a search-results page with your favorite keywords.

- ✔ **Press releases:** You may be able to find press releases related to your area of business. These are copyright free, and you can use them as you wish.

- ✔ **A Q&A area on your site:** This is a way to serve your site visitors *and* get keywords onto the site.

- ✔ **Forums or message boards:** With forums and message boards on your site, your visitors create the keywords for you.

- ✔ **Blogs:** Blogs — from the term *Weblogs* — provide another way to let people create content for you.

This list gives you a good idea of the sources of content, and the "Hunting for Other People's Content" section, later in this chapter, explores how you find, evaluate, and procure content from these sources.

Before I show you how to help yourself to someone else's content, I need to warn you about a critical legal issue: copyright law. You must have a working knowledge of copyright restrictions so that you can properly evaluate whether (and how) it's appropriate to use the content that you find. The next section gives you an overview of what you need to know, and this book's appendix goes into excruciating detail, if you're curious.

Understanding Copyright — It's Not Yours!

I'm constantly amazed at how few people understand copyright, even people who should know better. (I know a newspaper editor who thinks that just because he pays me to write a column, he *owns* the column and can do what he wants with it. He doesn't, because he doesn't have a contract that says so.)

When I speak to clients about adding content to a Web site, I sometimes hear something like this: "How about that magazine article I read last week? Let's put that up there!" Or maybe, "Such and such a site has some great information, let's use some of that."

That's called *copyright infringement*. It's against the law, and although serious harm is unlikely to befall you in most cases, you *can* get sued or prosecuted. So let me quickly summarize copyright law so that you have a better idea of what you can and can't use on your site:

- As soon as someone creates a work — writes an article, writes a song, composes a tune, or whatever — copyright is automatic. There's no need to register copyright; the creator owns the copyright whether or not it has been created. Most copyright works, in fact, are not registered, which is a good thing. If they were, the Library of Congress, which houses the Copyright Office and stores copyright registrations, would be the size of Alabama.

- If you don't see a copyright notice attached, it doesn't mean the work's copyright isn't owned by someone. Current copyright law does not require such notices.

- If someone owns the copyright, that person has the right to say what can be done with, um, copies. What this means is that you generally can't take an article you find in a newspaper, magazine, or Web site and use it without permission. (There are exceptions, which you find out about later in this chapter.)

- In the United States, certain kinds of copyright infringement are felonies. You may not only get sued but also get prosecuted.

- If you don't know whether you have the right to use something, assume that you *don't*.

- You can't just take something and rewrite it. *Derivative works* are also protected. If the result is clearly derived from the original, you could be in trouble.

- Copyright has to be expressly assigned. If you hire me to write an article for your Web site and don't get a contract saying that you own *all rights,* or that the work was a *work for hire,* you only have the right to place it on your Web site. I still have the right to use the article elsewhere.

A number of exceptions can prove *very* important when you're gathering content, so listen closely:

- **If it's really old, you can use it.** Copyright eventually expires. Anything created before 1921, for instance, is free for the taking.

- **If the guvmint created it, you can use it.** The U.S. Government spends millions of dollars creating *content*. This content is usually not copyright protected.

✔ **If it's donated, you can use it.** Authors often *want* you to use their materials. If they have given the public permission to use it, you can, um, use it.

✔ **It's only fair — *fair use* explained.** Copyright law has a *fair use* exception that allows you to use small parts of a work, without permission, under particular conditions.

I strongly suggest that you read this book's appendix to get the details on copyright, and make sure that you beg or borrow, but not steal, other people's work.

Hunting for Other People's Content

You've seen a list of different types of other people's content, I've warned you about copyright . . . it's time to get out there and grab some content. You're about to find some great places to get tons of content.

Remember the keywords!

When you're out on your content hunt, remember that the purpose is *keywords*. You're trying to add keywords to your site. You can do that several ways:

✔ Find content with the keywords already in it. You want content that has at least *some* of your keywords, though you'll often find it's not enough.

✔ Make minor edits to the content you get, to add more keywords. In some cases, you shouldn't edit the content because you'll be expected to use the content without changes. In other cases, you may be allowed to modify the content. You can, for instance, modify *open content* (described later in the chapter), and some syndicators allow it. As syndicator Feature-well says, "Clients can make minor edits to stories and photos, provided they do not modify or change the meaning, tone or general context of the articles. . . ." Thus you could replace a few words here and there with your keywords, as long as the article still makes sense and retains the same tone and context.

✔ "Chunk up" the article, breaking it into smaller, Web-friendly pieces and separating each piece with a heading (containing keywords, of course).

Newspapers often modify content they buy. A syndicated column you read in New York may be different from the same column run in a paper in Los Angeles, because newspapers will cut and modify for space reasons or because they don't like the way something is worded.

When adding content, you're generally interested in adding pages with a variety of keywords sprinkled throughout. Remember, if you have a rodent-racing site, you'll want lots of pages with the words *rodent, racing, race, event, mouse, rat,* and so on.

Product information

Does your Web site sell products that you buy from a wholesaler or manufacturer? If so, contact your source and find out what materials are available: brochures, spec sheets, technical documentation, or user manuals. Take a look at anything the manufacturer has available.

In many cases, the material may available in Adobe Acrobat PDF files. You can post these files on your site within seconds, and they will be indexed by some search engines — Google, for instance. However, the ideal approach is to also convert the work to HTML files because you have more opportunities to insert keywords — in the TITLE, DESCRIPTION, and KEYWORDS tags, and so on — and to stress keywords by putting them in bold, italic, <H> tags, and so on.

Web sites and e-mail newsletters

The Web is so full of content that it's about to sink (well, not your site obviously, or you wouldn't be reading this chapter). Why not grab a few articles you like from other sites or from the e-mail newsletters you subscribe to? In fact, you may want to go hunting to find articles for this very purpose.

If you ask nicely, many people are happy to let you use their content. In fact, as I explain in Chapter 13, many people use content syndication as a strategy for site promotion. They *want* people to use their stuff, as long as the sites using the material provide attribution — meaning they clearly state where the material is from and who wrote it, and provide a link back to the site of origin.

Asking for permission is quite easy. Simply contact the owner of the article you saw on a site or in a newsletter, and ask whether you can use it. I did this recently and, within *ten minutes,* got a positive response. Within 15 minutes, I had an article on my site that was loaded with keywords and that ranked very highly in the search engines in its own right. (I later realized that the author's page was ranking #3 for one of my critical keywords. Thus within minutes, I had a page that had the potential of ranking very highly for some important keywords. It hasn't reached #3 yet, but it will once I get the page's PageRank up.)

When you talk to the article's owner, make sure that you praise the article. (After all, you do like it, don't you, or you wouldn't be asking? There's too much good content out there to be using trash just to drop keywords into your site.) Also, clearly state that you will provide a bio at the bottom of the article and a link back to the owner's site.

Those of you who own your own sites have it easy. You can simply save the e-mail response from the article's author as evidence of permission to use the article. Those of you working for large corporations with legal departments have a bigger problem. Your lawyers, working under the principle of "common sense is dead," will expect you to get the article's author to sign a 32-page document providing permission, declaring that he or she has the right to give permission, and signing over exclusive and lifetime rights to the article and any spin-off toys or clothing derived from it. Sorry, I don't know how to help you here. I would tell you to just remember what Shakespeare said — "First thing we do, let's kill all the lawyers" — except I'm sure my publisher's legal department would complain.

Where can you find these articles? For Web site articles, search at a search site for sites that are likely to have the type of information you need. I suggest that you avoid sites that are directly competing. Also keep your eyes open for newsletters while you're doing your Web search, or look for appropriate newsletters at some of these sites:

- **Coollist:** www.coollist.com
- **EzineHub:** www.ezinehub.com
- **E-Zine-List:** www.meer.net/~johnl/e-zine-list
- **Ezine-Universe:** www.ezine-universe.com
- **listTool:** www.listtool.com
- **Low Bandwidth:** www.disobey.com/low
- **NewJour:** gort.ucsd.edu/newjour
- **Newsletter Access:** www.newsletteraccess.com
- **Tile.Net:** tile.net
- **Topica:** www.topica.com
- **WebScout Lists:** www.webscoutlists.com

Try searching for a combination of one of your keyword phrases and the words *article* and *newsletter* — for instance, rodent racing article and rodent racing newsletter.

You can also find articles at the syndication sites I tell you about in a moment.

How do you know who owns the copyright to the article? Here's a quick rule of thumb. If the article has an attribution attached to it, contact that person. For instance, many e-mail newsletters are either written by a single person (in which case you contact him or her) or have a variety of articles, each one with a bio and e-mail address (in which case you contact the author, not the newsletter itself). In the majority of cases, the author has given the newsletter one-time rights and still owns the copyright.

Some mechanisms used for syndicating content ensure that the search engines won't read the syndicated content! So you need to make sure you use the right technique. See "Content syndication sites," later in this chapter, for more information.

Government sources

I love this source, because it's *huge,* with a surprising range of information. In general, documents created by the U.S. Federal Government are in the public domain. Under the terms of Title 17 United States Code section 105, works created by U.S. Government departments do not have copyright protection.

However, you should be aware of some important exceptions:

- The government may still hold copyrights on works that have been given to the government — bequests or assignments of some kind.
- The law is a U.S. law, making U.S. Government works copyright-free. Most other governments hold copyrights on their works.
- In some cases, works that non-government agencies create on behalf of the government may or may not be protected by copyright — the law is not clear.
- Works created by the National Technical Information Service (NTIS) may have a limited, five-year copyright protection.
- The United States Postal Service is exempt from these regulations. The Postal Service can have copyright protection for its works. (It doesn't want people printing their own stamps!)
- In some cases, the government may publish works that were originally privately created works. Such documents are copyright protected.

Even with these exceptions, vast quantities of juicy government content are available. Now, don't think to yourself, "Oh, there probably aren't any government documents related to *my* area!" Maybe, maybe not. But where do you think all our tax billions go? The money can't *all* go to defense and schools. It has to be spent somehow, so some of it goes to creating vast amounts of Web content!

You can take this content and place it directly on your Web site. You'll find the content in Web pages or Adobe Acrobat PDF files. You may want to convert PDF files to Web pages for several reasons:

✔ Web pages load more quickly than PDF files.

✔ Although most major search engines now index PDF files, some systems don't.

✔ You can do more keywording in Web pages.

Not only will you find the sorts of documents useful for your purposes — text-heavy documents that the search engines can read — you'll also find other materials that may be useful for your site, such as videos.

Here are a few good places to find government materials:

✔ **FedWorld:** www.fedworld.gov

✔ **Government Printing Office:**

• Catalog of U.S. Government Publications: www.gpoaccess.gov/cgp

• New Electronic Titles: www.access.gpo.gov/su_docs/locators/net (contains some documents not yet in the Catalog of U.S. Government Publications database)

✔ **Library of Congress — Browse Government Resources:** lcweb.loc.gov/rr/news/extgovd.html

✔ **CIA's Electronic Reading Room:** www.foia.cia.gov

✔ **U.S. Department of State's Electronic Reading Room:** foia.state.gov

✔ **U.S. Historical Documents Archive:** www.ushda.org

✔ **FBI's Electronic Reading Room:** foia.fbi.gov

Content syndication sites

In the "Web sites and e-mail newsletters" section, earlier in this chapter, I discuss the idea of finding Web pages or e-mail newsletter articles you like and asking the owners for permission to use them. Well, here's a shortcut: Go to the content-syndication sites.

Content syndication sites are places where authors post their information so that site owners or newsletter editors can pick it up and use it for free. Why? Because, in return, you agree to place a short blurb at the bottom of the article, including a link back to the author's Web site.

Here are a few places to get you started in the wonderful world of content syndication:

- **Bull Marketer:** www.bullmarketer.com/free_content.htm
- **EZineArticles.com:** ezinearticles.com
- **FreeSticky.com:** www.freesticky.com
- **GoArticles.com:** www.goarticles.com
- **IdeaMarketers.com:** www.ideamarketers.com
- **The Open Directory Project's List of Content Providers:** dmoz.org/Computers/Software/Internet/Site_Management/Content_Management/Content_Providers
- **Purple Pages:** www.purplepages.ie
- **Stickysauce:** www.stickysauce.com
- **World Wide Information Outlet:** certificate.net

Some Web sites have their own *syndication areas* — libraries from which you can pick articles you want to use. Also, see Chapter 13, where I talk about syndicating your own content and point you to other syndication sites.

Make sure that when you grab articles from a content-syndication site, you're not using a competitor's article! All these articles have links back to the author's site, so you don't want to be sending traffic to the enemy.

Geeky stuff you must understand

I have to get into a little techno-geeky stuff right now, I'm afraid. I hate to do it, but if you don't understand this, you're just wasting your time with content syndication.

Many syndication systems use a simple piece of JavaScript to allow you to pull articles from their sites onto yours. For instance, take a look at this code I pulled from a site that syndicates news articles:

```
<script src="http://farmcentre.com/synd/synd.jsp?id=cfbmc">
            </script>
```

This piece of code tells the Web browser to grab the synd.jsp file from the farmcentre.com Web site. That file uses a JavaScript to insert the article into the Web page. Articles or other forms of content are automatically embedded other ways, too. They may be inserted using Java applets, and sometimes with an <iframe> tag.

None of these ways of embedding an article into your site does you any good with the search engines. As I explain in Chapter 6, the search engine bots *don't read JavaScript!* Nor do they read Java applets. And if they do read inside the

`<iframe>` tags, it doesn't help, because they follow the link that is used to pull the page into the frame and view that content as if it were on the origin Web site.

The `<iframe>` tag is used by Internet Explorer to place an internal frame inside a Web page. That frame contains information from another Web page, in this case a page on another Web site. Depending on how the iframe is set up, it can appear as if the information inside the frame is part of the original page — readers can't tell the difference.

So, the searchbot grabs the page and reads the source code. It sees the Java-Script (such as the example code we just saw) but ignores it, moving on to the next line. The syndicated article you wanted to place into the Web page *never gets placed into the page the searchbot reads!* All your time and energy placing content is wasted.

This all strikes me as quite humorous, really. Thousands of people are syndi-cating content or using syndicated content, partly for search engine reasons. People syndicating the content want to place their links on as many Web pages as possible for two reasons:

✔ So readers will see the links and click them.

✔ So the search engines will see the links and rank the home site higher.

And people using the syndicated content are doing so because they want content, stuffed with good keywords, for the search engines to read.

In many cases, both the syndicators and the people using syndicated content are wasting their time because the search engines aren't placing the content, aren't seeing the keywords, and aren't reading the links!

How do you avoid this problem?

✔ Don't use browser-side inclusion techniques, such as JavaScript, Java, or iframes.

✔ You can use server-side inclusion techniques, such as server includes, PHP, or ASP. If you're not sure whether a technique is server side or browser side, ask a knowledgeable geek — you want an inclusion tech-nique that loads the content into the page *before* it's sent to the browser or searchbot.

✔ Use manual inclusion techniques — that is, copy and paste the content into your pages directly. Plenty of content relies on manual inclusion, and you may even get content owners who are using automatic-inclusion techniques to agree to let you manually copy their content.

As long as you're aware of syndicated content's pitfalls and how to avoid them, as I explain here, it's quite possible to find syndicated content and make it work so that you reap the search engine benefits of having that content on your site.

Hosted-content services are companies that host the content on their sites along with a copy of your Web site template so that it looks like the content is on your site (unless you look in the browser's Location or Address bar, where you see the company's URL). The problem with such services is that the search engines are unlikely to pick up the content because they see the same articles duplicated over and over again on the same domain. Google, for instance, will probably keep one set and ignore the duplicates.

The problem with automatic updates

Another problem with content syndication sites involves *automatic updates.* Automatic updates allow the content owner to change the content immediately. For example, sites that provide weekly or monthly newsletters use automatic updates. This technique allows the content provider to update the content on dozens or hundreds of sites simply by changing the source file. The next time a page is loaded on one of the sites using the syndicated content, the new information appears.

But if you're adding content for keyword purposes, automatic updating may not be such a good thing. If you find an article with lots of nice keywords, it could be gone tomorrow. Manual inclusion techniques ensure that the article you placed remains in place, and also allow you to, for instance, break up the article into chunks by adding keyword-laden headings. (Although it's hard to say how likely a site owner who uses automatic updating will be to let you use manual inclusion, there is plenty of content out there.)

Traditional syndication services

Content syndication is nothing new. It's been around for a hundred years. (I just made that up, but it's probably true.) Much of what you read in your local newspapers is not written by the paper's staff; it comes from a syndication service.

Some syndication services will sell you content for your site. In general, this material should be better than the free syndicated content. However, much of the free stuff is pretty good, too, so you may not want to pay for syndicated material until you've exhausted your search for free content.

Here are a few places you can find commercial syndicated material:

- ✔ **AbleStable Syndication:** ablestable.com/content/syndication.htm
- ✔ **Featurewell:** www.featurewell.com (articles from $70)
- ✔ **MagPortal:** www.magportal.com
- ✔ **Moreover:** www.moreover.com
- ✔ **The Open Directory Project's List of Content Providers:** dmoz.org/Computers/Software/Internet/Site_Management/Content_Management/Content_Providers
- ✔ **OSKAR Consulting:** www.electroniccontent.com/conFinder.cfm?cat=beauty
- ✔ **Pages:** www.pagesmag.com ($195 per year for 60–70 new articles each month, plus a four-year archive)
- ✔ **Thomson Gale:** www.gale.com (kinda pricey; $10,000 for a subscription!)
- ✔ **United Media's uclick:** content.uclick.com
- ✔ **YellowBrix:** www.yellowbrix.com
- ✔ **Yahoo! News and Media Syndicates page:** dir.yahoo.com/Business_and_Economy/Business_to_Business/News_and_Media/Syndicates

Specialty syndication services provide content for particular industries. For example, Inman (www.inman.com) provides content for the real estate industry.

RSS syndication feeds

RSS is one of those geeky acronyms that nobody can define for certain. Some say it means *Really Simple Syndication;* others believe it means *Rich Site Summary,* or *RDF Site Summary.* What it stands for doesn't really matter. All you need to know is that RSS is the next big thing in content syndication.

RSS systems comprise two components:

- ✔ An RSS *feed,* a source of content of some kind
- ✔ An RSS *aggregator* (also known as a *news aggregator*), a system that takes the information from the feed and drops it into a Web page

For example, Google provides RSS feeds of its news headlines. You can install an RSS aggregator on your site and point it to a Google search. The page will then contain recent searches on news headlines, as you can see in Figure 8-1.

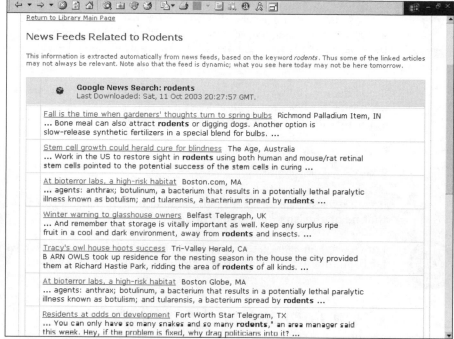

Figure 8-1:
A page
created
using an
RSS
aggregator,
zFeeder.
Look at all
those lovely
bolded
keywords!

What you need is an aggregator. Aggregators range from fairly simple to very complicated — and that's assuming you have some technical abilities in the first place. (If you don't, there's no range; they're all very complicated!)

Before you go to the trouble of getting an aggregator, decide whether there's enough suitable content to make it worthwhile. Although RSS will almost certainly be *very* big in the future, at the time of writing most of the RSS feeds tend to be a little geeky. So if your subject area is *macramé and knitting,* I suspect you may find a dearth of material at present. Also, often RSS feeds merely pass a link to material on another site, in which case you won't benefit much. Make sure that you're getting the actual material passed to your site. Check out these RSS feed sites:

- **Blogdex:** blogdex.net
- **Fagan Finder:** www.faganfinder.com/search/rss.shtml
- **Feedster:** www.feedster.com
- **Lockergnome:** rss.lockergnome.com
- **myRSS:** www.myrss.com
- **NewsKnowledge:** www.newsknowledge.com
- **Syndic8:** syndic8.com

Unlike the automated syndication techniques I mention earlier, which use Java-Scripts and other browser-side systems for inserting content, RSS aggregators generally use *server-side* techniques, so the content is inserted into the Web page *before* the search engines see it. That's what we call in the search engine business a *good thing*.

If you decide you want to go ahead with RSS, you need an aggregator. Try searching for *news aggregator* or *rss aggregator,* and check out the following software directories (or ask your favorite geek to do so for you):

- ✔ **freshmeat:** freshmeat.net
- ✔ **SourceForge.net:** sourceforge.net

If your geek has never heard of freshmeat or SourceForge, it's just possible that he or she isn't quite geeky enough.

I have used an aggregator called zFeeder (formerly zvonFeeds), which was fairly simple to work with. You can find it at zvonnews.sourceforge.net.

Open content and copyleft

Have you heard of open-source software? It's software that is created through the contributions of multiple individuals who agree to allow pretty much anyone to use the software, at no charge. Another movement that doesn't get quite the same attention as open-source software is the *open content* movement. Open content is, as explained on the Open Content List Web site, "content (books, articles, documentation, images, databases, and so on) that is 'freely available for modification, use, and redistribution under a license similar to those used by the Open Source / Free Software community.'"

Open content relies on what has become known as *copyleft*. Under copyleft, the owner of a copyrighted work doesn't release it into the public domain. Instead, he or she releases the work for public modification, with the understanding that anyone using the work must agree to not claim original authorship and to release all derivative works under the same conditions.

Stacks of information are released under copyleft. Start at these sites:

- ✔ **Creative Commons:** creativecommons.org
- ✔ **Open Content List:** www.opencontentlist.com
- ✔ **The Open Directory Project's Open Content page:** dmoz.org/Computers/Open_Source/Open_Content

You really should check out open content, in particular the open content encyclopedias, which have information on just about anything. You can find these encyclopedias on the Open Directory Project's Open Content page.

Watch for competitors' information. Some companies use open content as a way to get their links out onto the Web.

Search pages

Flip back to Figure 8-1, the search page I showed you in the "RSS syndication feeds" section, earlier in the chapter. As you can see in the figure, the great thing about such search pages is that they have the exact keywords you define, liberally scattered throughout. When you conduct a search in a search engine — whether you're searching Web sites, a directory of magazine articles, or news headlines — what does the search engine return? Matches for your keywords.

In Figure 8-1, you can see that the keyword *rodents* appears throughout the page, and even better, it's in bold text.

RSS provides one way to insert searches — in particular, searches of news headlines — into your pages. Even though the page's content will change continually, you don't have to worry about the content changing to a page that doesn't contain your keywords, because the content is a reflection of the keywords you provide. You may also be able to find search pages that you can manually copy and paste. Sites that contain large numbers of articles and a search function may be good candidates. Run a search, and then copy the results and paste them into a Web page.

Make sure that the links in the search results still work and that they open the results in a new window. (You don't want to push people away from your site.) You'll probably also want to check with the site owner to make sure that this is okay. In many cases, site owners will be fine with it; again, it's more links to their site!

Press releases

The nice thing about press releases is that you can use them without permission. The purpose of a press release is to "send it out and see who picks it up." You don't need to contact the owner of the press release, because there's already an implied agreement that you can simply take the release and post it wherever you want (unchanged and in its entirety, of course).

You may be able to find press releases that have the keywords you want, are relevant to your site in some way, and are not released by competitors. For instance, if you're in the business of running rodent-racing events, companies selling rodent-racing harnesses and other gear are not direct competitors and may well have press releases you can use.

Where do you find these press releases? Try searching for press releases at a search engine. Combine the search term with some keywords, such as *rodent racing press release*. You can also find press releases at press release sites, such as these:

- **Hot Product News:** www.hotproductnews.com
- **Internet News Bureau:** www.internetnewsbureau.com
- **M2PressWIRE:** www.presswire.net
- **Online Press Releases:** www.onlinepressreleases.com
- **PR Newswire:** prnewswire.com
- **PR Web:** www.prweb.com
- **USANews:** www.usanews.net

You might even subscribe to some of these press release services so you get relevant press releases sent to you as soon as they are published.

Q&A areas

After you get sufficient traffic to your site, you may want to set up a Question and Answer (Q&A) or FAQ (Frequently Asked Questions) area on your site. Visitors to your site can ask questions — providing you with keyword-laden questions in many cases — and you can answer them.

A number of free and low-cost software tools automate the creation and management of such areas. Search the utility sites, such as resourceindex.com, for these tools, and find a friendly geek if you need help installing a tool.

Make sure the search engines can read pages created by any tool you install on your site, such as the FAQ tool or the BBS and blog tools I tell you about next. Find a tool you like and then find out if Google indexes the pages in the demo or sample sites. If not, ask the software author to point you to a demo that *does* have indexed pages.

Message boards

Message board areas can be very powerful, in more than one way. Setting up a message board — also known as a forum or Bulletin Board System (BBS) — allows your site visitors to place keywords in your site for you! A message board often draws traffic, bringing people in purely for the conversation.

Own a site about kayaks? As you sleep, visitors will leave messages with the word *kayak* in them, over and over. Does your site sell rodent supplies? While you go about your daily business, your visitors will leave messages containing words such as *rodent, mouse,* and *rat.* Over time, this can build up to hundreds of pages with many thousands of keywords.

BBS systems — even really cool ones with lots of features, such as the ability to post photos — are cheap, often free, in fact. They're relatively easy to set up even for low-level geeks. Don't underestimate this technique; if you have a lot of traffic on your Web site, a BBS can be a great way to build huge amounts of content. Search for terms such as *bbs software* and *forum software.*

Blogs

Blogs are sort of like diaries. They're systems that allow someone to write any kind of twaddle — er, musings — they want and publish this nonsense (um, literature) directly to a Web site. My cynicism aside, you can find some very interesting blogs out there (or so I'm told).

Blogs provide another way to allow your site visitors to create content for you. On your rodent-racing Web site, for instance, you can provide a blog tool and allow anyone to set up a blogging account. Make sure that you use the *right* blog tool. It has to be one that creates pages that are readable by the search engines. Search for terms such as *blog software* and *blog tool.*

You can use a tool such as Blogger (www.blogger.com), which is owned by Google and hosted on its servers. You can integrate Blogger into your Web site, which means that you can automatically insert any blog page that's created.

If you use any tool that allows visitors to post messages on your site, you should monitor the messages and delete inappropriate messages. Many search engine marketers use such tools to post messages with links pointing back to their sites.

Part III
Adding Your Site to the Indexes and Directories

The 5th Wave   By Rich Tennant

"Look, I've already launched a search for 'reanimated babe cadavers' three times and nothing came up!"

In this part . . .

Getting your Web site indexed by the search engines and directories should be easy. Let them know the URL and wait for them to add it, right? Wrong. Sure, you can submit information about your site to the search engines, but they probably won't index it.

In this part, I explain what you need to do to get your site into the major search engines. (**Hint:** You need to make it easy for the search engines to find your site on their own.) I also explain how to work with the two major search directories: Yahoo! (easy, just pay) and the Open Directory Project (easy, and free, but you may have to keep trying).

This part also tells you how to find important but lesser-known systems and how they can help you. (Sure, most searches are carried out through the major systems, but the specialized systems can often provide valuable, highly targeted traffic.)

Chapter 9

Getting Your Pages into the Search Engines

*A*fter you've built your Web pages, the next question is how do you get them into the search systems? That's what this chapter and the next chapter explain. In this chapter, I talk about how to get your pages into the search engines, and in Chapter 10, I explain how to get your site listed with the search directories.

Many site owners are confused about how they get their Web sites into search engines. They assume that to submit or register their sites, they go to a search engine's Web site, provide the URL to one (or all) of their pages, and wait for the search engine to come along and index the pages. The truth, as this chapter explains, is more complicated.

Why Won't They Index My Pages?

It's frustrating when you can't seem to get search engines to index your site. With some search engines, you have to pay before you can submit your URL (as I cover later in this chapter). Other search engines enable you to submit your URL for free, but doing so doesn't seem to make any difference; your site is not picked up.

Here are a few reasons why search engines are not as helpful as we'd like them to be:

- ✔ **Most search engines have fairly small indexes.** Although Google and Yahoo! are very big systems — Google has well over 4 billion pages — the other systems are relatively small — Teoma has only about 1.5 billion. And most systems are smaller still; Gigablast, for instance, contains 200 million pages. The smaller systems don't care about getting every page they can find into the index; that's simply not the game they're playing.

- ✔ **Some systems want you to pay to get into the search engine.** They either don't accept URLs for free or actively discourage people from submitting URLs for free, in order to encourage people to pay. I look at this practice in the "Using Paid Inclusion" section, later in this chapter.

- ✔ **Some systems, in particular Google, believe that they can maintain the quality of their indexes by focusing on Web pages that have links pointing to them.** These search engines would rather find your pages themselves than have you submit the pages.

When I say that a page is in a search engine's index, it doesn't mean the search engine has read and indexed the entire page. In many cases, the search engine has never even read the page but knows where the page is based on links it has seen in pages that it *has* read. And even if a search engine has read a page, it may not have read the entire page.

Linking Your Site for Inclusion

In Chapters 12 and 13, I talk about the importance of — and how to get — links pointing from other sites to yours. The more links you have pointing at your site, the more important the search engines will think your pages are.

Links are also important because they provide a way for the search engines to find your site. Without links, you *might* get your site into the search engine's indexes, but chances are you won't. And getting into the most important index, Google's, is much quicker through linking than through registration. I've had sites picked up and indexed by Google within two or three days of having put up a link on another site. If you simply submit your URL to Google, you may have to wait weeks for it to index your site (if it ever does).

But one or two links sometimes aren't enough for some search engines. They are for Google, however. If Google sees a link to your site on another site that it's already indexing, it will probably visit your site and index that, too. But the smaller systems are far choosier and may not visit your site even if they do see a link to it. So the more links you have pointing to your site the better. Eventually, the smaller systems will get sick of tripping over links to your site and come see what the fuss is all about.

Don't think your work is done when you create a site and then submit a page or two to the search engines. Building links from other sites is an essential part of the process. It's frustrating and requires tremendous patience, but that's the way it works!

Submitting Directly to the Major Systems

The next few sections take a quick look at the major systems and whether or not you can submit your site directly to them. The systems I discuss are the ones introduced in Chapter 1: the major search systems that are important in their own right, or important feeders that provide search results to other search sites.

Just because you submit a site doesn't mean you'll get picked up. But the process of submitting your site is quick and easy, so what do you have to lose?

Are you sure it won't do any harm?

Will submitting directly to the search engines, or submitting many pages over and over, harm your search engine position? Will the search engines get annoyed and penalize your pages? No — and here's why.

Imagine that your Rodent Racing Web site is sitting at the top of page two for a popular search term in a particular search engine. You feel this ranking isn't good enough, so you go to the search engine, run the search, and then grab the URLs of all the pages that turn up on the first results page. You then submit those URLs to the search engine over and over and over again, perhaps using a submission program. You keep doing this for days, until the search engines get so annoyed they remove all those pages, pushing your page to the top! Simple, eh? Too simple, in fact, which is why that tactic doesn't work.

However, having said that, I should note that you do need to be aware of some potential repercussions. Systems that are repeating submissions to an egregious degree may be blocked. The search engine may identify your system's IP address (the unique number identifying your computer on the Internet) and then block you from submitting or even using the search engine. If the IP address used by the program submitting URLs is the same as the IP address at which your Web site is hosted, your site could be penalized. These situations are rare, though, because the IP numbers used by such submission programs and the associated Web sites are usually different. What is far more common is that the search engines simply block the submission program from submitting more than a certain number of URLs at a time.

Submitting for free

The following systems accept free URL submissions. Note that in some cases, they won't accept more than a specific number of submissions: one a day, three a day, or whatever. The systems may suggest that you don't provide more than one URL. In that case, give them the URL of a page that is linked well throughout your site, and the search engines will find the other pages when they crawl the site.

Here are some systems where you can submit your site for free:

- **Google:** `www.google.com/addurl.html`
- **Yahoo! Web Search:** `submit.search.yahoo.com/free/request`; you have to create a Yahoo! account before you can submit.
- **MSN:** At the time of writing, MSN uses Yahoo! search results, but it's preparing to drop Yahoo and replace it with its own index (perhaps late 2004). The MSNbot is currently crawling the Web, building this index, but not accepting direct submissions. You can find information at `search.msn.com/msnbot.htm`. Sometimes MSN lets people in to play with the beta version of the system; try here: `techpreview.search.msn.com/`.
- **Zeal (if you have a noncommercial Web site):** `zeal.com/website/add_start.jhtml`

You may want to check out Grub, too (`www.grub.org`). The goal of the Grub project is to reach a stage where distributed crawling can update an index containing every page on the Web, every day. Right now, a second-tier search engine called WiseNut uses the data, but in the future, the data will be used for other purposes. To submit to Grub, you have to download the Grub distributed-crawling program to your system and let Grub use your system as part of the project. You can define which of your pages you want included in the index. If you uninstall the Grub program, your pages may not be reindexed.

You'll notice that of the major systems mentioned in Chapter 1, I haven't yet discussed Yahoo! Directory, the Open Directory Project, and Teoma/Ask Jeeves. Yahoo! Directory and the Open Directory Project are directory systems, so I cover those in Chapter 10. Teoma/Ask Jeeves doesn't allow any free submissions, but it does have a paid-inclusion system, which I discuss in the "Using Paid Inclusion" section, later in this chapter.

If a search engine doesn't provide a way for you to submit a URL, that doesn't mean you can't get into the search engine. You need lots of links pointing to your site so the search engine will find it, and a fair amount of patience, but it definitely does happen. And just because the search engine *does* provide a way for you to submit a URL doesn't mean you *will* get into the search engine. You need lots of links pointing to the site.

Using Paid Inclusion

Paid-inclusion programs (such as Yahoo's Site Match) provide you with the privilege of paying to have a search engine index your pages. You pay the search engine a fee — $15 a year, $49 a year, or whatever *per URL* — and the search engine guarantees to index your pages within a certain time (generally 48 to 72 hours), promises to come back frequently (generally every 48 hours) to reindex, and guarantees that your pages will remain in the index for the full term of the agreement (usually a year).

I don't like the idea of paid inclusion; it strikes me as a bit of a scam. The Federal Trade Commission doesn't like it much either, and consumer advocate complaints have targeted paid inclusion based on the federal law that "prohibits unfair or deceptive acts or practices in or affecting commerce [such as] a representation, omission, or practice that is likely to mislead the consumer acting reasonably in the circumstances, to the consumer's detriment."

The argument is over whether paid inclusions are, in effect, ads. The search engines say they're not; you're simply paying for an improved service in getting your URLs into the index, thereby improving the index. For dynamic sites, this is true because it is nearly impossible to crawl a dynamic site. (See Chapter 7 for more on why this is so.)

But from the consumer's perspective, paid-inclusion ads are misleading. If a search engine has a complex algorithm designed to provide accurate, relevant search results but then allows sites to partially bypass the algorithm, how is that not misleading to searchers? The search engines say that the paid-inclusion pages still have to compete on the same terms with all the other pages in the index and are not ranked any higher based on their payment status. That may be true, but paid-inclusion pages definitely *are* going to rank higher than the pages that are *not* in the index because their owners haven't paid!

Some paid-inclusion programs allow site owners to add enhancements to their listings such as logos, icons, and "taglines."

Note: The founders of Google *also* find paid-inclusion to be misleading and have refused to allow the search engine to use such programs.

Deciding whether to use paid inclusion

If you're trying to decide whether or not to use paid inclusion, consider the following points:

- ✔ Teoma/Ask Jeeves and Yahoo!, have paid-inclusion programs; a number of the other sites sell paid inclusion for feeder systems — AltaVista and FAST/AlltheWeb sell Yahoo!'s Site Match services, for instance.

- ✔ To submit a single URL to all the preceding systems' paid-inclusion programs, the cost is $79 a year.

- ✔ To submit the second and subsequent URL, the cost is $120 a year (see the details in "The paid-inclusion systems," later in this chapter).

- ✔ You may get stuck paying the search engines their paid-inclusion fees year after year.

- ✔ If you have a really good linking strategy, you may get these search engines to index your site without having to pay them. A large number of high-quality links into your site will help ensure you get picked up.

- ✔ If you don't have a good linking strategy, your pages probably won't rank well anyway. Paid inclusion gets you into the index, but it doesn't affect your position in the index, so you may be paying to be on a page that few people read.

Some people like paid inclusion because of the speedy updates. You can tweak pages and see the results in your search engine rank within a few days. But again, each paid-inclusion program accounts for only a small proportion of the overall search engine results anyway.

Here's an interesting conundrum. All the major search engines that use paid-inclusion programs also add pages to the index for free. Three of the four accept free submissions — though on their free-submission pages, they try to steer you toward paid inclusion — and all their searchbots add pages that they find as they're crawling the Web. If these large systems (which have over a billion pages in their indexes) limited their indexes to only paid inclusions, they would quickly go out of business. So, a few important questions about paid inclusion:

- ✔ If you pay to have your pages indexed, what happens when the agreement period expires? Presumably, the search engines remove your pages. They have to, or the paid-inclusion program more or less collapses, doesn't it? That means the search engines, in effect, hold you hostage, removing pages that might otherwise have been indexed automatically by their searchbots!

- ✔ What's to stop you from indexing a single page using paid inclusion, a page that contains lots of links to your other pages (a sitemap page, for instance), to make sure the search engines find all your pages? The search engines want you to submit multiple pages via the paid-inclusion program, so it would be against their interests to do this. Are the search engines disabling the normal algorithm for paid-inclusion pages to ensure they aren't picked up for free? I don't know.

- ✔ If, in its normal course of travel, the searchbot runs across pages that you have paid to have included, will it index those pages and flag them as no longer requiring payment? I dunno. Will the search engine refund your money for the rest of the submission period? Rather unlikely.

The paid-inclusion systems

If you're interested in paid inclusion, here's a little information about the major players:

- ✔ **AltaVista:** 48-hour addition to the index, daily reindexing. For six months, you pay $39 for the first URL, $29 each for two to ten URLs, and $19 for each one thereafter. Sign up at www.altavista.com/web/express_incl.

- ✔ **Yahoo! Site Match:** Yahoo! don't say how quickly the pages are added to the index, but they're re-indexed every 48 hours. The cost is $49 for the first URL, $29 for the second to tenth, and $10 for every additional URL, *plus* it charges 15 cents every time someone clicks through to your site. Site Match feeds the Yahoo! index, which is also used by AltaVista, AlltheWeb, and others.

- ✔ **Teoma/Ask Jeeves:** Pages added within a week and reindexed every week. For one year, you pay $30 for the first URL and $18 for each one thereafter. Sign up at sitesubmit.ask.com.

The search engines using paid inclusion sell the service through resellers who may have slightly different pricing and services. Some of the major resellers are Position Technologies (www.positiontech.com), Lycos (insite.lycos.com), ineedhits (ink.ineedhits.com), and Network Solutions (www.netsol.com).

As you can see from the preceding list, paid inclusion can get expensive. A 20-page Web site would cost $782 a year if you choose to list your site with the two paid-inclusion systems, before Yahoo!'s click charges. And remember, these systems currently amount to less than 25 percent of the world's search results because Google doesn't offer paid-inclusion programs.

Using trusted feeds

Another form of paid inclusion is known as a *trusted feed* — a sort of *en masse* paid inclusion. Trusted feeds are sometimes used by companies with dynamic Web sites (see Chapter 6 for more on what makes sites dynamic) and are generally intended for large numbers of pages, 500 or more. With a trusted-feed program, you don't pay to have your pages included, but you do pay for every click on a link to one of those pages, $0.25 or more per click.

Both of the paid-inclusion services I mention in the preceding section also have trusted-feed programs. You can get data into the search engines two ways:

- ✔ Provide a list of URLs in a text file.

- ✔ Provide an Excel spreadsheet containing, for each page, the URL, page title, DESCRIPTION meta tag, KEYWORDS meta tag, and the page content.

Providing the data in an Excel spreadsheet allows you to submit data to the search engines so they don't have to crawl your Web site to pick it up. It also allows you to submit the relevant data — ignoring irrelevant page content — which raises the question, "Isn't this just a legal form of cloaking?" (Cloaking is a technique for showing a searchbot a different page from the one a site visitor would see, and it's frowned upon by the search engines. You can read about cloaking in Chapter 7.)

The same resellers who sell paid inclusion also sell trusted feeds, and will help you build your data feed.

Submitting to the Secondary Systems

You can also submit your site to smaller systems with perhaps a few hundred million pages in their indexes — sometimes far fewer. The disadvantage with these systems is that they are relatively little used, compared to the big systems discussed earlier in the chapter. (However, some are still fairly popular sites. ExactSeek, for instance, is ranked by Alexa as the 1,600th most popular Web site.) Many search engine professionals ignore the smaller systems altogether. So if your site is ranked in these systems, you have less competition because they're so small. Here are a couple secondary systems that are worth submitting to:

- ✔ **ExactSeek:** www.exactseek.com/add.html
- ✔ **Gigablast:** www.gigablast.com/addurl

I've provided a list of additional search engines at my site, www.SearchEngine Bulletin.com, and you can find more, including regional sites, listed on the following pages:

- ✔ www.searchenginewatch.com/links/article.php/2156161
- ✔ www.dir-search.com
- ✔ www.allsearchengines.com
- ✔ www.searchengines.com/generalKids.html (search engines for kids)
- ✔ www.searchengines.com/worldUSCan.html (regional search engines)
- ✔ dir.yahoo.com/Computers_and_Internet/Internet/World_Wide_ Web/Searching_the_Web/Search_Engines_and_Directories/

Some of the smaller search engines try to encourage you to pay for a submission. Don't. Unless you know for sure otherwise, you can safely assume that the amount of traffic you are likely to get is probably not worth the payment.

Many smaller search sites don't have their own searchbots; they get the data from other systems such as the Open Directory Project (which feeds around 350 different systems). So, sometimes you'll run across search sites to which you can't submit directly.

If you plan to submit your site to many search engines, you may want to use a programmable keyboard or a text-replacement utility or macro program such as ShortKeys (www.shortkeys.com), which can make entering repetitive data much quicker:

- ✔ With a programmable keyboard, you can assign a string of text — URL, e-mail address, and so on — to a single key, so all you need to do to enter your e-mail address, for instance, is to press F11.
- ✔ A text-replacement utility replaces a short string of text with something else. To enter your e-mail address, for instance, you might just type **em**.

A few sites require that you submit your site with a username and password. Most sites require at least an e-mail address, and some also require that you respond to a confirmation e-mail before they will add your site to the list. Don't use your regular e-mail address! Use a throwaway address because you'll receive a lot of spam.

Using Registration Services and Software Programs

You can also submit your pages to hundreds of search engines by using a submission service or program. Many free services are available, but some of them are out-of-date — they've been sitting out on the Internet running automatically for a few years now and haven't kept up with changes in the search engine scene.

Many of the free services are definitely on the *lite* side. They're provided by companies that hope that you'll spring for a fee-based full service. For example, one well-known service, AdPro (www.addpro.com), provides free submission to the following search engines: ABACHO, Acoon, Aewi, Cipinet, Entireweb, ExactSeek, Find Once, Fyberation, Google, Infomak, Kunani, ScrubTheWeb, Searchit, SplatSearch, Subjex, SurfGopher, Walhello, and WotBot. (Note that ABACHO and Acoon are German search engines, and Aewi is no longer in business.) AdPro also has a paid service that submits to 120 search engines. For $29.95 a year, it manually submits your site to the top search engines and uses a submission program to submit to 120 other services.

Another popular submission system is provided by ineedhits (www.ineedhits.com), which submits a URL to 300 search engines for as little as $2.50. Many of these submission services are available; search for *search engine submission service,* and you'll find a gazillion of them.

Will you get much traffic from these 300 search engines? Probably not, but submitting to them can't hurt. Note also that some submission services increase their submit count by including all the services that are fed by the systems they submit to. For instance, if a service submits to Yahoo!, that's multiple submissions because Yahoo! feeds AltaVista, AlltheWeb, Lycos, Terra.com, HotBot, Overture, InfoSpace, Excite, and more.

Many software programs are available, as well. Here are a few of the more popular ones:

- **Dynamic Submission**, which you can find at www.dynamicsubmission.com. (See Figure 9-1.) I like this program because it's easy and quick to use.

- **SubmitWolf**, at www.submitwolf.com.

- **WebPosition Gold**, at www.webposition.com. (Okay, this program does have some limited submission tools, but it's really more useful for checking search engine positions. See Chapter 18 for more on that score.)

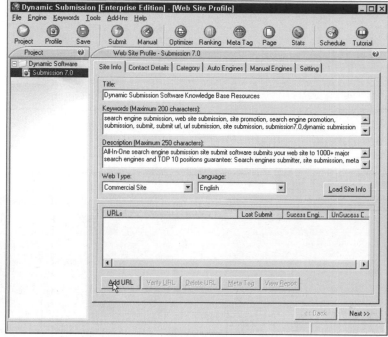

Figure 9-1:
The
Dynamic
Submission
mass-
registration
tool.

The big advantage of these software programs is that you only pay once rather than pay for a service every time you use it.

Although automated tools are handy, submitting a URL by hand is the best option, if you have the time. You can't guarantee that an automated tool completes the correct fields, or that if a response to an e-mail is required, it happens. But if you're submitting to 300 little-used search engines, by all means use an automated tool!

Chapter 10

Submitting to the Directories

*I*n Chapter 9, you look at getting your site into the search engines. In this chapter, you look at getting your site into the directories. The major directories are very important to a search strategy, although they can be rather frustrating to work with. Compared to search engines, the overall process of working with directories is very different — and in some ways it's simpler . . . but in other ways not. There aren't many of them though — just a handful of directories of any real significance.

Understanding Search Directories (Vs. Search Engines)

Before you starting working with directories, it's helpful to know a few basics about what directories are — and are *not*. Search directories don't operate like the search engines:

- The directories don't send "bots" out onto the Web looking for Web sites to add.

- The directories don't read and store information from Web pages within a site.

- Because the directories don't read and store information, they don't base search results on the contents of the Web pages.

Unlike search engines, the search directories also don't index Web *pages;* they index Web *sites.* Each site is assigned to a particular *category.* Within the categories, the directory's index contains just a little information about each site — not much more than a name, title, and description. The result is categorized lists of Web sites — and that's really what the search directories are all about.

Not too long ago, Yahoo! was based around its directory. In fact, look at Figure 10-1 for an example of what Yahoo! looked like early in 1998 (courtesy of a wonderful service called the WayBackMachine, which you can find at www. archive.org). The idea behind Yahoo! was a categorized directory of Web sites that people could browse. You could click links to drill-down through the directory and find what you needed, similar in a way to flipping through a Yellow Pages directory. Although you could use the Search box to search the categories, site titles, and site descriptions, the Search tool was nothing like the Yahoo! search tool of today, which can hunt for your search term everywhere on the Web (through, at the time of writing, Google).

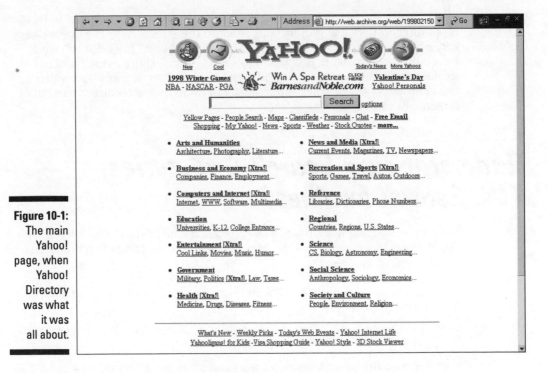

Figure 10-1:
The main
Yahoo!
page, when
Yahoo!
Directory
was what
it was
all about.

But Yahoo! made an enormous mistake. In fact, the image in Figure 10-1 is from a time at which Yahoo! was at its peak, a time when most of the world's Web searches were carried out through its site . . . just a few months before Google began operations. Yahoo! evidently hadn't fully realized the weaknesses of the directory system until it was too late. These weaknesses include the following:

✔ **Directories provide no way for someone to search individual pages within a site.** The perfect fit for your information needs may be sitting somewhere on a site that is included in a directory, but there's no way to know because the directory doesn't index individual pages.

✔ **Categorization is necessarily limited.** Sites are rarely about a single topic; even if they appear to be, single topics can be broken down into smaller subtopics. By forcing people to find a site by category and by keyword in a very limited amount of text — a description and title — the directories are obviously very restrictive.

✔ **Hand-built directories are necessarily limited in size.** *Hand-built* directories, such as Yahoo! Directory and the Open Directory, add a site to their directories only after a real live human editor has reviewed the site. With hundreds of millions of Web sites, there's no way a human-powered system could keep up.

✔ **Hand-built directories can also get very out-of-date.** Yahoo! Directory contains some extremely old and out-of-date information that simply wouldn't be present in an index that is automatically reindexed every few days or weeks. (Yahoo! spiders the sites in its index for broken links and dead sites, but if the site's purpose has changed, Yahoo! may not realize that fact.)

The proof of directories' weaknesses is in the pudding: Google took over and now is the dominant search system on the Web. (To be fair, Yahoo! helped Google by integrating Google results into Yahoo! searches, for several years, though in the summer of 2004, it dropped Google and began using its own index.

The old Yahoo! site directory is still there, but it's virtually hidden to many visitors. If you have your computer monitor set to a resolution of 800 x 600 (as perhaps 50 percent of computer users do at this point), then the directory is "below the fold," to use a newspaper term; you have to scroll down the main page to see it. Even if you use a higher resolution, you still may not see the directory (depending on the browser you are using and the number of toolbars you have open). Yahoo! has most definitely de-emphasized the role of the directory in its search services.

Why Are Directories So Significant?

I don't want to sound like *I'm* de-emphasizing the search directories! They're still very significant, for a number of reasons:

✔ Yahoo! Directory is part of the Yahoo! search system, one of the world's most popular search sites. As such, it still gets a lot of traffic. You can access it directly at `dir.yahoo.com`, and some people do access it from the Yahoo! main page. In addition, when you use the Search the Web box at the top, Yahoo! produces search engine results as well as a tab at the top of the page that takes you to matching directory results. Yahoo! claims that 230 million *unique users* visit Yahoo! Directory each month (though Yahoo! probably actually means 230 *unique visits,* which is a very different thing).

✔ The Open Directory Project feeds results to Google Directory, which is part of the world's *most popular* search site.

✔ The Open Directory Project also feeds results to literally hundreds of other sites (well over 300), large and small; many of these sites are crawled by the major search engines (such as Google), so a link from the Open Directory Project can show up as links from many other sites, too.

✔ Links in the major directories help provide "context" to the search engines — if your site is in the category in the Open Directory Project, for instance, the search engines know that the site has something to do with playing with rodents. The directory presence helps search engines index your site and may help your site rank higher for some search terms.

By the way, don't underestimate the Open Directory Project just because you've never heard of it . . . or because the submission forms are often broken or unreliable. Data from this system is widely spread across the Internet, and has often been used to kick-start major search systems. Yahoo!, for instance, once used data from the Open Directory Project (which, incidentally, is owned by AOL/Netscape).

Submitting to the Search Directories

The previous chapter has what some may find an unusual message: "Sure, you can submit to the search engines, but it may not do you any good." Search engines really like links to your site, and having links to your site is often the best way to get into the search engines.

But the search directories don't care about links, and the only way to get into search directories is to *submit* to them. And you can forget automated submission programs for the major directories — there's no way to use them. Submissions must be entered into Yahoo! and the Open Directory Project "by hand."

Submitting to Yahoo! Directory

Once free, submissions to Yahoo! Directory used to be very difficult. Surveys showed that people who had managed to get their sites listed in the directory had to try multiple times over a matter of months. Well, I've got good news and bad. The good news is that you can now get your site listed in Yahoo! Directory within about a week. Of all the major search systems, getting into Yahoo! Directory is easiest; Yahoo! guarantees to review your site within seven business days. They're not guaranteeing to include your site, by the way, only to review it and add it if it's appropriate, but in general, most people don't have many problems. If your site is a functioning site without a lot of broken links; if it's in English (assuming you're submitting to the main directory and not a regional directory); if the site is designed for multiple browser types (they expressly exclude Java-only sites); and if you select an appropriate category, Yahoo! will almost certainly accept it.

The bad news is it's probably going to cost you $299 a year for the privilege ($600 for adult sites). It *is* free if you have a noncommercial site, but for any kind of commercial venture, you'll have to cough up the cash. (Note, however, that Yahoo! Directory still contains many sites that predate the paid-listing policy and do not require payment.)

Is listing in Yahoo! Directory worth $299? Hard to say, but there are some good reasons to do so:

- ✔ It seems likely that getting into Yahoo! Directory also ensures that you get into the Yahoo! Web Search (though I've been unable to find any verification of this idea).

- ✔ It's crawled by Google's searchbot — Google will note the link, and it may help your PageRank a little (as explained in Chapter 12).

- ✔ The search engines will use the directory to help them categorize your site.

- ✔ Many people, as I mentioned earlier, *do* use the directory.

- ✔ After your site is in the directory, you may be able to place a cheap ad at the top of your category. (Some category sponsors are paying as little as $25 per month.)

The 1-2-3's of getting listed

Here's how to get listed:

1. **Find a credit card — preferably yours or that of someone who has given you permission to spend $299 (or is it $600?).**

2. **To make sure that your site isn't already included, open your browser and go to** dir.yahoo.com. **After the page has loaded, search for your site by typing your domain name into the Search box and clicking Search.**

   If you have total control over your site, this step isn't necessary. Of course, you'll know if your site is already listed. But if, for example, you inherited it from another department in the company you work for, who knows — it may already be there.

3. **Return to the Yahoo! Directory main page, and browse through the categories looking for the best match for your site.**

   You can find tips on choosing a category in the next section, "Picking a category."

4. **When you've found a category into which you want to place your site, look for a link that says something like *Suggest a Site,* or perhaps a promotional box of some kind (see Figure 10-2 for an example).**

   The link is probably somewhere in the top right of the page.

5. **Click the link and follow the instructions; you'll have to enter a site description, contact and billing information, and so on.**

Picking a category

Because of the sheer volume of categories, picking a category is not as simple as it might seem. Yahoo! Directory has 14 major categories, and many thousands of subcategories. But understanding a few points about hunting for and submitting to a category can make the process a little smoother.

Look for one of these links.

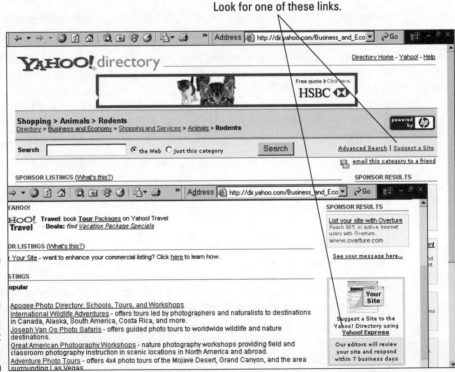

Figure 10-2:
Look for one of these links to submit your site.

First, you need to choose a fairly specific category. You can't submit a site to a category or subcategory if it only holds other subcategories. For instance, you can't submit a site to the Business & Economy category. It's just too broad. Rather, you have to drill down further into the subcategories and find a category that's specific enough to contain actual Web sites.

You'll probably find that your site could perhaps fit into several categories, so you're going to have to dig around for a while and pick the most appropriate category. Although discouraged, it *is* possible to put a single site into multiple categories, but of course you'll have to pay for each category. (And Yahoo! doesn't like doing this, anyway; it can take time and effort to persuade them to allow you to do so.)

One good strategy is to look for your competitors; what categories are they assigned to? If you find a category with a whole bunch of companies similar to yours, you've probably found the right one.

Note, by the way, that as you move through Yahoo! Directory, you'll see that some category names have an @ sign at the end, such as Graduate Programs@, Booksellers@, Intranet@, and so on. These are cross-references to categories under different branches of the directory. For instance, if you browse down the directory to Recreation > Travel, you see a link to Tour Operators@; click this link, and you jump over to > > > Tour Operators. In fact virtually all Web sites that sell or promote a product end up somewhere under Business and Economy, even if they are cross-linked from other parts of the directory.

Note also that you have to actually be *inside* a category before you can add a page. This is a little confusing perhaps. When you first search in the directory, Yahoo! displays a page that contains a list of categories and a whole bunch of Web sites that match your search, but from various different categories (see Figure 10-3). Thus you are not actually inside a category at this point, so can't add a page here. You see links that will take you into specific categories.

Submitting to the Open Directory Project

Submitting to the Open Directory Project is a little easier in some ways than submitting to Yahoo! Directory, but more difficult in one important way. Yes, the Open Directory Project is free, and yes, you can submit much more quickly. But the problem is there's no guarantee that your site will be listed. I've seen sites get into the Open Directory Project within a week or two of submission . . . and others that waited months without ever getting in. (If that happens, you should try resubmitting.) In addition, the submission forms sometimes don't seem to work!

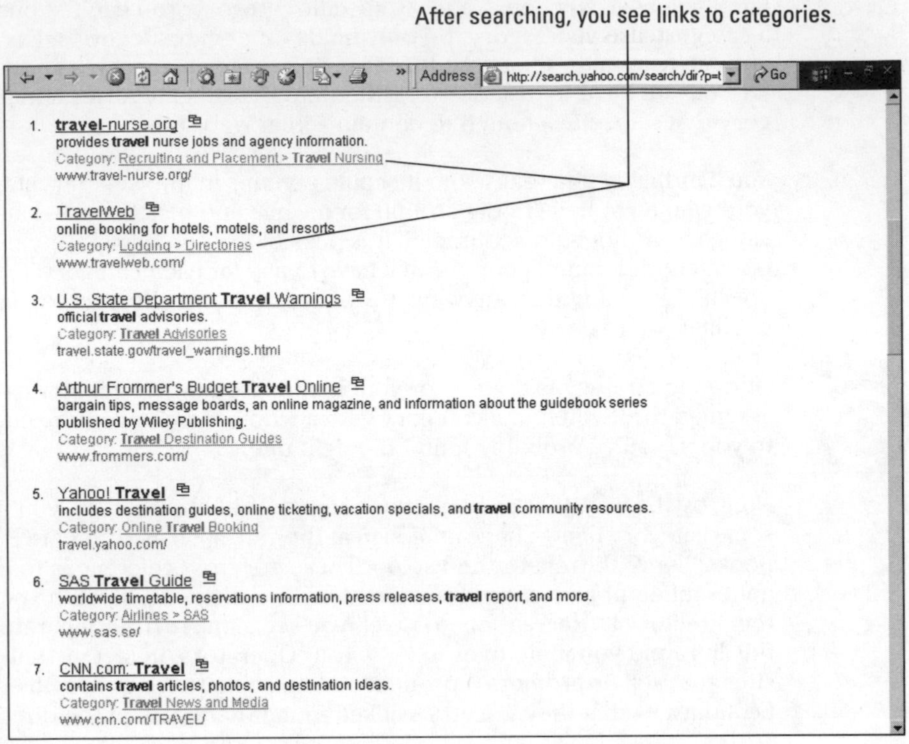

After searching, you see links to categories.

1. **travel**-nurse.org
   provides **travel** nurse jobs and agency information.
   Category: Recruiting and Placement > **Travel** Nursing
   www.travel-nurse.org/

2. TravelWeb
   online booking for hotels, motels, and resorts.
   Category: Lodging > Directories
   www.travelweb.com/

3. U.S. State Department **Travel** Warnings
   official **travel** advisories.
   Category: **Travel** Advisories
   travel.state.gov/travel_warnings.html

4. Arthur Frommer's Budget **Travel** Online
   bargain tips, message boards, an online magazine, and information about the guidebook series
   published by Wiley Publishing.
   Category: **Travel** Destination Guides
   www.frommers.com/

5. Yahoo! **Travel**
   includes destination guides, online ticketing, vacation specials, and **travel** community resources.
   Category: Online **Travel** Booking
   travel.yahoo.com/

6. SAS **Travel** Guide
   worldwide timetable, reservations information, press releases, **travel** report, and more.
   Category: Airlines > SAS
   www.sas.se/

7. CNN.com: **Travel**
   contains **travel** articles, photos, and destination ideas.
   Category: **Travel** News and Media
   www.cnn.com/TRAVEL/

Figure 10-3:
After searching at Yahoo! Directory, you see links to directory categories.

But don't give up. As I make abundantly clear, both earlier in this chapter and in Chapter 1, the Open Directory Project is very important. Here's how to submit:

1. **In your browser, go to** `www.dmoz.org`.

   The Open Directory Project home page appears.

2. **Find a suitable category for your site; see "Picking a category," earlier in this chapter.**

3. **Click the Suggest URL link at the top of the page.**

4. **Follow the (fairly simple) directions.**

Submitting to the Open Directory Project is much easier than doing so to Yahoo! Directory. You simply enter your home page's URL, a short title, a 25- to 30-word description for the site, and your e-mail address. That's it. Then you wait.

Give it six to eight weeks, and if your site doesn't appear in the index, try again. You might also visit www.resource-zone.com, where you can find forums hosted by Open Directory Project editors who may be able to help you.

Submitting to Second-Tier Directories

There are many *second-tier* directories — smallish directories with nowhere near the significance of Yahoo! Directory or the Open Directory Project — that can help you a little if you're willing to spend a couple of hours registering your site with them.

Unlike search engines, directories can be "crawled" by a searchbot. Directories, remember, are categorized collections of sites that you can browse. If you can browse by clicking links to drill down through the directory, then so can a searchbot. In fact, the major search engines, including Google, index many small directories. If you have a link in one of these directories and Google sees it, that can help your Google standing, as explained in Chapter 12.

Finding second-tier directories

There are hundreds of directories, though you don't want to spend much time with most of them. Many of the directories you find are using data from the Open Directory Project, so you have, in effect, already submitted to them. (You did submit to ODP, didn't you?) Often these sites have a little Open Directory Project box, like the one shown in Figure 10-4, near the bottom of the page. This box will soon become familiar as you dig around looking for directories. But sometimes a site's relationship to the ODP isn't so clear.

Figure 10-4:
This box means the data comes from the Open Directory Project.

> Help build the largest human-edited directory on the web
> Submit a Site - Open Directory Project - Become an Editor

I've provided a list of second-tier directories at my Web site (`www.Search EngineBulletin.com`). You can also find more directories at some of these sites:

- `www.searchengines.com`
- `www.dir-search.com`
- The Search Engines and Directories category in the Yahoo! Directory. (Go to `dir.yahoo.com` and search for *search engines and directories* to find a huge list.)

Don't pay! . . . Maybe

Don't bother paying to register with these second-tier systems. As with search engines, the directory owners are also trying to get site owners to pay to be placed into the index. For example, JoeAnt wants a $39.99 one-time fee to take your information. In most cases, the listing simply isn't worth the fee. Regard being listed in these directories as cheap additional links, not as something you need to spend a lot of money on.

On the other hand, you may run across directories that you feel really *are* of value. Business.com (`www.business.com`) is a great example of a very important second-tier directory, integrated into busy sites such as BusinessWeek Online (`www.businessweek.com`, the online companion to *Business Week* magazine). Being in such directories may bring sufficient traffic to your site to be worthwhile.

Chapter 11

Buried Treasure — More Great Places to Submit Your Site

1 n Chapters 9 and 10, you find out about the places where you can register your site — the major search systems such as Google and the Open Directory Project, and secondary systems such as ExactSeek and Business.com. Some of the sites you find out about in this chapter are more important than the secondary systems and, in some cases, even more important than the major search systems. That's right, some companies do more business from the sites I discuss in this chapter than from the major search engines.

Don't forget the Yellow Pages sites, which handle billions of searches each year. Although most businesses probably won't want to pay for an ad on a Yellow Pages site (if you have a business phone line, you've already got a free listing), these are search systems, and many businesses use them very profitably. In general, if you've found the paper Yellow Pages to be worthwhile, you may find online Yellow Pages useful, too.

Keeping a Landscape Log

I recommend that you keep track of what you discover during your online research. You'll come across small directories related to your area of business, newsgroups, Web-based forums, mailing-list discussion groups, private sites created by interested individuals, competitors . . . all sorts of things that can help promote your site.

In effect, you're mapping the Internet landscape, the area of the Internet in which your business operates. You need to keep the information you gather so you can use it after your research is complete. Maybe you find some directories that you want to register with. Or you discover some e-mail newsletters that you want to work with when you have the time. For instance, you may want to contact newsletters to see if they will do a review of your site or your products. (There's more to promoting a site than just working with the search engines!)

Your landscape log doesn't have to be complicated. It can be a Microsoft Word document or maybe an Excel spreadsheet. If you want to get really organized, you can use an ACT or Access database. I suggest that you keep the following information:

- **Site name**
- **Company name (if different from the site name)**
- **URL**
- **PageRank:** I explain PageRank in Google in Chapter 12. It's a good indication of the value of any link you might get from the site. In general, the higher the rank, the more valuable the link.
- **Alexa Traffic Rank:** When you visit a site, look at the traffic ranking noted on the Alexa Toolbar. (I suggest that you load this toolbar in Chapter 1.) This ranking provides a good indication of how much traffic the site gets so you can decide if some kind of cooperative venture is worthwhile.
- **Contact name:** If you can find a contact name, it's useful to have.
- **Contact e-mail address**
- **Notes:** Write a quick description of your impression of the site and how it might help you.
- **Actions:** Keep track of when you contact the site (to ask for a link, for example).

I'm not just talking about the research you do while looking for specialized directories. Whenever you work online and uncover competitors, potential partners, useful resources, and so on, you should store that information somewhere for later use.

Finding the Specialized Directories

For just about every subject you can imagine, someone is running a specialized search directory. Although specialized directories get very little traffic when compared to the Googles and Yahoo!s of the world, the traffic they do get is highly targeted, just the people you want to attract. And such directories are often very popular with your target audience.

Here's an example of how to search for a specialized directory. Suppose that you're promoting your rodent-racing Web site. Go to Google and type `rodent racing directory`. Hmmm, for some reason Google doesn't find any directories related to rodent racing. Strange. Okay, try `rodent directory`. Now you're getting somewhere! I did this search and found several useful sites:

- ✔ **The IRD — International Rodentfancy Directory:** "An international listing of PET rodent breeders, shelters, vets, stores, pet sitters and more! This service is brought to you by Rodentfancy.com and the Rat and Mouse Fanciers for Excellence . . . free to your business or service's listing to the directory!" This site's home page has a PageRank of 5 and an Alexa traffic rank of 302,000.

- ✔ **NetVet's Electronic Zoo:** This is a big list of links to rodent-related sites, though mostly related to research (the Digital Atlas of Mouse Embryology and the Cybermouse Project, for instance). But with a PageRank of 6 and an Alexa traffic rank of under 5,600, it might be worth your trying to get listed. Perhaps you can suggest that your site is related to research into cardiovascular performance of rodents under stress.

- ✔ **Rodent Resources at the National Center for Research Resources:** Hmm, this is another rodent-research site, but with an Alexa traffic rank of 284 and a PageRank of 9. Getting listed in this directory would be very useful. (Maybe it's time to apply for a research grant.)

- ✔ **The Rodent Breeders List:** This directory strikes me as one of those "not very pleasant, but somebody's got to do it" things. Still, if you breed rodents for your races, you may want to get onto this list.

When you do a search for a specialty directory, your search results will include the specialty directories you need, but mixed in with them, you'll also find results from the Yahoo! Directory, Google Directory, and the Open Directory Project. If you want, you can clear out the clutter by searching like this:

```
rodent directory -inurl:yahoo.com -inurl:google.com -inurl:dmoz.org
```

This search phrase tells Google to look for pages with the words *rodent* and *directory,* but to ignore any pages that have yahoo.com, google.com, or dmoz. org (the Open Directory Project) in their URLs.

Note that some of the specialty directories you find actually *pull* data from the Open Directory Project. For instance, I found the Rodents Directory, which is part of Directory.NET (`www.directory.net/Recreation/Pets/Rodents`). This directory looked very large and professional, but upon further investigation, I discovered it was using the Open Directory Project data. You certainly want to be listed in this rodent directory, but in order to get into the directory, you need to get into the Open Directory Project itself, as I explain in Chapter 10.

Hundreds of sites use Open Directory Project information, so you're bound to run into them now and then. How can you tell when a site is pulling data from the Open Directory Project? Here are a few signs to look for:

✔ Although it's a little-known site, it seems to have a lot of data, covering a huge range of subjects.

✔ The directory seems to be structured in the familiar table of categories and subcategories.

✔ The real giveaway is usually at the bottom of the page, where you'll find a box with links to the Open Directory Project, along with a note crediting that organization. (See Figure 11-1.)

With a traffic rank of almost 18,000, Directory.net is definitely not a top-level search system . . .

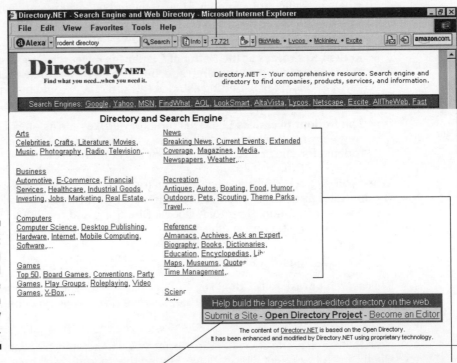

Figure 11-1: Identifying data pulled from the Open Directory Project.

Here's what gives it away — the attribution to the Open Directory Project.

. . . but still, it has a huge amount of information.

You may also want to search for these directories by using the term *index*. Although this term is not used as commonly as *directory,* some sites do use it. For instance, when I searched for photography index, I found the Nature Photo Index (www.naturepix.com), which includes a directory of Web sites related to nature photography.

More ways to find directories

You can use other methods to track down specialty directories. In fact, as you get to know the Internet landscape around your business, you'll run into these directories eventually. People mention them in discussion groups, for instance, or you'll find links to them on other Web sites.

I also like browsing for these directories in the major directories, Yahoo! and the Open Directory Project. Yahoo! Directory (dir.yahoo.com) has many subcategories for directories. It doesn't have one for rodent racing, which apparently gets no respect, but it certainly has directories for many other topics, such as the following:

- ✔ Snowboarding > Web Directories
- ✔ Photography > Web Directories
- ✔ Radio Stations > Web Directories
- ✔ Arts > Web Directories
- ✔ Transgendered > Web Directories
- ✔ Comics and Animations > Web Directories

For some reason, Yahoo! Directory also has subcategories simply called Directories. (No, I don't know the difference between a Web Directories subcategory and a Directories subcategory.) Here's a sampling of the Directories subcategory:

- ✔ Travel and Transportation > Directories
- ✔ Business and Economy > Directories
- ✔ Reference > Directories
- ✔ Haunted Houses > Directories
- ✔ Ethnic Studies > Directories

Pay attention while you're working in Yahoo!, or you may find yourself in the Yahoo! Search results area rather than the Yahoo! Directory. Note the tab at the top of the page. When the Web tab is highlighted, you're in Yahoo! Search; when the Directory tab is highlighted, you're in the Yahoo! Directory.

The best way to find the Web Directories or Directories subcategories is simply to go to the Yahoo! Directory and browse for suitable categories for your Web site. Each time you find a suitable category, search the page for the word *directory* to see if the page includes a link to a Web Directory or Directory subcategory. (You can also use the Search box; search for `haunted houses directory`, and one of the resulting links will be to *Haunted Houses > Directories*.)

Yahoo! currently has almost 1,400 of these directory subcategories, representing many thousands of directory Web sites. I found links to 13 directories of haunted houses (a number that one might almost imagine is intentional); 13 directories of humor sites; 9 directories of sites related to transgendering; 7 directories of sites that provide electronic greeting cards; and 6 directories of fitness Web sites.

This grossly unscientific survey suggests to me that probably almost 14,000 directory sites are listed in Yahoo! So chances are good that several may be good candidates for listing your site.

The Open Directory Project also lists thousands of directories. Again, browse through the directory (at `www.dmoz.org`) looking for appropriate categories, and then search the page for the word *directories*. Or search for an appropriate directory: *golf directories, golf directory, rodent directories, rodent directory, transgender directories, transgender directory,* and so on. (Yes, searching on *directories* and *directory* will provide different results.)

When you find a directory, see what's in it. Don't just ask for a link and move on. Dig around, see what you can find, and add information to your landscape log. The directory will contain links to other sites that may also have their own directories.

Local directories

You can also find local directories — directories of businesses in your area. These local directories are often good places to get listed. They are easy to get into and can provide more site categorization clues for the search engines, and they often have high PageRanks.

It's easy to find such directories. Search for a placename and the term *directory* — `colorado directory`, for instance, or `denver directory`. And look in Yahoo!'s and the Open Directory Project's regional categories.

Why bother with directories?

Why should you care about these directories? Here are a few reasons:

- ✔ **They provide another channel to your site from the search engines.** When someone searches on, say, fitness, your Rodent Chasing for Cardiovascular Health site may not appear, but Buzzle.com and AtoZfitness.com might. If you're listed in those directories, maybe the searcher will find you.

- ✔ **Some of the pages at these directory sites have very good PageRanks.** Links from pages with high PageRanks pass on part of the PageRank to *your* site, helping you rise in the search engines. For instance, one of the directory pages I looked at on the AtoZfitness.com site had a PageRank of 5, which is very good. (For the lowdown on PageRank, check out Chapter 12.)

- ✔ **As a general principle, links are good.** Almost all links help to boost your PageRank, but in addition, links increase your chances of getting found by the search engines. The more links to your site, the more often search bots will stumble across your site and index it.

- ✔ **Some of these directory sites get a lot of traffic.** Buzzle.com, for instance, is more or less the world's 1,700th most popular Web site. I know that sounds like a big number, but with hundreds of millions of users online, and millions of Web sites, that's not bad. Some of these directories may be able to send you some really good traffic.

Getting the link

After you've found a directory, you want to get the link. In some cases, you have to e-mail someone at the directory and ask. Many of these little directories are run by individuals and are often pretty crudely built. The problem you may run into is that it may take some time for the owner to get around to adding the link — the directory is just a hobby in many cases, after all.

Some directories have automated systems. Look for a Submit Your Site link, or maybe Add URL, Add Your Site, or something similar. The site may provide a form in which you enter your information. Some directories review the information before adding it to the directory, and in other, less common, situations, your information may post directly to the site.

By the way, some of these directories may ask you to pay to be added to the directory or give you preferential treatment if you pay.

Should you pay?

Generally, no.

Why not?

Look, it sometimes seems like everyone's trying to get you to pay these days. Every time you try to get a link somewhere, someone's asking for money. Buzzle.com, for example, a portal with all sorts of directories, wants you to pay $59 (regularly $99, though I'm not sure what or when regular is). That gets you into the index within seven days and gets you preferential placement.

The term *portal* is an Internet-geek term that, roughly translated, means "We've got all sorts of stuff on our site like news, and weather, and you know, *communities,* and, like, stuff, and we still have some of our dotcom cash left, which should keep us going a few more months while we try to figure out how to make money, and heck, if we don't, Uncle Joe still wants me to come work for him in his furniture store."

Of course that means Buzzle.com has to have listings over which you can have preferential placement; in other words, you *can* get in for free. Scroll down the page a little, and you'll find the free Basic Submission.

I recommend that you do *not* pay for these placements, at least to begin with. In *most* cases, they simply aren't worth spending $60, $100, or more for the link. It's worth spending a few moments getting a free link, though. If a site asks you to pay, dig around and see if you can find a free-placement link. If not, just move on. (If the site can guarantee that you'll be on a page with a PageRank of 6 or 7 or more, the fee may be worth it. See Chapter 12 for more information about PageRank.)

At some point, it might, perhaps, be worthwhile to *consider* thinking about paying for such placements, but generally only if you know the site is capable of sending you valuable traffic.

You don't have to pay

Luckily, you may find that some of the best directories are free. Take, for instance, the model rocket business. Hundreds of model rocket sites are on the Web, often run by individuals or families. (See the site shown in Figure 11-2.) Many of these sites have link pages. Although these sites don't get huge numbers of visitors, they *do* get the right visitors (people interested in model rockets) and often have pretty good PageRanks.

Most of these sites will give you a free listing, just for the asking. Look for a contact e-mail address somewhere.

Figure 11-2:
Okay, so it's ugly and doesn't get a huge amount of traffic. But it does have a reasonable PageRank, and if you ask nicely, the site may give you a link. (It probably won't give me a link now, but maybe you'll get one.)

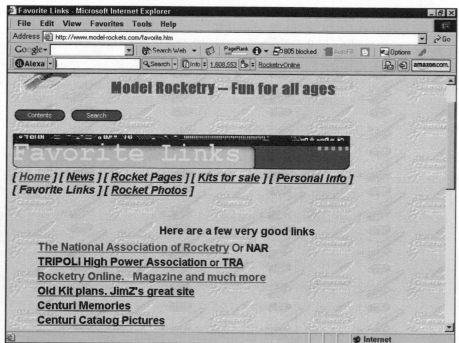

Working with the Yellow Pages

The Yellow Pages companies don't know what's about to hit them. Yellow Pages are incredibly profitable — the biggest Yellow Pages companies make billions of dollars each year, with profits of many hundreds of millions. They're real cash cows, but they're about to get steamrollered.

It won't happen this year, or next year. But pretty soon the shakeup will begin. Millions of computer-literate, Internet-loving people no longer pick up a Yellow Pages book or, perhaps, pick one up once or twice a year, compared with several times a month in the pre-Internet days. Five or ten years from now, the number of people using the book will be declining precipitously, and businesses will realize it. Google is already experimenting with geographic searches, and in a few years, online searches for local businesses will be as convenient for searchers as using the paper Yellow Pages — better, actually.

The Yellow Pages companies don't fully appreciate the changes that are about to hit them. They have, however, started their foray into the Internet. In fact, several Yellow Pages sites are incredibly important already. It may make sense for you to list your Web site with the Yellow Pages sites, especially if your business already buys Yellow Pages ads.

You rarely hear much about the Yellow Pages sites in discussions about search engines, but they *are* search engines . . . directories, anyway. And they're incredibly important ones, too. Billions of searches are carried out every year through the Yellow Pages sites.

The following are the largest Yellow Pages sites (the numbers in parentheses are the Alexa traffic ranks, indicating the sites' overall popularity):

- **Yahoo! Yellow Pages (1):** yp.yahoo.com
- **InfoSpace (184):** www.infospace.com
- **WorldPages.com (424):** www.worldpages.com
- **SBC SMARTPages (646):** smartpages.com
- **BellSouth RealPages.com (1,210):** www.realpages.com
- **Yell.com (1,296):** yell.com
- **YellowPages.com (1,595):** www.yellowpages.com
- **DexOnline.com (1,651):** www.dexonline.com
- **Verizon SuperPages (18,797):** superpages.com
- **Yellowbook.com (22,002):** www.yellowbook.com
- **Yellow.com (28,944):** www.yellow.com

The advantages to using Yellow Pages sites? They generate lots of local searches. If you own a shoe shop, for example, potential customers are more likely to find you through a Yellow Pages site than through a search engine.

The disadvantages? They're expensive. Basic listings are free because the basic listings come from the paper Yellow Pages, and all business phone customers get a free basic listing. But these basic listings don't have links to your Web site, so however useful they are for generating phone calls, they won't generate clicks. For that, you'll have to pay. An ad like the one shown in Figure 11-3, for instance, will cost you $300 a year on YellowPages.com. On the real Yellow Pages sites, the ones owned by the companies publishing Yellow Pages directories, ads can often be much more.

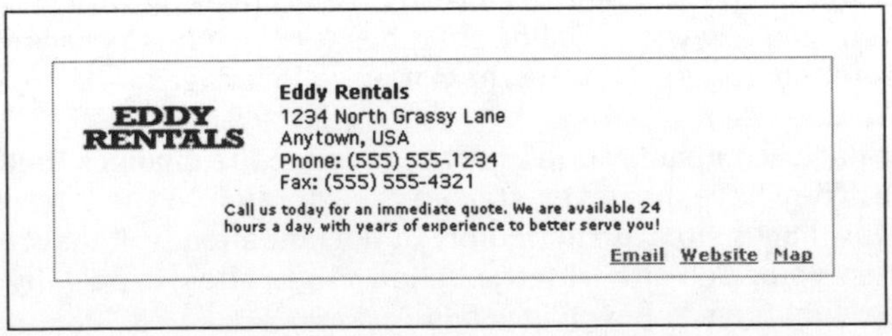

Figure 11-3: $300 a year. Is it worth it? Sorry, I really don't know!

EDDY RENTALS

Eddy Rentals
1234 North Grassy Lane
Anytown, USA
Phone: (555) 555-1234
Fax: (555) 555-4321

Call us today for an immediate quote. We are available 24 hours a day, with years of experience to better serve you!

Email Website Map

Getting into the Yellow Pages

You can get your business into a Yellow Pages site three ways:

- ✔ **Get a business phone line.** You'll get your free listing in the local Yellow Pages book, which also gets you your listing in the online Yellow Pages. As with the book, this is just a simple listing, with no extras.

- ✔ **Buy a listing or ad through your local Yellow Pages rep.** This is the same guy selling you space in the paper book.

- ✔ **Sign up directly through the Web site.**

The Yellow Pages companies share listings. If you have a business phone in Colorado, your listing is in a QwestDex paper book, ends up on DexOnline.com, and also ends up in the Verizon SuperPages site, as shown in Figure 11-4.

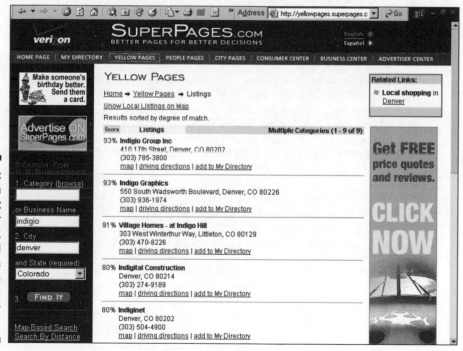

Figure 11-4: Verizon doesn't cover Colorado, but it still carries Colorado listings in its Yellow Pages.

I recommend that if your company already buys Yellow Pages ads and your business is *geo-specific* — that is, you're trying to attract buyers in a particular area — you should look into using the Yellow Pages. Talk to your rep. The rep should be able to tell you how many searches are carried out in the company's online Yellow Pages, in a particular category and a particular region, each month. From that information, you may be able to decide if purchasing an ad makes sense. The online Yellow Pages companies sell a variety of services, such as the following (you can see some in Figure 11-5):

✔ A link from the listing in the online Yellow Pages to your Web site

✔ An e-mail link

✔ A page with detailed information, such as a map to your location, information about your products and services, payment options, and so on

✔ A link to a picture of your ad that appears in the paper Yellow Pages

✔ A pop-up promo box that appears when someone points at an icon, and that can be modified whenever you want through an online-management system

✔ A link to a coupon that customers can print

As I've already mentioned, these ads can be pricey. You pay by the month for each component — maybe $30 a month for a link to your Web site, $30 for a detailed information page, $20 for an e-mail link, and so on. (Rates vary among companies.) Such advertising probably makes sense if you are a dedicated advertiser in the paper Yellow Pages and find it works for you. The online version may work, too. Dedicated users of the Yellow Pages are moving online, and the Yellow Pages companies are spending millions of dollars in an effort to encourage people to use their sites.

You can buy ads directly from some of the Yellow Pages sites. You can sign up online at, for instance, YellowPages.com. But this isn't a *real* Yellow Pages site. It's not owned or operated by a company that makes Yellow Page books. It's also ugly and hard to use. (I'm shy, and don't like to upset anyone, so I won't tell you what I really think about the site.) You can also buy ads at Yell.com, though this site predominantly targets the U.K. market. (Prices are in pounds sterling, despite the fact that the directory also covers the United States.) Some of the bigger sites don't take orders online directly. You can request a quote online, but your information is probably sent to a real-live rep who then calls you. (Traditional Yellow Pages companies often have agreements with the sales-reps unions that make direct online sales impossible.)

Click here to view an image of the ad in the Yellow Pages book.

Click here to go to
a company's Web site. ⎯

Click here to view details
about this company.

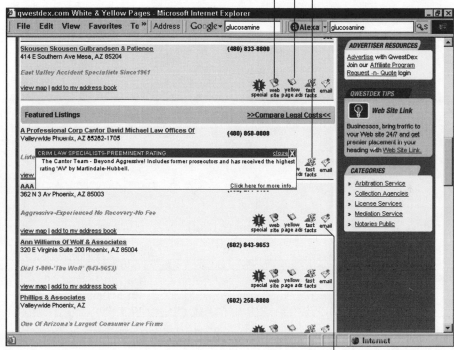

Figure 11-5:
Some of the
new ad
features on
the Dex
Online.com
Web site.

Click here to send an e-mail to the company.

Part IV
After You've Submitted

The 5th Wave — By Rich Tennant

"So far our Web presence has been pretty good. We've gotten some orders, a few inquiries and nine guys who want to date our logo."

In this part . . .

Submitting your site to the search engines isn't enough. It doesn't guarantee that they'll include your site, and it doesn't guarantee that your site will rank well. So this part of the book is essential to your success. In particular, you must understand the value of links pointing to your Web site.

Search engines use links to find your site, to figure out what your site is about, and to estimate how valuable your site is. Search engine optimization without a link campaign is like looking for a job without a résumé: You may make contact, but you won't close the deal. In this part, you discover the different ways in which search engines use links, and then you find out how to get those all-important incoming links.

But this part of the book has more. You find out about the shopping directories, specialized systems that index commercial products (and, in a few cases, services) — from Froogle and Google Catalogs, to Shopping.com and Yahoo! Shopping. If you're selling online, you must know about these systems.

Finally, this part provides information that helps you make the most of a pay-per-click (PPC) advertising campaign. Billions of dollars are being spent on *paid placement* search results. Many companies use these ads very successfully, while others lose money. Read this part to find out how to be part of the right group!

Chapter 12

Using Link Popularity to Boost Your Position

In This Chapter

▶ Understanding how search engines calculate value

▶ Building Web site hubs

▶ Identifying links that aren't links

▶ Using keywords in links

Thousands of site owners have experienced the frustration of not being able to get search engines to index their sites. You build a Web site, you do your best to optimize it for the search engines, you register in the search engines, and then nothing much happens. Little or no traffic turns up at your site, your pages don't rank well in the search engines, and in some cases, you can't even find your pages in the search engines. What's going on?

Here's the opposite scenario. You have an existing site, and you find a few other sites to link to it. You make no changes to the pages themselves, yet all of a sudden you notice your pages jump up in the search engines.

There's a lot of confusion about links and their relationship to Web sites. Most site owners don't even realize that links have a bearing on their search engine positions. Surely all you need to do is register your page in a search engine and it will be indexed, right? Maybe, maybe not. And if it is, it may not be ranked highly.

This chapter takes the confusion out of links by showing you the ways in which links can help you, and the things you need to know in order to make them work.

Why Search Engines Like Links

A few years ago, pretty much all you had to do to get your site listed in a search engine — and maybe even ranked well — was to register with the search engine. Then along came Google in 1998, and that all changed. Google decided to use the links pointing at a site as another factor in determining if the site was a good match for a search. Each link to a site was a vote for the site, and the more votes the site received, the better a site was regarded by Google.

To rank well today, you need to use links to *vote* the site up in the search engines. Links pointing to a Web page do several things:

- ✓ **Links make it easier for search engines to find the page.** As the searchbots travel around the Web, they follow links. They index a page, follow the links on that page to other pages, index those pages, follow the links on those pages, and so on. The more links to a page, the more likely the page is picked up and indexed by the search engines, and the more quickly it happens.

- ✓ **Search engines use the number of links pointing to a page as an indication of the page's value.** If lots of pages link to your page, the search engines place a greater value on your page than pages with few links pointing to them. If you have lots of links from sites that are themselves linked to by many other sites, search engines conclude that your site must *really* be important. (Google calls this value the page's PageRank, but Google is not the only search engine to use links as an indication of value.)

- ✓ **Links provide information to the search engines about the page they're pointing to.** The link text often contains keywords that search engines can use to glean additional information about your page. The theme of the site that is pointing to your site also gives search engines an indication of the theme of your site. For example, if you have links from hundreds of rodent-related Web sites, it's a good bet that your site has something to do with rodents.

- ✓ **Links not only bring searchbots to a page, but also bring *people* to the page.** The whole purpose of your search engine campaign is to bring people to your site, right?

Links are very important. Sometimes they mean the difference between being indexed by a search engine and not being indexed, and between being ranked well in a search engine and not being ranked well. In this chapter, I delve into this subject, a topic often broadly known as *link popularity,* to give you a good understanding of what links are all about. In the next chapter, you discover *how* to get other sites to link to yours.

Backlinks are an integral part of the optimization of your Web site. A *backlink* — this may surprise you — is a link back to your site. Search engines look at backlinks to figure out what your site is about and how important it is. Links aren't something detached from your site; they're an integral part *of* your site. Think of your Web site in terms of a regional map: Your site is the major city, and the backlinks are the roads bringing traffic into the city. A geographer looking at the map wouldn't regard the city and roads as separate entities; they are all *part* of the *same* economic and social system. So don't think of the links pointing to your site as something "out there;" they are a critical part of your site. Here's an indication of just how important Google considers links to be: The original name of the Google search engine, in January of 1996 (before it was officially launched), was *BackRub,* so named for its ability to analyze backlinks.

The search engines are trying to figure out what site or page is the best match for a search. As you discover later in this chapter, search engines use links as one way to determine this. As with content though (discussed in Chapter 8), using the number of links to and from a site to measure significance is an imperfect method. A page can conceivably be the best page on a particular subject, yet have few links to it. Just because I publish a page today, doesn't mean it's worse than a page that was published five years ago and now has many links to it. However, search engines have difficulty figuring out what the searcher needs, so they have to use what information is available to them. Using links is a way of recruiting Web site owners to help point out useful sites and pages. The strategy is imperfect, but that's the search engine world we're living in.

Understanding Page Value and PageRank

Search engines assign a value to your site based on the links pointing to it. The most popular term for this kind of ranking is *PageRank,* which is used by Google. The PageRank is a value that Google gives to a page, based on the number and type of links into the page.

PageRank is used frequently in the search engine optimization field for several reasons. The primary reason is that Google is the world's most important search engine and will remain the most important search engine for the foreseeable future.

You could be forgiven for thinking that the term PageRank comes from the idea of, well, ranking pages. Google claims, however, that it comes from the name of one of the founders of Google and authors of the original PageRank document, Larry Page. The truth is probably somewhere in between. (Otherwise why isn't it the PageBrinRank?)

Another reason why PageRank is such a hot topic for SEO types is that you don't need a Ph.D. to figure out the PageRank for a page. The Google Toolbar — the handy little tool I show you how to download in Chapter 1 — shows you the PageRank of the page currently loaded in your browser. (Okay, strictly speaking that's not true, as you find out later in this chapter, but it does give you an indication of what the PageRank is.)

We also have a good idea of how PageRank is calculated. Sergey Brin and Lawrence Page, founders of Google, published a paper about the algorithm while at Stanford University. It's unclear whether the algorithm used by Google is exactly the same as the one they published, but it's likely to be similar.

Although this section focuses on PageRank, other search engines use similar rankings, and the things you do with links that boost your PageRank also help boost your site with other search engines.

PageRank — one part of the equation

Keep in mind that the PageRank value is just one part of how Google determines which pages to show you when you search for something. I want to stress that point because so many people get really hung up on PageRank. A low PageRank is often an indicator of problems, and a high PageRank is an indicator that you're doing something right, but PageRank itself is just a small part of how Google ranks your pages.

When you type a search term into Google and click Search, Google starts looking through its database for pages with the words you've typed. Then it examines each page to decide which pages are most relevant to your search. Google considers many characteristics: what the <TITLE> tag says, how the keywords are treated (are they bold or italic or in bulleted lists?), where the keywords sit on the page, and so on. It *also* considers PageRank. Clearly it's possible for a page with a low PageRank to rank higher than one with a high PageRank in some searches. When that happens, it simply means that the value provided by the high PageRank isn't enough to outweigh the value of all the other characteristics of the page that Google considered.

I like to think of PageRank as a tiebreaker. Imagine a situation in which you have a page that, using all other forms of measurement, ranks as equally well as a competitor's page. Google has looked at both pages, found the same number of keywords in the same sorts of positions, and thinks both pages are equally good matches for a particular keyword search. However, your competitor's page has a PageRank that is higher than your page. Which page will rank higher in a Google search for that keyword? Your competitor's.

Remember that it all comes down to what the searcher is searching for. A page that ranks well for one keyword or keyword phrase may rank poorly for another.

Here's what Google says about PageRank:

> "The heart of our software is PageRank(tm), a system for ranking web pages developed by our founders Larry Page and Sergey Brin at Stanford University. And while we have dozens of engineers working to improve every aspect of Google on a daily basis, PageRank continues to provide the basis for all of our web search tools."

So Google claims that PageRank *is* in use and *is* important. (Some form of the algorithm is in use, anyway; it's likely that the current algorithm is not quite the same as the original, but it's probably similar.) But you need to keep its significance in perspective. It's still only part of the story.

The PageRank algorithm

I want to quickly show you the PageRank algorithm; but don't worry, I'm not going to get hung up on it. In fact, you really don't need to be able to read and follow it, as I explain in a moment. Here it is:

$$PR (A) = (1 - d) + d (PR (t1) / C (t1) + ... + PR (tn) / C (tn))$$

Where:

PR = PageRank
A = Web page A
d = A damping factor, usually set to 0.85
t1...tn = Pages linking to Web page A
C = The number of outbound links from page tn

I could explain all this to you, honestly I could. But I don't want to. And furthermore, I don't have to because you don't need to be able to read the algorithm. For instance, do you recognize this equation?

$$F_{ij} = G \frac{M_i M_j}{D_{ij}^2}$$

Don't think you can kid me, I know you don't know what this is. (Well, okay, maybe you do, but I'll bet over 95 percent of my readers don't.) It is the Law of Universal Gravitation, which explains how gravity works. I can't explain this equation to you, but I really don't care, because I've been using gravity for some time now, without the benefit of understanding the jumble of letters. The other day, for instance, while walking down the street, someone shoved a flyer into my hand. After walking on, glancing at the flyer, and realizing that I didn't want it in my hand, I held it over a trash can, opened my hand, and used gravity to remove it from my hand and deposit it into the trash can. Simple.

If you want all the nasty, complicated details about PageRank, you can find a number of sources of information online. One description of PageRank that I like is at the WebWorkshop site (`www.webworkshop.net/pagerank.html`). This site also provides a calculator that shows you the effect on PageRank of linking between pages in your site. Or you can get the lowdown on PageRank from the horse's mouth: Read *The PageRank Citation Ranking: Bringing Order to the Web* by Sergey Brin and Lawrence Page, the founders of Google. (Search on the document's title at Google.)

Rather than take you through the PageRank algorithm step by step, here are a few key points that explain more or less how it works:

- ✔ **As soon as a page enters the Google index, it has an intrinsic PageRank.** Admittedly, the PageRank is very small, but it's there.

- ✔ **A page has a PageRank only if it's indexed by Google.** Links to your site from pages that have not yet been indexed are effectively worthless, as far as PageRank goes.

- ✔ **When you place a link on a page, pointing to another page, the page with the link is *voting* for the page it's pointing to.** These votes are how PageRank increases. As a page gets more and more links into it, its PageRank grows.

- ✔ **Linking to another page doesn't reduce the PageRank of the origin page, but it does increase the PageRank of the receiving page.** It's sort of like a company's shareholders meeting, at which people with more shares have more votes. They don't lose their shares when they vote. But the more shares they have, the more votes they can place.

- ✔ **Pages with no links out of them are wasting PageRank; they don't get to vote for other pages.** Because the inherent PageRank of a page is not terribly high, this isn't normally a problem. It becomes a problem if you have a large number of links to dangling pages of this kind. Or it can be a problem if you have a dangling page with a high PageRank. Though rare, this could happen if you have a page that many external sites link to that then links directly to an area of your site that won't benefit from PageRank, such as a complex e-commerce catalog system that Google can't index or an external e-commerce system hosted on another site. Unless the page links to other pages inside your Web site, it won't be voting for those pages and thus won't be able to raise their PageRank.

✔ **A single link from a dangling page can channel that PageRank back into your site.** Make sure that all your pages have at least one link back into the site. (This usually isn't a problem because most sites are built with common navigation bars and often text links at the bottom of the page.)

✔ **You can increase a site's overall PageRank two ways:**

   • Increase the number of pages in the site (although it's a small increase because the inherent PageRank of a new page is low)

   • Get links to the site from outside.

✔ **The page receiving the inbound link gets the greatest gain.** Thus, ideally, you want links into your most important pages — pages you want ranked in the search engines. PageRank is then spread through links to other pages in the site, but these secondary pages get less of the boost.

It's important to understand that Web sites don't have PageRanks, Web *pages* have PageRanks. It's possible for the home page of a site to have a high Page-Rank, while internal pages have very low ranks. Here are a couple of important implications from this:

✔ **You can vote large amounts of PageRank through your site with a single link.** A page with a PageRank of 5 can pass that on to another page as long as it doesn't split the vote by linking to other pages.

When I use the term *pass,* I use it in the sense of passing on a virus, not passing a baton. You can pass PageRank from page to page; linking from page A to page B passes PageRank from A to B in the same way that person A may pass a cold to person B. Person A doesn't get rid of the cold when he passes it to B, he's still got it. And page A still has its PageRank when it passes PageRank on to page B.

✔ **You can ensure PageRank is well distributed around your Web site by including lots of links.** Linking every page to every other page is the most efficient way to ensure even PageRank around the site.

Huge sites = greater PageRank

Because every page is born with a PageRank (as soon as Google finds it, anyway), the more pages in your site, the greater the site's intrinsic PageRank. If you create a linking structure that links all your pages well, you'll be providing your pages with a high PageRank simply because you have many pages.

However, don't think of this as a search engine strategy. You'd need a huge number of pages to make a difference. If you own or manage a site that already has hundreds of thousands of pages just because that's *what you do,* consider yourself lucky. But don't build hundreds of thousands of pages just to boost PageRank.

This fact does provide another reason for Web sites to retain old pages, perhaps in archives. A news site, for instance, should probably keep all news articles, even very old ones. Of course, massive repositories of data often have high PageRanks for another reason: because many other sites link to the data. Remove pages, and you'll lose the links.

Measuring PageRank

How can you discover a page's PageRank? You can use the Google Toolbar. (I explain in a moment why you can never find out the *true* PageRank.) As I mention in Chapter 1, you should install the Google Toolbar (available for download at `toolbar.google.com`). Each time you open a page in Internet Explorer 5.0 or later, you see the page's PageRank in a bar, as shown in Figure 12-1. If the bar is all white, the PageRank is 0. If it's all green, the PageRank is 10. You can estimate PageRank simply by looking at the position of the green bar, or you can point at the bar, and a pop-up appears with the PageRank number.

If the PageRank component isn't on your toolbar, click the Options button to open the Toolbar Options dialog box, check the PageRank check box, and click OK.

Figure 12-1:
The PageRank bar on the Google Toolbar shows the page's PageRank.

Here are a few things to understand about this toolbar:

- **Sometimes the bar is gray.** Sometimes when you look at the bar, it's grayed out. Some people believe that this means Google is somehow penalizing the site, that it's withholding PageRank. I've never seen this happen, though. (You can get penalized, but that's generally not what's going on here.) I believe the bar is simply buggy, and that PageRank is just not being passed to the bar for some reason. Every time I've seen the bar grayed out, I've been able to open the Web page in another browser window (you may have to try two or three) and view the PageRank.

✔ **Sometimes the toolbar guesses.** Sometimes the toolbar guesses a page's PageRank. You may occasionally find a PageRank being reported for a page that isn't even in the Google index. It seems that Google may be coming up with a PageRank for a page on the fly, based on the PageRank of other pages in the site that have already been indexed.

Also, note that Google has various data centers around the world, and because they're not all in sync, with data varying among them, it's possible for one person looking at a page's PageRank to see one number, while someone else sees another number.

✔ **A white bar is not a penalty.** Another common PageRank myth is that Google penalizes pages by giving them PageRanks of 0. That is, if you see a page with a PageRank of 0, something is wrong with the page, and if you link to the page, *your* Web page may be penalized, too. This is simply not true. *Most* of the world's Web pages show a PageRank of 0. That's not to say that Google won't take away PageRank if it wants to penalize a page or site for some reason. I'm just saying that there's no way to know if it's a penalty or if it's simply a page with few valuable links pointing in.

✔ **Zero is not zero, and ten is not ten!** Although commonly referred to as PageRank, and even labeled as such, the number you see in the Google Toolbar is not the page's actual PageRank. It's simply a number indicating the approximate position of the page on the PageRank range. Therefore, pages never have a PageRank of 0, even though most pages show 0 on the toolbar, and a page with a rank of, say, 2 might actually have a PageRank of 25 or 100.

The true PageRank scale is probably a logarithmic scale. Thus, the distance between PageRank 5 and 6 is much greater than the difference between 2 and 3. The consensus of opinion among people who like to discuss these things is that the PageRank shown on the toolbar is probably on a logarithmic scale with a base of around 5 or 6, or perhaps even lower.

Suppose, for a moment, that the base is actually 5. That means that a page with a PageRank of 0 shown on the toolbar may have an actual PageRank somewhere between a fraction of 1 and just under 5. If the PageRank shown is 1, the page may have a rank between 5 and just under 25; if 2 is shown, the number may be between 25 and just under 125, and so on. A page with a rank of 9 or 10 shown on the toolbar most likely has a true PageRank in the millions. With base 5, for instance, the toolbar PageRank numbers would represent true PageRanks, as shown in Table 12-1.

Table 12-1	Pure Conjecture — What Toolbar PageRanks Would Represent if PageRank Were a Logarithmic Scale Using Base 5
Toolbar PageRank	*True PageRank*
0	0 – 5
1	5 – 25
2	25 – 125
3	125 – 625
4	625 – 3,125
5	3,125 – 15,625
6	15,625 – 78,125
7	78,125 – 390,625
8	390,625 – 1,953,125
9	1,953,125 – 9,765,625
10	9,765,625 – 48,828,125

The maximum possible PageRank, and thus this scale, continually change as Google recalculates PageRank. As pages are added to the index, the PageRank has to go up.

How can you be sure that the numbers on the toolbar are not the true Page-Rank? The PageRank algorithm simply doesn't work on a scale of 1 to 10, on a Web that contains billions of Web pages. And, perhaps more practically, it's not logical to assume that sites such as Yahoo! and Google have PageRanks just slightly above small privately owned sites. I have pages with ranks of 6 or 7, for instance, whereas the BBC Web site, the world's 25th most popular Web site according to Alexa, has a PageRank of 9. It's not reasonable to assume that its true PageRank is just 50 percent greater than pages on one of my little sites.

Here are two important points to remember about the PageRank shown on the Google Toolbar:

✔ Two pages with the same PageRank shown on the toolbar may actually have very different true PageRanks, with one having a PageRank of a fifth or sixth, or maybe a quarter, of the other.

✔ It gets progressively harder to push a page to the next PageRank level on the toolbar. Getting a page to 1 or 2 is pretty easy, but to push it to 3 or 4 is much harder (though certainly possible), and to push it to the higher levels is very difficult indeed. To get to 8 or above is rare.

Leaking PageRank

It's possible for PageRank to *leak* out of a site, despite the fact that pages don't lose PageRank when they link to other pages. Here's how.

As you've seen, each time you link from one page to another, the origin page is voting for the recipient page. Thus a link from one page in your site to another page in your site is a vote for that other page. If you link to a page on another site, you're voting for another site's page rather than your site's page.

Suppose that you have a page with a PageRank of 10,000 and it has 40 links on it. Each link is getting a PageRank vote of 250 (250 × 40 = 10,000). Now suppose that half the links on the page are external. In that case, you're taking 5,000 votes and pointing to pages out of your site rather than inside your site. So PageRank leaks in the sense that your overall site PageRank is lower.

As a general rule, you should worry more about getting backlinks to your site from appropriate Web sites than about how much PageRank is leaking through your outgoing links. You can build PageRank quickly by using the techniques in Chapter 13, and in most cases, worrying about outgoing links won't save you much PageRank. Still, you can do two simple things to help reduce *rank leak:*

- ✔ If you have a page with lots of outgoing links, make sure it also has links to the other pages in your site. You'll be splitting the vote that way between outgoing and internal links, instead of passing all of it on through outgoing links.

- ✔ Ideally, you want the page with the external links to be one with a low PageRank, reducing the outgoing votes. You can do that by minimizing the number of links from other pages on your site into the link page.

Page relevance

Page relevance is harder to measure. The idea is that a link from a page that is related in some way to your page is more valuable than a link from a page that is entirely unrelated. A link to your rodent-racing site from a Web site that is also related to rodent racing is more valuable than, say, a link from your aunt Edna's personal Web site.

The problem with PageRank is that it's independent of keywords. The value is a number derived from links pointing at a page, but it has no relation whatsoever to a specific keyword. Just because a page has a high PageRank doesn't mean it's the type of page you're looking for when you search for a particular keyword.

Thus, the search engines add something else to the mix: *relevance,* or *context.* The major search engines are attempting to do this sort of analysis by matching keywords. In effect, the search engines are trying to create what have been termed *context-sensitive PageRanks* or *topic-sensitive PageRanks.* A topic-sensitive PageRank is dependent on a particular topic. Rather than counting any and all links, only links from relevant Web sites are included.

One way the search engines are probably trying to do this sort of thing is by using the Open Directory Project directory to provide some context. Because Web sites listed in the directory have been put into categories, it gives the search engines a starting point to figure out what keywords and sites relate to what categories.

Because the search engines use the Open Directory Project and Yahoo! Directory to help figure out what category you're related to, this is yet another reason why it's important to be in these two directories.

This discussion is getting complicated now, and you really don't need to know the details. But if you want to read a little geek stuff related to relevance or context, search for a paper entitled *Topic-Sensitive PageRank,* by Taher Haveliwala of Stanford University.

My feeling is that this sort of technology isn't as advanced as many believe or as advanced as the search engines want us to believe. Still, people in the search engine business swear that links from related sites are more valuable than links from unrelated sites. Or, to be more precise, links from sites that a search engine *thinks* are related are more valuable than those from sites that a search engine *thinks* are unrelated. Because the technology is imprecise, search engines don't always get it right. The fact is that no search engine really knows for sure if one site is related to another; it can only guess. As with everything else, relevance is just one ingredient in the mix.

Don't let anyone tell you that links from unrelated sites have no value. A link from an unrelated site helps search engines find your pages, boosts PageRank, and may even bring visitors to your site. These links just won't have the extra boost provided by relevance.

As I discuss in more detail in Chapter 13, the ideal link is one from a related Web site, not just any old Web site you can convince to link to you. The most powerful link *hubs* — networks of interlinked Web sites — are those that are tightly focused on a particular topic. The search engines respect that, want to uncover such situations, and rank the target sites more highly, and are probably getting better every day at doing so.

Hubs and Neighborhoods

Search engines are also looking for what may be thought of as Web *neighborhoods* or *communities* or *hubs* — groups of Web sites related to a particular subject, and the sites that appear to be most central. If you're positioned in the middle of a cloud or web of Web sites related to a particular subject, that's a good thing.

Imagine a chart showing the world's rodent-racing Web sites and how they're connected. In this chart, you have little boxes representing all the various Web sites and lines connecting the boxes showing links between the sites. (Figure 12-2 gives an example of such a chart.) Some of the boxes seem to be sitting by themselves — very few links are going out, and very few are coming in. Other boxes have lots of links going out of them, but few other boxes are linking back to them. Now imagine your rodent-racing site. It seems to be the hub; your box has lots of links going out, and lots of links coming in. That would look pretty important on a chart. Wouldn't you think the search engines would find that interesting? In fact, search engines are trying to figure out this sort of thing all the time, so if you can build links to turn your site into a hub, that's a great thing!

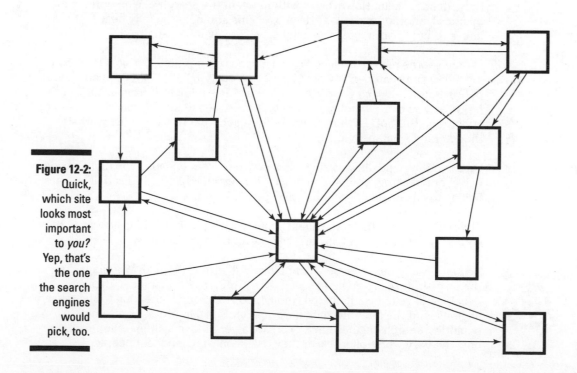

Figure 12-2:
Quick, which site looks most important to *you?* Yep, that's the one the search engines would pick, too.

Avoiding Links with No Value

Some links have no value:

- ✔ If a page isn't in Google, the links from the page have no value. Google doesn't know about them, after all. (On the other hand, those pages may be in *other* search engines, so the links do have value on those engine's rankings.)

- ✔ If a page is what Google regards as a *link farm* (described in a moment), Google may know about the page but decide to exclude it from the index.

When site owners figured out that links were valuable, they started playing tricks to boost incoming links to their sites. Some tricks were so egregious that the search engines decided they were totally unacceptable. The trick you hear about most often is the *link farm,* an automated system that allows site owners to very quickly create thousands of incoming links, by joining with thousands of other site owners to exchange links. Another trick is to create hundreds of shadow domains, and link them all into one.

The search engines don't like link farms and will exclude link-farm pages if they identify them. However, as with much in the search-engine-optimization business, another myth has arisen over this subject. You may hear that if a link is found to your site from a link farm, you will be penalized.

Let me set the record straight: Search engines do not penalize sites for incoming links. They can't, or it would encourage dirty tricks. Want to push a competitor's site down so your site can beat it? Then link to it from as many link farms as you can. Obviously it wouldn't make sense for the search engines to encourage this sort of thing, so links from such pages won't hurt your site — though they won't help it, either.

On the other hand, links *to* such sites may hurt you. Because you do have control over links from your site to others, if a search engine decides that you are linking to a bad neighborhood, it may penalize you.

The bottom line is that you should avoid working with link farms because they could potentially harm you, and they won't help you anyway.

 Do search engines ever penalize? Sure. But with billions of Web pages in the large indexes (Google has well over 4 billion, for instance), these penalties have to be automated (though you can report cheating to the search engines, and the offending site may be reviewed). In order to automate penalties, search engines have to create a very loose system that penalizes only the very worst offenses, or they risk penalizing innocent people.

The proof is that if you spend time searching through the major search engines, you will find many pages that clearly break the rules, yet which are still included in the indexes.

Identifying links that aren't links

I've seen this happen many times. Someone gets a link to his site from another site with a high PageRank, perhaps a perfectly related site, and is excited: That's a great vote for his site, isn't it? Then some jerk, perhaps someone like me, has to burst his bubble and point out that, actually, no, it's not going to have the slightest effect on his site because it turns out the link is not a link. When is a link not a link? In cases such as these:

- ✔ The link has been created in such a manner that the search engines can't read it.

- ✔ The link points somewhere else, perhaps to a program on someone else's Web site, which then forwards the browser to your site.

Here are some examples. Take a look at this link:

```
http://ad.doubleclick.net/clk;6523085;7971444;q?http:
            //www.yoursite.com
```

This link passes through an ad server hosted by an advertising company called DoubleClick. When someone clicks this link, perhaps on a banner ad, a message is sent to a program on the ad.doubleclick.net ad server, which logs the click and then forwards the browser to www.yourdomain.com. You may think this is a link to www.yourdomain.com, and it may work like one, but as far as the search engine is concerned, it's really a link to ad.doubleclick.net.

Here's another example. Suppose the person creating a link to your site doesn't want the search engine to be able to read it. This person may be trying to get as many incoming links as possible while avoiding outgoing links, so he does something like this:

```
<SCRIPT LANGUAGE="JavaScript">
<!--
document.write("Visit <A HREF='http://www.yourdomain.com/'>
Joe's Rodent Racing site here</A>.")
//-->
</SCRIPT>
```

The author is using a JavaScript to write the link onto the page. You can see the link, other visitors can see it, and the link works when clicked upon. But search engines won't read the JavaScript, and they won't know there's a link there. What appears to be a perfectly normal link on a Web page is invisible to the search engines. So it does your site no good as far as PageRank or any other link-popularity algorithm goes.

Here's another form of link that the search engines can't read:

```
<A HREF="#" class=results onclick="window.open('searchresult-
templ.php?CS=cddzdzdrzfzpzpdc&SRCH=134893378&YD=0.88&RK=
3&PID=16&URL=yourdomain.com','merch','Height=' +
screen.availHeight + ',Width=' + screen.availWidth +
',left=0,top=0,scrollbars=yes,status=yes,toolbar=yes,
directories=yes,menubar=yes,location=yes,resizable=yes',
false)";>Everything About Rodent Racing!</A>
```

This is a real link tag, an `<A>` tag. However, it doesn't use the `HREF=` attribute to point to a Web page. Rather, it uses a JavaScript `onclick` event handler to make it work. The JavaScript runs a program that, in this case, loads the page into another window. Again, the link will work in most browsers, but search engines won't see it.

Incidentally, it's also possible to do the reverse: to make links appear to the search engines to be links to your site when actually they're links to another site. For instance, look at the following link, created by a system called Links4Trade.com (which you find out about in Chapter 13):

```
<A HREF="http://www.yourdomain.com?cid=33003&refid=
139782&link=www%2Eyourdomain%2Ecom" onClick="return
rewrite(this);" class="">Joe's Rodent Racing</A>
```

This link starts off well, showing `yourdomain.com` as the page being linked to. In fact, if you took the URL from the `HREF=` and pasted it into a browser, it would work properly. However, when someone clicks the link, the JavaScript `onClick` event handler runs, taking the domain and passing it through to a JavaScript function called `rewrite`. Because the search engines don't read JavaScripts, they don't see what *really* happens when someone clicks the link. (In this example, the click runs through a program on the Links4Trade.com site, which is used to track how many people use the link.) The search engines *think* it's a link to your site, and I guess it is in a sense, but it has to pass through a program on a different site first.

Some links are more valuable than others

It seems likely that search engines — and Google in particular — regard some links as more valuable than others. And it seems very likely to me that they — and Google in particular — will tighten up the way they regard links. Because the search engines keep their techniques secret, the following practices may already be in use or could be soon:

✔ Links inside paragraphs of text are regarded as more valuable than links in large lists or links set apart from text.

✔ The search engines could compare incoming links with outgoing links, and downgrade a page or site if it appears to be doing a lot of reciprocal linking from link pages.

✔ Links pointing to a page inside a site might be valued more highly than links to the home page.

✔ Outgoing links concentrated on a few pages might be valued less than links spread around a site.

Inserting Keywords into Links

As Chapter 4 makes abundantly clear, keywords in your pages are very important. But keywords *outside* your pages can also affect the page results. That is, the keywords in *links* pointing to your site are very important. If hundreds of links around the world point to one of your pages and all these links contain the words *rodent racing,* then Google and, presumably, other search engines will get the idea that your pages are somehow related to rodent racing. It actually makes a lot of sense if you think about it. If hundreds of site owners create links pointing to your site, and, in effect, say, "This site I'm pointing to is about rodent racing," then Google is being given a darn good clue regarding what your site is about! In effect, Google has recruited site owners to tell it what other owners' sites are about.

Link text, in geek terminology, is known as *anchor* text. The link tag is an <A> tag, and the A stands for *anchor.* Thus you may, if you hang around in geek company, hear links referred to as *anchors.*

Listen to this, from Sergey Brin and Lawrence Page, founders of Google:

> ". . . anchors often provide more accurate descriptions of web pages than the pages themselves . . . This idea of propagating anchor text to the page it refers to was implemented in the World Wide Web Worm [a search engine that pre-dates Google] especially because it helps search non-text information, and expands the search coverage with fewer downloaded documents. We use anchor propagation mostly because anchor text can help provide better quality results."

> (*The Anatomy of a Large-Scale Hypertextual Web Search Engine,* 1998)

In other words, Google and other search engines use links to get an idea of what the pages are about. Links can even help search engines figure out what a document is about if they can't read it for some reason (though that's not really our primary concern here).

Now, wait a second. This is important. If a link pointing to your site can be used to describe to a search engine what your site is about, you'd better do all you can to make sure the link says what you want it to say! Even if you don't own the site pointing to the one you're trying to optimize or are trying to get another site owner or site manager to link to your site, it's in your interest to try to get the right keywords into the link!

As you browse the Web, take a close look at links on the sites you visit. Now that you know how critical it is to add keywords to links, you'll see that many links provide relatively little value to the sites they're pointing to. Sure, a link is better than no link, but a bad link could be better still. Here are some of the problems you'll see:

- **Image links (buttons or banners linking to sites):** Search engines can't read images, so they're not getting keywords from them. (You should add keywords to the ALT attributes to the image, but ALT text isn't weighted by the search engines as highly as link text.)

- **One- or two-word links, such as company names:** In most cases, company names don't help you in the search engines. You need to use the keywords your potential visitors and clients are using.

- **Combinations of descriptions and *click here* links:** For instance: *For more information on rodent racing — rats, mice, gerbils, and any other kind of rodent racing — click here.* Wow, what a waste! All the keywords are there, they just have no link on them! Remember, click-here links are a total waste of hyperlink space.

Link text is incredibly important; don't waste this valuable resource!

A Few Basic Rules about Links

You know that links are valuable and can help boost your position in the search engines. But what sorts of links? Let me quickly summarize:

- Links from sites that are related are often more valuable than links from sites that aren't related. (Because the relevancy software is almost certainly imprecise, this is not always the case.)

- Links from pages with high PageRanks are much more valuable than from pages with low PageRanks.

- Virtually all incoming links to your site have some kind of value, even if the pages have a very low PageRank or are not contextual. It may not be much of a value, but it's there.

✔ The more links on a page that point to your site, the lower the value of the link to your site because the vote is being shared. Thus, in some cases, a link from a low-PageRank page with no other links may actually be more valuable than a link from a high-PageRank page with many links.

✔ Links are even more valuable when they include keywords in them because keywords tell the search engines what the referenced site is all about.

✔ A link strategy that positions your site as an authority, or a *hub,* in a Web community or neighborhood can be a powerful way to get the attention of the search engines.

Chapter 13

Finding Sites to Link to Yours

*I*n Chapter 12, I explain the value of linking — why your site needs to have *backlinks,* links from other sites pointing to it. Now you have the problem of finding those sites.

Chapter 12 gives you some basic criteria. You need links from pages that are already indexed by the search engines. Pages with high PageRanks are more valuable than those with low PageRanks. Links from related sites may be more valuable, and so on. However, when searching for links, you probably don't want to be too fussy to start with. Focus on links that make sense from a subject-matter perspective. Find links from sites that are related in some way to yours, and link only to sites that can be of use to visitors to your site. If a site seems to fit this criteria, don't turn it down just because it doesn't appear to have much of a PageRank.

Use this chapter to go get links, and things will start happening. Your site will get more traffic, it will get picked up by the search engines, and you may find your pages rising in the search engine ranks.

Controlling Your Links

Before you run off to look for links, think about what you want those links to *say.* In Chapter 12, I talk about how keywords in links are tremendously important. The position of a page in the search engines depends not only on the text within that page, but also on text on other pages that refer to that page — that is, the text in the links.

For instance, suppose your rodent-racing company is called Robertson Ellington. (These were the names of your first two racing rats, and they still have a special place in your heart. And you've always felt that the name has a distinguished ring to it.) You could ask people to give you links like this:

Robertson Ellington
Everything you ever wanted to know about rodent racing — rodent-racing schedules, directions to rodent-racing tracks, rodent-racing clubs, and anything else you can imagine related to rodent racing

You got a few useful keywords into the description, but the link — Robertson Ellington — is the problem. The link text contains no keywords that count — are people searching for `Robertson Ellington`, or are they searching for `rodent racing`?

A better strategy is to change the link to include keywords. Keep the blurb below the link, but change the link to something like this:

Rodent Racing — rats, stoats, mice, and all sorts of other rodent racing

Here are some strategies for creating link text:

- Start the link with the primary keyword or keyword phrase.

- Add a few other keywords if you want.

- Try to repeat the primary keyword or keyword phrase once in the link.

- Mix in a few other words.

You need to control the links as much as possible. You can do this a number of ways, but you won't always be successful:

- Provide a *Link to Us* page at your Web site. On this page, provide suggested links to your site — include the entire HTML tag so people can grab the information and drop it into their sites.

  Remember that although links on logos and image buttons may be pretty, they don't help you in the search engines as much as text links do. You can add ALT text to the image, but ALT text is not as valuable as link text. Some site owners now distribute HTML code that creates not only image links but also small text links right below the images.

- When you contact people and ask them for links, provide them with the actual link you'd like to use.

✔ As soon as someone tells you he or she has placed a link, check it to see if the link says what you want. Immediately contact that person if it doesn't. He or she is more likely to change the link at that point than weeks or months later.

✔ Occasionally use a link-checking tool to find out who is linking to you and to see how the link appears. If necessary, contact the other party and ask if the link can be changed. (I mention some link-checking tools later in this chapter.)

Whenever possible, *you* should define what a link pointing to your site looks like, rather than leave it up to the person who owns the other site. Of course, you can't force someone to create links the way you want them, but sometimes if you ask nicely. . . .

Always use the `www.` portion of your URL when creating links to your site; `http://www.yourdomain.com` and not just `http://yourdomain.com`. Search engines regard the two addresses as different, even though in most cases they are actually pointing to the same page. So if you use both URLs, you are, in effect, "splitting the vote" for your Web site. The search engines will see a lower link popularity (see Chapter 12 for a discussion of how links are "votes").

Generating Links, Step-by-Step

Here is a quick summary of additional ways to get links; I describe them in detail next:

✔ **Register with search directories.** Yahoo! Directory, the Open Directory Project, specialty directories, and so on are not only important in their own right, but also provide links that other search engines read.

✔ **Ask friends and family.** Get everyone you know to add a link.

✔ **Ask employees.** Ask employees to mention you.

✔ **Contact association sites.** Contact any professional or business association of which you're a member and ask for a link.

✔ **Contact manufacturers' Web sites.** Ask the manufacturers of any products you sell to place a link on their sites.

✔ **Contact companies you do business with.** Get on their client lists.

✔ **Ask to be a featured client.** I've seen sites get high PageRanks by being linked to from sites that feature them.

✔ **Submit to announcement sites and newsletters.** Such as URLwire (`www.urlwire.com`).

- ✔ **Send out press releases.** Sending out press releases, even if distributed through the free systems, can sometimes get you links.

- ✔ **Promote something on your site.** If you have something really useful, let people know about it!

- ✔ **Find sites linking to your competition.** If other sites link to your competition, they may link to you, too.

- ✔ **Ask other sites for links.** During your online travels, you may stumble across sites that really should mention your site, as a benefit to their visitors.

- ✔ **Make reciprocal link requests.** Ask other site owners to link to you, in exchange for a link to them.

- ✔ **Respond to reciprocal link requests.** Eventually, other people will start asking you to link swap.

- ✔ **Search for** `keyword add url`. You can find sites with links pages this way.

- ✔ **Use link-building software and services.** Try using a link-exchange program or service to speed up the process.

- ✔ **Contact e-mail newsletters.** Find appropriate e-mail newsletters and send them information about your site.

- ✔ **Create a blog.** Many blog sites are read by search engines.

- ✔ **Mention your site in discussion groups.** Leave messages about your site in appropriate forums, with links to the site.

- ✔ **Pursue offline PR.** Getting mentioned in print often translates into being mentioned on the Web.

- ✔ **Give away content.** If you have lots of content, syndicate it.

- ✔ **Apply for online awards.** Sign up for site awards.

- ✔ **Advertise.** Sometimes ads provide useful links.

- ✔ **Use a service or buy links.** Some services sell links from high-PageRank sites.

- ✔ **Just wait.** Eventually links will appear, but you must prime the pump first.

These link-building strategies are ranked by priority in a very general way. One of the first things you should do is to ask friends and family for links, and one of the last is just waiting. However, in between these first and last strategies, the priority will vary from business to business, person to person. You may feel that a strategy lower down on this list is important to do right away.

The next sections look at each of these link-generation methods.

Register with search directories

In Chapter 10, I discuss getting links from directories, the Yahoo! Directory and the Open Directory Project. And in Chapter 11, I tell you about getting links from specialty directories. Links from directories are important not only because people will find you when searching at the various directories, but also because search engines often spider these directories.

Google, for instance, spiders both Yahoo! and the Open Directory Project. And the Open Directory Project results are syndicated to hundreds of smaller search engines, many of which are also read by Google. These links are also highly relevant because they're categorized within the directories; as you find out in Chapter 12, the search engines like relevant links. So if you haven't registered with the directories, you should probably consider that the first step in your link campaign. (For more info on submitting to the directories, see Chapter 10.)

Ask friends and family

Ask everyone you know to give you a link. Many people now have their own Web sites or blogs — Weblogs, which I discuss in more detail later in this chapter. Ask everyone you can think of to mention your site. Send them a short e-mail detailing what you'd like them to say. You may want to create a little bit of HTML that they can paste straight into their pages, perhaps with a link to a logo stored on your Web site so the logo appears in their pages. If you do this, you get to control the link text to ensure that it has keywords in it: *The best damn rodent racing site on the Web,* for instance, rather than *Click here to visit my friend's site.*

Ask employees

Employees often provide a significant number of links back to their employer's Web site, often by accident. In particular, employees often mention their employer in discussion groups that get picked up by the search engines. So why not send an e-mail to all your employees, asking them to link to the company's site from their Web sites and blogs and to mention you in discussion groups. Again, you might give them a piece of HTML including an embedded logo.

You can also ask them to include a link to your site in the signature of their e-mails. The signature is the blurb you see at the bottom of e-mail messages, often containing contact information. Ask them to add a full link — not just `www.domainname.com`, but `http://www.domainname.com`. That way, whenever they post messages via e-mail to discussion groups, the link may be picked up by search engines. And you can also ask them to always use a signature with the link when posting via non-e-mail methods, such as posting to Web-based discussion groups.

Of course, some employers don't want their employees talking about them in discussion groups because they're scared what the employees will say. If that's your situation, I can't do much to help you, except suggest that you read *Figuring Out Why Your Employees Hate You For Dummies* by I. M. N. Ogre.

Contact association sites

Association sites are a much-overlooked source of free and useful links. Contact any professional or business association of which you're a member and ask for a link. Are you in the local Better Business Bureau? The Lions Club or Rotary Club? How about the Rodent Lovers Association of America, or the Association for Professional Rodent Competitions? Many such sites have member directories and may even have special links pages for their members' Web sites.

Contact manufacturers' Web sites

Another overlooked source of links are manufacturers' Web sites. If you sell products, ask the manufacturer to place a link from its site to yours. I know one business that sells several million dollar's worth of a particular toy that it gets from a single retailer. The link from the retailer, which does not sell direct, brings the company *most* of its business. This is a valuable link in itself, but because the manufacturer is a well-known national company that gets plenty of traffic, the manufacturer's Web site has a PageRank of 5 on its main page (which actually could be much higher if the company knew what it was doing). The link to the retailer is on the manufacturer's home page, so not only does the link bring plenty of business, but it also gets plenty of attention from the search engines.

Contact companies you do business with

Many companies maintain client lists. Check with all the firms you do business with and make sure that you're on their lists.

Ask to be a featured client

While looking at a competitor's Web site for a client, I noticed that the competing site had a surprisingly high PageRank even though it was a small site that appeared to be linked to from only one place, www.inman.com, which is a site that syndicates content to real-estate sites.

It turned out that the competitor was linked to directly from one of Inman's highest PageRanked pages. Inman was using the client as an example of one of its customers.

If you're using someone's services — for Web hosting, e-mail services, syndication services, or whatever — you may want to contact the site and ask if *you* can be the featured client. Hey, someone's going to be, so it might as well be you.

Submit to announcement sites and newsletters

Though not as popular as they used to be, a number of site-announcement Web sites and e-mail newsletters still exist. (The newsletters usually end up published on the Web, too.) Some of these services are *very* influential because they are either very popular (USAToday.com's Hot Sites, for instance) or are read by many journalists.

Check out URLwire (www.urlwire.com), for instance. This service claims to have over 125,000 readers, of whom 6,500 are journalists and site reviewers who get the e-mail newsletter. You have to pay for this service, from $300 to $1,000 to get into one of the announcements, but other announcement services are generally free.

Unfortunately, getting you site into the announcements can be difficult because of stiff competition! In fact, some announcement sites don't accept submissions — Yahoo! Picks, for instance, doesn't take suggestions. Sometimes to get picked up by these sites, you need to be mentioned in another influential announcement service, such as URLwire. However, if you *can* get in, the effect can be huge. Not only do you get a link from a site that is undoubtedly well indexed, but you probably also get picked up by many other sites and newsletters. URLwire in particular (no, I'm not getting a kickback!) is incredibly influential.

Here are a few places to try:

- ✔ **USAToday.com's Hot Sites:** `www.usatoday.com/tech/webguide/front.htm`
- ✔ **URLwire:** `www.urlwire.com`
- ✔ **Yahoo! Picks:** `picks.yahoo.com/picks`

These announcement services used to be abundant, but unfortunately most have died off.

Send out press releases

Does your company publish press releases? You should distribute these as widely as possible. Press releases often turn up on Web sites anyway, but even if you submit press releases through a large service such as PR News-wire (`prnewswire.com`), you should also distribute them through the free and low-cost distribution services, which will quite likely get them placed onto other Web sites. You may want to write a few quick press releases and send them out through the free-distribution services, just to see if you can generate some links.

These are the free/low-cost services that I know of:

- ✔ **PR Web:** `ww1.prweb.com/login.php`
- ✔ **WorldAnnounce:** `www.worldannounce.com`
- ✔ **PRESSLine:** `www.us.pressline.com`
- ✔ **pressbox:** `www.pressbox.co.uk`

You may want to create your own list of press-release distribution e-mail addresses and Web pages. For instance, look for industry journals in your field that accept press releases.

Make sure that the press release includes your URL at least twice, preferably three or four times. For instance, include it once in the header, once in the contact information at the bottom, and a couple of times in the text. And use a full link: `http://www.yourdomainname.com` rather than just `yourdomainname.com`.

The URL should be clickable. That is, it should appear in a Web page as a real link that can be clicked. You don't have a lot of control over this with a free distribution service. Just create a full URL and hope for the best. (If you're working with fee-based press-release services, talk to them to find out how to make sure your URLs are clickable links.)

Promote something on your site

One of the most powerful link-building techniques is to place something very useful on your site and then make sure everyone knows about it. I've included a little story in the section "How Links Build Links," at the end of this chapter. It shows how links can accumulate — how, in the right conditions, one link leads to another, which leads to another, and so on. In this true story, the site had something that many people really liked — a directory of glossaries and technical dictionaries. Over 2,000 sites link to this site, all because the site owner provided something people really wanted and appreciated.

Find sites linking to your competition

If a site links to your competition, it may be willing to link to you, too. Find out who links to competing sites and then ask them if they'll link to yours. In some cases, the links will be link-exchange links, which I look at in the section "Respond to reciprocal link requests," but in many cases, they'll just be sites providing useful information to their readers. If your competitors' sites are useful, and (I'm assuming) yours is too, you've got a good chance of being listed.

So how do you find out who links to your competitors? You can do this a number of ways, as described in the next few sections. I list the methods in order of the number of links that you're likely to find, from the least to the most.

Google Toolbar

The Google Toolbar — the one I show you how to download in Chapter 1 — has a Backward Links command. Open your competitor's home page, click the little blue i button on the toolbar, and then select Backward Links from the drop-down menu. This feature generally shows pages with a PageRank of 4 or more; it doesn't show all the links in Google's index. (Sometimes lower-ranked pages seem to sneak through.) It also shows links to that page, not links to all the pages on the site.

If you don't see the i button on the toolbar, click the Options button, and check the Page Info Menu check box on the Options tab of the Toolbar Options dialog box.

Google search

Search for `link:domainname.com` in Google or in the search box in the Google Toolbar.

Alexa Toolbar

The Alexa Toolbar has a similar tool. Select a page at a competitor's site (which doesn't have to be the home page), click the little downward-pointing triangle on the Info button, and an information box opens. At the bottom of the box, you see a line that says something like *See 7,419 sites that link here.* Click this link to open a page on the Alexa site listing all the links.

Link popularity sites

Online tools, such as LinkPopularity.com, can help you find links. Enter the competitor's URL and click the search button, and LinkPopularity.com searches Google, AltaVista, and HotBot for you.

Another service I like is the tool at Marketleap (www.marketleap.com/publinkpop), which searches for links at AlltheWeb, Google, AltaVista, HotBot, and MSN.

Many such tools are available. Search for link popularity tools, and you'll find them.

Link popularity software

A number of link-popularity software tools are available that you can run on your computer. I like a program called LinkSurvey, which you can find at www.antssoft.com. This great little tool, shown in Figure 13-1, lets you enter all your competitors' URLs. You can define whether you want to find links to any page in the domain or links only to the specified page, and then search up to 15 search engines. It even has a built-in Web browser, so in its list of pages linking to your competitors, you can click a link to quickly see what that page looks like. The program even highlights the link within the page. You can export everything you find to a Microsoft Excel spreadsheet.

Another interesting link-analysis tool I've run into recently is OptiLink (www.optitext.com), which not only finds links to a specified site, but also reviews the link text. As I explain in Chapter 12, the text in the links pointing to your site is incredibly important; this tool gives you an idea not only of how many links point to a site, but of how valuable they are.

Asking for the link

How do you ask for the link? Nicely. Send an informal, chatty message. Don't make it sound like some kind of form letter that half a billion other people have received. This should be a personal contact between a real person, you, and another real person, the owner or manager of the other site. Give this person a reason to link to your site. Explain what your site does and why it would be of use to the other site's visitors.

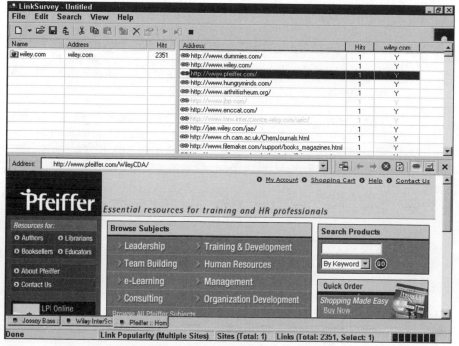

Figure 13-1:
The
LinkSurvey
link-
popularity
tool in
action.

Ask other sites for links

During your travels online, you'll run across sites that provide lists of links
for visitors, and maybe your site should be listed, too. For instance, while
working for a client that had a site related to a particular disease, I found
sites that had short lists of links to sites about that disease; obviously my
client should also have been in those lists.

Approach these sites the same way you would approach the sites linking to
your competitors: Send an informal note asking for a link.

Make reciprocal link requests

A reciprocal link is one that you obtain in exchange for another. You ask site
owners and managers to link to your site, and you in turn promise to link to
theirs.

Reciprocal linking, if done right, can help you in two ways:

- ✔ The search engines see nice, keyworded links coming into your site from appropriate, relevant sites.
- ✔ You link to appropriate, relevant sites too. (In Chapter 12, I discuss the concept of hubs or value networks.)

If reciprocal linking is not done right, the value you gain is not as great. If you get links from any site you can, without regard to whether the sites are of use to your visitors or whether your site is of use to theirs, search engines won't regard them as relevant links.

Reciprocal linking is different from the previous technique of asking to be added to a list, although plenty of overlap exists. With the previous technique, you don't need to offer a link in exchange because the link list is a service to the other site's visitors. However, sometimes (often?) site owners respond with, "Sure, but will you link to us, too?" In this case, you've just found yourself in a reciprocal linking position.

Relevant or contextual links are more valuable than nonrelevant, noncontextual links. Links to your rodent-racing sites from *other* rodent-racing sites are far more valuable than links from sites about Satan worship or *Star Trek*.

Reciprocal linking is a popular method for obtaining links to your site. Find a site that appears to be in an area similar to yours — that is, attracts the same sort of people you want to attract and involves a related subject area — and then contact the owner and ask for a link.

Making the contact

Before you contact others to ask for reciprocal links, link from your site to their sites. Find a page from which it would make sense to link. If possible, avoid the use of *links pages* (which I discuss next). Rather, find a spot on your site where a link to the other site would *fit,* a position in which it would make sense from a visitor's point of view. Keyword the link nicely. (Do unto others as you would have them do unto you.)

Then contact the site owner. Let the site owner know that you've added the link *and* that you've keyworded it. In fact, why not explain keyworded links and their purpose? Doing so will probably make it easier to persuade the site owner to give you the type of keyworded link you want. Provide the URL to the page on which the link sits. You might even explain why you try to avoid the use of links pages.

Then ask for a reciprocal link and suggest a page on which it would make sense. You're better off *not* being on a links page if you can avoid it.

Should you use links pages?

You've undoubtedly seen links pages all over the place — pages with titles such as *Useful Links, Useful Resources, Visit Our Friends,* and so on. To be honest (I say that when I'm about to upset people), these pages don't generate much traffic to your Web site. How often do you find useful links useful, or useful resources particularly, er, resourceful? Not very often, I bet. People simply don't use them. And having tested link-exchange software that measures the amount of traffic going through the links pages, I can tell you that they don't generate much traffic to Web sites. (I discuss link-exchange software later in this chapter.)

You may hear the term *link-exchange.* In many quarters, this practice is frowned upon because it implies that the site owners simply want to accumulate as many links as possible and don't really care about the type of sites they're working with. It also implies the use of a links page. On the other hand, *reciprocal linking* implies to many people a more circumspect methodology, in which links are carefully considered and placed throughout the site.

However, as I explain at the beginning of Chapter 12, you have three reasons to get links to a Web site. One is to get traffic through the links, and I've pretty much killed that idea for the typical *links page.* The other reasons are to help search engines find your site and to push up your PageRank, and links pages *can* do that, the proof being that it's possible to find sites that have a decent PageRank, perhaps 4 or 5, that have very few links apart from reciprocal links.

However, you are far better off *not* using links pages because of the following problems:

- ✔ **Search engines may already downgrade links from such pages.** A link from an ordinary page is likely to be more valuable than a link from a links page.

- ✔ **Links pages often have dozens or even hundreds of links on them.** Remember that the more links on a page, the lower the vote for each outgoing link.

- ✔ **Links pages may be further downgraded in the future.** If someone at Google or Yahoo! decides that removing the effect of links pages from their algorithms will improve search results — and there's good reason to think that it would have this effect — you could one day wake up and discover that all the links to your site from links pages no longer have *any* value.

I'm not saying that you should never use links pages. Life is an exercise in compromise, and, to be honest, a really good reciprocal-link campaign can be incredibly time consuming. However, the ideal situation would be to do the following:

✔ Scatter links to other sites around your site, in locations that make sense.

✔ Encourage site owners linking back to you to do the same. Start educating the other sites you work with! (In fact, tell them to run out and buy this book; better still, tell them to buy ten copies of this book, for colleagues, friends, and family.)

✔ Avoid having large numbers of links on one page.

✔ Avoid calling a page a *links* page. You might try using *resource* page, although I suspect this title is also overused.

Some people claim that search engines don't index these links pages. This simply is not true. They often (usually?) do, and the proof is in the pudding:

✔ Go to Google and search for these terms (make sure that you include the quotation marks): `"visit our friends"` (I found 123,000 pages), `"link exchange"` (8,170), and `"links page"` (over 3 million). Sure, not all the pages you find are links pages, but many are.

✔ Go to links pages and check to see if they're in the Google cache, or use the `site:domain.com/filename -llllll` search command to see if they're in the Google index. They often are.

✔ When you visit links pages, look at the Google Toolbar. You'll often see that they have a PageRank. However, I should reiterate: Links from links pages probably do not have the value of links from normal pages.

Finding high-PageRank links

Ideally, you want links from pages with high PageRanks. Now, you may hear that you should focus on links from sites that are related to you, not from sites with high PageRanks. That's partially true. Although relatively little traffic goes through link exchanges, remember that links from related sites are more valuable than links from unrelated sites. Links to your rodent-racing site from other rodent-related sites will probably be more valuable, in terms of PageRank, than links from unrelated sites about music or Viagra. (On the other hand, I wouldn't be surprised if links from sites about horse racing or car racing are more valuable.)

The best strategy is to get links that are related to you *from pages with high PageRanks!* Thems the facts, ma'am, and it doesn't matter how many politically correct statements people want to make about not worrying about PageRank. The fact is, PageRank *does* matter.

I'm not implying that you should turn down links from pages with low Page-Ranks, but what if you could search for pages with a high PageRank, and then go after them? If you're looking for reciprocal-link partners anyway, you might as well use a search technique that uncovers sites with high PageRanks, for several reasons:

✔ If a page has a high PageRank, it either has lots of links to it or a small number of links from other pages with high PageRanks (or both). This means that search engines are more likely to find and reindex the page, thus are more likely to find and follow the link to *your* page.

✔ For obvious reasons, people are more likely to follow the links to your page, too.

✔ The vote from the high-PageRank page counts for more than the vote from a low-PageRank page.

Here are some ways to find pages with high PageRanks:

✔ **Use the Backward Links command on the Google Toolbar or the** `links:domainname.com` **search syntax.** (Both techniques are discussed in "Find sites linking to your competition," earlier in this chapter.) These techniques find only high-PageRank pages, 4 or above. So you can look for pages linking to a competitor and know that the pages have a decent PageRank.

✔ **Look in the Google Directory.** Go to `directory.google.com` and browse through the directory until you find an appropriate category. Notice that each entry near the top of the category is shown with a green and gray bar in the left column. The longer the green part of the bar, the higher the PageRank.

These techniques will help you find sites with high PageRanks, but that doesn't necessarily mean the pages on which your links will be placed will have high PageRanks. However, I ran across a PageRank club: the High PR Link Club (`www.highprlinkclub.com`). The owner, Rick Katz, spends hours searching for sites that have link-exchange pages that have PageRanks of 4 or above. Club members have access to a categorized directory of these sites, containing the site title, the URL, a description, the PageRank of the link-exchange page, and the site-owner contact information. Yes, links pages are not ideal, but perhaps you can convince the site owner to place a link elsewhere.

I tried this service (it's $97 a year), and within ten minutes, I found 45 sites that seemed to be appropriate for one of the sites I was currently working on. Nineteen of them had a PR of 5, three had a PR of 6, and 23 had a PR of 4. It's better to spend your time trying to get links from 45 pages with high PageRanks of 4, 5, and 6, than from a couple of hundred pages with PageRanks of 0.

Respond to reciprocal link requests

Eventually, other sites will start asking *you* to link swap. Remember, ideally you should treat your outgoing links like gold and link only to relevant sites that will be of use to your visitors.

Search for keyword add url

Go to Google and search for something like this:

```
"rodent racing" +"add url"
```

Google searches for all the pages with the term *rodent racing* and the term *add url*. You'll find sites that are related to your subject and have pages on which you can add links, as shown in Figure 13-2. (For some inexplicable reason, you won't find much with `"rodent racing" +"add url"`, but you will find plenty with, for instance, `"boating" +"add url"` or `"psychology" +"add url"`.)

You can also try these searches:

```
"rodent racing" +"add a url"
"rodent racing" +"add link"
"rodent racing" +"add a link"
"rodent racing" +"add site"
"rodent racing" +"add a site"
"rodent racing" +"suggest url"
"rodent racing" +"suggest a url"
"rodent racing" +"suggest link"
"rodent racing" +"suggest a link"
"rodent racing" +"suggest site"
"rodent racing" +"suggest a site"
```

However, these are not always high-quality links. In general, the search engines don't really like this sort of linking, and the word on the street is that links from such pages probably don't have the same value that you'd get from links that are personally placed.

Use link-building software and services

Link-building campaigns are LTT: laborious, tedious, and time-consuming. (I love making up acronyms; I'm just hoping this one takes off.) You have to find sites, add links on your site to the sites you want to exchange with, contact the owners, wait to see if they respond, try again when they don't, check to see if they actually add the links, and so on. It's a helluva lot of work.

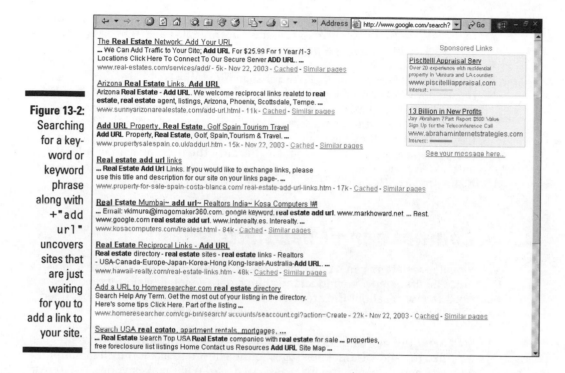

Figure 13-2: Searching for a keyword or keyword phrase along with +"add url" uncovers sites that are just waiting for you to add a link to your site.

Some programs and online services can help you automate the process. They usually help you search for appropriate sites to work with, assist you in contacting the owners, and even create your links pages for you. A number of computer programs are available; perhaps the best known are Zeus (www. cyber-robotics.com) and ARELIS (www.axandra.com/arelis). Some people find the online services easier to work with, but you have to pay a monthly fee to use them (in some cases a few hundred bucks a year).

These programs and services can be used or misused. You can easily use these systems to amass a large number of links in a hurry, without regard to relevance or context. Or you can use them to assist you in a careful campaign to garner links from sites that really make sense.

One free service is LinkPartners (www.linkpartners.com), a huge directory of people who want to exchange links. This service is associated with a pay service called LinksManager (www.linksmanager.com), which automates the process of contacting the site owners and verifying that the link-exchange partners have actually placed links on their pages. If you get a request for a link through LinksManager and accept the exchange, LinksManager does the work for you, adding the links to both your pages and the link-exchange partner's pages. It even automatically uploads the links pages to your Web site.

Another service I've used is Links4Trade (`links4trade.com`), which is similar to LinksManager, but it currently creates only a single page. (LinksManager creates a series of categorized pages.)

Some purists feel that using link-exchange programs is cheating, and indeed these services are walking a fine line between valid linking that the search engines accept and automated link-generation systems that the search engines hate. I've spoken with the owners of both LinksManager and Links4Trade, and they both tell me they have spoken with Google and been told that the way the programs are managed is acceptable. Because the programs are not totally automated and require some manual oversight and management, they're okay. Again, the proof is that these pages *are* indexed by Google.

Contact e-mail newsletters

E-mail newsletters can be an incredibly powerful method for getting the word out. The first step is to find all the appropriate e-mail newsletters, publications that write about the area in which you operate. After you've identified some newsletters, here are some ways you can work with them:

- **Send the newsletters a short announcement introducing your site.** I like to send informal messages to the editors to ask if they'll mention the site and then give them a reason to do so. What makes your site interesting or useful to the newsletter readers?

- **Consider buying small ads in the newsletters.** Some ads are cheap, and if the newsletter is highly targeted, buying an ad may be worthwhile. Make sure that you know how many people subscribe to the newsletter. (Lots of little newsletters with very few subscribers may charge pricey ad rates!)

- **Offer some kind of cooperative campaign.** For example, provide a special offer for newsletter readers or put together a contest to give away your products.

- **Write articles for the newsletters.** I cover this topic in more detail in "Got Content? Syndicate It," later in this chapter.

Create a blog

The term *blog* is derived from *Weblog* and covers everything from the utterly pointless ramblings of people who have a lot to say about nothing, to very interesting and widely read musings on just about everything. Many blog sites are indexed by the search engines, so links in these blogs get read and followed. You can set up a blog for yourself, family, employees, or whomever.

Perhaps the best known blog site is Blogger (`blogger.com`), which is owned by Google. Do you think Blogger gets spidered by Google?! Blogger provides tools that allow you to quickly set up and maintain a blog.

Other blog sites include JoeUser.com (`www.joeuser.com`), 20six (`www.20six.co.uk`), TheSpoke.com (Microsoft's new blog site), TheBlogSite.com, and blog.com (`www.blog.com`). But you can also use tools to set up blogs very quickly; look in the Weblogs Compendium tools list to find one (`www.lights.com/weblogs/hosting.html`).

You want to find a service that is being indexed by the search engines, so if you find a tool you are interested in, find examples of blogs using that tool and check to see if they're in the Google index.

Mention your site in discussion groups

Many discussion groups are indexed by the search engines. You need to find a discussion group that publishes messages on the Web, so an e-mail-based discussion group that does not archive the messages in Web pages won't help you.

Whenever you leave a message in the discussion group, make sure that you use a message signature that has a link to your site and also mention the link in the message itself.

Sometimes URLs in messages and signatures are read as links, and sometimes they aren't. If you type `http://www.yourdomain.com/` in a message, the software processing the message can handle the URL in one of two ways:

✔ It can enter the URL into the page as simple text.

✔ It can convert the URL to a true HTML link (`<A HREF=" http://www.yourdomain.com"> http://www.yourdomain.com/ </A>`).

If the URL is *not* converted to a true link, it won't be regarded as a link by the search engines.

Pursue offline PR

Getting mentioned in print often translates into being mentioned on the Web. If you can get publications to write about and review your site, not only do many people see the link in print — and perhaps visit your site — but often your link ends up online in a Web version of the article.

Give away content

Several of my clients have vast quantities of content on their Web sites. It's just sitting there, available to anyone who visits. So why not take the content *to* the visitors before they reach your site? Placing the content on other Web sites is a powerful way not only to build links back to your site but also to get your name out there — to "brand" yourself or your company.

I cover this topic in more detail a little later in this chapter, in the section "Got Content? Syndicate It!" because you need to be aware of several technical issues.

Apply for online awards

Getting someone to give an award to your site used to be a popular technique for getting links. But it reached the point at which it was possible to get an award for just about any complete-piece-of-junk Web site because the sites giving out the awards were more interested in getting links *back to their sites*. Those who win awards place the award images on their Web sites, so the images are linked back to the sites giving the awards.

Award sites are less common now, but a few still exist, such as `www.favourite websiteawards.com`. Awards with some real heft behind them are probably harder to get these days, but if you think your site is well designed or has some kind of unusual or special function, you may have a chance to get one.

Advertise

You may want to consider advertising in order to get links to your site. However, you need to consider a couple of issues first:

- ✔ Advertising is often grossly overpriced. It may be much too expensive to justify just for a link.

- ✔ Advertising links often don't count as links to your site. Rather, they're links to the advertising company, which runs a program that forwards the visitor's browser to your site. Search engines won't see the link as a link to your site. (See Chapter 12 for more information.)

In some cases, buying ads on a site to get a link does make sense. For instance, if many of your clients visit a particular Web site, and it's possible to get a low-cost ad on that site, it may be worthwhile to buy an ad to both brand your company and get a link that will be read by the search engines. And remember, it's a very relevant link, coming from a site important to your business.

Use a service or buy links

I can't stress enough that link campaigns can be very laborious, tedious, and time-consuming. You may be better off paying someone to do the work for you. Some of these services simply run the link-acquisition campaign for you. Others already have an inventory of ad space on thousands of sites and charge you to place a link on a set number. One company I saw claimed it would put links on 250 sites for $99. Another company I ran into claims it can place links on sites of a particular PageRank, too. One company, for instance, claims to be able to sell you a link on a PageRank 8 site for $799. (A PageRank 4 page is just $29.) I have no idea how legitimate such services are.

However, remember that the vote from a page is shared among all the pages it links to, so the more ads that are sold, the less the value of each ad. You should know exactly what page the link will be placed on, and you should be able to view the page. In general, buying links like this is probably not a great idea. Consider it a form of advertising that should be evaluated as such. How much of an impact will the ad have on bringing more visitors to your site?

Many companies do this sort of work; two firms that first come to mind are the Web Link Alliance (www.weblinkalliance.com) and Linking Matters (www.linkingmatters.com).

I'm not endorsing any of the companies I'm mentioning here. I'm just providing them as examples so you can see the types of services available.

If you're interested in such a service, search for link popularity and link building at a major search engine. Make sure that you understand what you're getting into. As you have seen, you can use many methods to get links to a site, but they don't all provide the same value. Are you working with a company that will find really good links from popular sites that are relevant to yours? Or a company that will use an automated link-exchange tool to gather links from anywhere it can? There's a real difference!

Remember, a link campaign can be incredibly LTT — you know, laborious, tedious, and time-consuming — so don't be surprised if a firm quotes, say, $2,000 to get you 30 links. It may be a reasonable price, assuming the firm is doing it the right way.

Just wait

I'm not really recommending that you sit and wait as a way to build links, but the fact is that if you're doing lots of other things — sending out press releases, getting mentioned in papers and magazines, contacting e-mail newsletters to do product giveaways, and so on — even if you're not actively looking for links, you'll gather links anyway. You've got to prime the pump first; then things seem to just take off.

Consider having a *Link to Us* page on your site, as I discuss in Chapter 12, on which you can provide logos and suggest HTML text that people can drop onto their sites.

Fuggetaboutit

Don't bother getting links in guest books, FFA (Free For All) pages, and link farms, for the following reasons:

- ✔ Many Web sites contain guest book pages, and one early link-building technique was to add a link to your Web site in every guest book you could find. The search engines know all about this technique, so although many guest books are indexed, links from them probably have very little value in most search engines.

- ✔ Free For All pages are automated directories to which you can add a link. They bring virtually no traffic to your site, are a great way to generate a lot of spam (when you register you have to provide an e-mail address), and don't help you in the search engines.

- ✔ Link farms are highly automated link-exchange systems designed to generate thousands of links very quickly. Don't get involved with link farms. Not only will they not help you, but if you link to a link farm or host a link-farm page on your site, you may get penalized in the search engines.

The search engines don't like these kinds of things, so save your time, energy, and money.

Got Content? Syndicate It!

I discuss one aspect of syndication in Chapter 8: using syndicated content to bulk up your Web site. Now, it's time to look at the flip side: taking your content and syndicating it to other Web sites and e-mail newsletters.

E-mail newsletters don't help your search engine position because search engines don't read them (although that could change at any time). However, most e-mail newsletters are placed into Web archives — that is, they become Web pages — which often *are* indexed by search engines. Furthermore, newsletter readers sometimes post articles from the newsletters on their sites or come directly to your site.

Suppose that you're trying to compare load and no-load mutual funds. Go to Google and search for the term `load vs. no load`. When I tried this search, I saw the search results shown in Figure 13-3. The four entries I've pointed to in the figure are actually the same article, written by the same man, promoting the same Web site . . . but appearing on *different* Web sites (none of them his, by the way).

What has this man, Ulli Niemann, done? He hasn't managed to get his own Web site onto the first page for this search, but he has managed to get his work onto the first page. People clicking one of the entries have a very good chance of seeing his name and his work and a link to his site at `www.successful-investment.com`. See how well this campaign has worked? Now he's got a link in a book, too.

Figure 13-3: The four entries I've pointed to are articles written by the same man, syndicated to different Web sites.

At the end of the day, it's not all about search engines, it's about getting the word out about your Web site, through whatever method that works.

Some site owners use this form of syndication as the *only* type of promotion they do, and it can work incredibly well. They write articles and distribute them as widely as possible. But many sites already have a lot of content. Why not give it away and use it as a technique to grab more search engine positions, generate links to your site, and brand your site and company?

Another huge advantage to using syndication is that the links you get back to your site are from relevant sites. Remember, the search engines like *relevant*. Ulli Niemann is an investment advisor, so what sorts of sites do you think are carrying his articles? Finance and investment sites!

Four ways to syndicate

You can syndicate content four ways. The trick, however, is that some of the methods don't help you one lick in terms of getting your site noticed by search engines! In some cases, it's possible to syndicate content and *not* benefit from those links pointing to your site, depending on how the content is distributed. The following list details the four main syndication categories:

- ✔ **Browser-side inclusion:** Many syndicators employ browser-side content inclusion through the use of JavaScripts; a JavaScript in a Web page pulls the article off the syndicating site. The problem is that JavaScripts are run by the Web browser itself. The page loads, and then the browser runs the JavaScripts. Searchbots, however, don't run JavaScripts. Googlebot, when indexing the page, will ignore the JavaScript and thus won't see the content and won't see the link to your site in the content. Although site visitors will see the links, and some will click them, you won't get the benefit of the link popularity in the search engines.

- ✔ **Hosted content:** Some content syndicators, generally those *selling* content, host the content on their own servers, and the sites using the content link to it. The problem with this method is that if you host content for, say, 50 sites, you don't get the benefit of 50 links in the search engines. Google sees that you have the same article 50 times, and ignores 49 of them.

- ✔ **Manual inclusion:** This method works well for the search engines; they see the content and the links to your site. But the problem is that you're relying on the owner of the other site to manually place the content into the page.

- ✔ **Server-side inclusion:** You can do server-side inclusions a number of ways, such as by using INCLUDE commands, running PHP or ASP scripts, and using a relatively new method, RSS feeds. The advantage is that the search engines *will* see your content and the links back to your site. The disadvantage is that the methods are more complicated to use than either manual or browser-side inclusion.

To ensure that the search engines see links to your Web site, you simply can't use the first or second methods. That leaves the last two, of which the third, manual inclusion, is easiest and by far the most common.

If you want to syndicate your content, prepare the articles carefully. I suggest that you produce each article in two forms: in plain text for text newsletters, and in HTML for HTML newsletters and Web sites. Make the HTML version simple so it can be taken and dropped into any other Web page.

It is possible to make a JavaScript-style syndication give you at least one link that is readable by the search engines. Typically, syndicators ask users to drop a piece of JavaScript into their pages. Of course, you can ask them to drop a piece of HTML that includes a JavaScript inside it. For instance, instead of using this:

```
<SCRIPT LANGUAGE="JavaScript" src="http://www.
         ronaldsrodents.com/content/article.js"></SCRIPT>
```

you can use this:

```
<SCRIPT LANGUAGE="JavaScript" src="http://www.ronaldsrodents.
         com/content/article.js"></SCRIPT><P><STRONG>
         Article provided by <A HREF="http://
         ronaldsrodents.com>Ronald's Rodents</A>. Visit us
         for more great articles on rodent racing.</P>
```

Getting the most out of syndication

If you're going to syndicate your work, you should consider the following points when creating your articles:

- ✔ Every article should contain your site name near the top of the article. In the HTML version, put a site logo near the top and include a link on the logo back to your site.

- ✔ If you can find a way to work a link to your site into the article, all the better. You can do it a couple of times maybe, but don't overdo it. Perhaps link to another article on your site for more information. In the HTML version, make sure the link text has useful keywords.

- ✔ At the bottom of the article, include an attribution or bio box, including a keyworded link back to your site and, in the HTML version, a logo with a link on it. (Don't forget to use ALT text in the <IMG> tag.)

You'll want to set up a library area on your Web site where people can access the articles. In the library, you should post certain conditions:

✔ Consider putting limits on the number of articles that can be used without contacting you first. For example, site owners can use up to five articles, and if they want more, they must get permission.

✔ State clearly that you retain copyright of the article and make clear the following conditions:

• The user cannot change the content.

• All logos, attributions, copyright notices, and links must remain.

• Links must remain standard HTML <A> tags and cannot be converted to another form of link.

Getting the word out

When you have your articles ready, you need to get them into the hands of people who can use them. First, you need to register with as many syndication directories as possible. Here's a huge list, partially compiled with the help of Ulli Niemann:

✔ www.allnetarticles.com

✔ www.amazines.com

✔ www.articlecity.com

✔ www.authorconnection.com

✔ www.boazepublishing.biz

✔ www.bullmarketer.com/free_content_syndicated1.htm

✔ www.certificate.net

✔ www.clickforcontent.com

✔ www.connectionteam.com/sources.htm

✔ www.content-wire.com/Online/Syndication.cfm?ccs=111&cs=1696

✔ www.debt-consolidation-directory.com

✔ www.electroniccontent.com/conFinder.cfm

✔ www.ezinearticles.com

✔ www.ezine-writer.com.au

✔ www.family-content.com

- www.freesticky.com/stickyweb
- www.freesticky.com/stickyweb/submitselfsyndicate.asp
- www.goarticles.com
- www.gold-investor.com
- www.greekshares.com
- www.ideamarketers.com
- www.investnewz.com
- www.jogena.com
- www.magportal.com
- www.makingprofit.com
- www.marketing-seek.com
- www.netterweb.com
- www.shoppingwithwomen.com
- www.stickysauce.com/dcd
- www.teenanalyst.com
- www.top7business.com/submit
- www.ultimateprofits.com
- www.usanews.net/todays_releases.htm
- www.vectorcentral.com
- www.webcollage.com/html/index.asp
- www.webmomz.com
- www.webpronews.com
- www.web-source.net/syndicator.htm
- www.windstormcomputing.com/pubs/free-ezine-content
- www.womans-net.com
- www.writers-and-publishers.com

Here are a few more ideas for getting the articles out:

- Make sure that visitors to your site know the library is available.
- Directly contact sites and e-mail newsletters that may benefit from your content.
- Include information about available materials in any e-mails you send and in your printed materials.

Syndicating utilities

A number of companies have done a tremendous job at building truly huge numbers of incoming links by giving away Web site utilities. One that comes to mind is the *Atomz Express Search* free search component from Atomz (`www.atomz.com`). Every site using this program has at least one link, probably several, back to the Atomz.com site. I just used LinkSurvey and found about 6,000 links to Atomz.com. Another company with a huge number of incoming links is MapQuest (`www.mapquest.com`). Because it distributes maps, both paid and free, and because all those maps include links back to the home site, thousands of links around the Web point to MapQuest.com.

This technique has worked incredibly well for many technology companies but can also work for others with a little imagination. Whatever you give away, whether it's clip art, videos, flash animations, or PDF documents, make sure you include links back to your site. For instance, your rodent-racing site could distribute a utility for handicapping mice and rats. (I don't mean to physically damage them; I mean to calculate the race handicap.) The utility would have a link back to your site — nicely keyworded — providing you with lots of great backlinks for search engines to read.

Using RSS

Grabbing content from RSS feeds, as I explain in Chapter 8, is relatively easy. Creating content is a bit more complicated. Is it currently worthwhile for syndication purposes? Perhaps, but probably not quite yet for most Web sites. (Keep watching, though, things are going to change quickly.) At present, I suggest that you use the manual form of syndication first.

As I mention in Chapter 8, RSS is one of those geeky acronyms whose real meaning no one has really nailed down. Some stump for *Really Simple Syndication,* while others swear it means *Rich Site Summary,* or *RDF Site Summary.* It's worth keeping an eye on no matter what RSS actually stands for.

If you really want to syndicate using RSS, you have some research to do. A good place to start is Lockergnome's RSS Resource (`rss.lockergnome.com`), which contains several articles to help you get started. Good luck. Better still, have your company geek or geek friend do all this for you, if you're not a geek yourself.

After you have set up your RSS feeds (do you like the way I jumped?), register the RSS feeds with as many RSS directories as you can, such as the following:

- ✔ **Blog Universe:** www.bloguniverse.com
- ✔ **blogarama:** blogarama.com
- ✔ **Blogdex:** blogdex.com
- ✔ **Blogdigger:** www.blogdigger.com
- ✔ **BlogSearchEngine.com:** www.blogsearchengine.com
- ✔ **BlogShares:** www.blogshares.com
- ✔ **BlogStreet:** www.blogstreet.com
- ✔ **Blogwise:** www.blogwise.com
- ✔ **Bloogz:** www.bloogz.com
- ✔ **DayPop:** www.daypop.com
- ✔ **Feedster:** feedster.com
- ✔ **Lockergnome's RSS Resource Site:** rss.lockergnome.com
- ✔ **NewsIsFree:** newsisfree.com
- ✔ **SearchEngineBlog.com:** www.searchengineblog.com
- ✔ **Syndic8:** syndic8.com
- ✔ **Waypath:** www.waypath.com

This is geeky stuff, so if you're proud of yourself when you manage to program the VCR for a show on later tonight, but have problems with a show next week, you may not want to touch this stuff.

Who's Going to Do All This Work?!

Wow, finding sites to link to yours is a lot of work. As I said before, it's very LTT. It's also not, shall we say, high rent work. How do you get all this done? Assuming you're not using a link-acquisition firm, here are some options:

- ✔ Do you have kids? If not, get some. It's a little drastic, but after you've spent a week or two doing this stuff, it may not seem so bad.
- ✔ Do your neighbors or employees have kids?
- ✔ Do your siblings have kids?
- ✔ Local schools and colleges definitely have kids, so you may want to find one or two who will do a few hours of work each evening.

How Links Build Links

I want to share a story that provides a wonderful illustration of how a link campaign can work. It shows how you can build links, PageRank, and traffic, all at the same time, the old fashioned way. I found this story in one of Webmaster-World's discussion groups. As the author of the story puts it, we should remember how the "Internet started and what it was supposed to be all about: sharing information." The search engines want you to remember this, too.

If you want to read the full story, you can find it here: `www.webmasterworld.com/forum10/626.htm`.

The story is from an Aussie called *Woz*. Once upon a time, Woz had a site called Glossarist (`www.glossarist.com`), a directory of glossaries and topical dictionaries. This was a hobby for Woz, and he had done little to promote the site.

But one sunny day — July 26, 2003 — he noticed a 4,000 percent increase in traffic. (For the math challenged among you, traffic on that day was 40 times greater than the day before!) It appears that the site was mentioned in the ResearchBuzz e-mail newsletter and Web site (`www.researchbuzz.com`), by the fairy godmother, Tara Calishain. ResearchBuzz is, not surprisingly, a resource for people interested in research. It's the sort of site that would be interested in a directory of glossaries and topical dictionaries.

The very next day, a wonderfully bright and sunny day, Glossarist was picked up by The Scout Report (`scout.wisc.edu/Reports/ScoutReport/2001/scout-010727.html`), which, perhaps a little more surprisingly, is a "weekly publication offering a selection of new and newly discovered Internet resources of interest to researchers and educators." (And you thought it was something to do with youth activities.)

Then on August 9, a *really* sunny day, the site was mentioned in USAToday. com's Hot Sites (`www.usatoday.com/tech/2001-08-09-hotsites.htm`). I've had one of my sites mentioned in *USA Today,* and believe me, your traffic really spikes when that happens!

By the middle of August, Woz wuz able to identify links from over 200 sites — "libraries and student-resource pages from schools and universities, translation sites, business reference sites, writers sites, information architecture sites, and so on." He also got a lot of traffic from newsletters that had been forwarded from subscribers to friends and colleagues (both ResearchBuzz and The Scout Report are very popular e-mail newsletters); not only did site owners find out about him through these e-mails, but many visitors also came to his site through the e-mail links.

All this publicity was great, providing his site with a lot of traffic through those links and also making it more likely that his site would be found and indexed by the search engines. But it also boosted his site's PageRank. By mid-August, the Glossarist PageRank had reached 3; by the end of August, it was 8, which is an excellent PageRank for what is really a hobby site, created by a single person without a marketing budget! (I just checked, and it's currently showing a PageRank of 7, which is still very good.)

By the end of August, he had around 300 links. I recently checked and found 2,219 links to this site! And, as Woz claims, he didn't request a single one of these links.

Don't underestimate the power of this kind of grass-roots promotion. It can be tremendously powerful. One link can set off a chain reaction, in the way that a single link in ResearchBuzz did.

Chapter 14

Using the Shopping Directories and Retailers

In This Chapter

▶ Finding the shopping directories

▶ Selling directly from third-party merchant sites

▶ Creating your datafeed files

*I*f your Web site is an e-commerce site, you have more places at which you can register. There's a whole 'nother category of search engines — shopping directories. These are giant catalogs of products. Search for *digital camera,* for instance, and you see a page with pictures of cameras, their prices, links to the appropriate Web sites, and so on. (A few of these services, such as NexTag, list services as well as products.)

Most of these directories expect you to pay, but not all of them do. Froogle, Google's product directory, is completely free, for example. In general, the ones that *do* expect you to pay charge only when someone clicks a link to visit your site, so these directories may be worth experimenting with.

I begin this chapter by talking about the different systems that are available and end by providing you with a little help on preparing your data for the directories.

Finding the Shopping Directories

The following directories are probably the most important shopping directories that you will want to research. Go to each one and try to find information about signing up and uploading your data. In some cases, that process is simple — the directory wants you to join, so you find a link that says something like Sell on Our Site, or Merchant Info. Sometimes you have to dig a little deeper because the information is not clearly visible; you may need to use the Contact Us link and ask someone about signing up.

- **Google Catalogs:** `catalogs.google.com`
- **Froogle:** `www.froogle.com`
- **Yahoo! Shopping:** `shopping.yahoo.com`
- **Shopping.com:** `www.shopping.com`
- **PriceGrabber.com:** `www.pricegrabber.com`
- **BizRate:** `www.bizrate.com`
- **NexTag:** `www.nextag.com`
- **Price Watch:** `www.pricewatch.com`
- **PriceSCAN:** `www.pricescan.com`

Most of these systems expect you to pay if you want to play — generally you pay each time someone clicks a link to your site. Some let you list your products, and receive traffic, at no cost. Here is a rundown of the three types of systems:

- **Free:** You have no direct control over your position, but you don't have to pay for any traffic you get from the site. Google Catalogs and Froogle are of this type.
- **Pay per click, fixed fee:** Yahoo! Shopping is of this type. You don't have any control over position because there's no bidding (as there is with the following type); you pay a fixed fee per click.
- **Pay-per-click bidding:** Most of the other systems charge per click, but have bidding systems that help determine your position on search-results pages. (As you may expect, merchants with the highest bids are listed first on the page.)

I think there's a good chance that the fixed-fee systems will eventually become bidding systems.

What will you pay for the PPC (pay-per-click) systems?

- In most cases, PPC systems don't charge a listing fee.
- You have to begin by funding your account — typically $50 to $250, which goes toward paying for your clicks.
- You pay each time someone clicks your link. Clicks vary in price, generally from ten cents up.

✔ In systems that accept bids, there's a minimum click rate, but the actual rate is dependent on how many people are bidding and their pain threshold; in some cases, clicks could even cost several dollars.

✔ You may be charged other fees, such as a fee to place a store logo next to your listing. (Some of the PPC systems give these logos to the highest bidders free.)

Google Catalogs

Here's a simple one. A *very* simple one. If your company publishes a catalog of some kind (pretty much any kind), get it to Google Catalogs right away. Visit catalogs.google.com and click the Info For Catalog Vendors link. The page that appears provides the address to which you should send your catalog. Simply add this address to your subscriber list so Google Catalogs gets the next edition (and make sure it never drops off the list!); drop a copy of the current edition in the mail; and then e-mail Google letting it know.

Google claims to scan every catalog it receives within a few days. It also OCRs them; that's a new verb derived from *Optical Character Recognition*. This means the text in the catalog is converted from images to computer text that can be searched.

Take a look at Figure 14-1. This is the beginning of the Consumer Electronics category. The figure shows images of catalog covers. Under each cover is the catalog name, a short description of the contents, the edition, and a link to the company's Web site. Of course, you should always make sure your catalog includes your site's URL in a prominent position, but this is one more good reason to do so.

Click a catalog, and you're inside that catalog, as shown in Figure 14-2. One more click, and you're reading a catalog page (shown in Figure 14-3). The controls at the top let you move through the catalog page by page, or you can search for a particular word.

At the time of writing, Google Catalogs is in *beta*. It's not on the main Google site, though for a while in the summer of 2003 it was incorporated into Amazon. com. Eventually, you may see more of Google Catalogs — certainly on the main Google site and perhaps elsewhere. However, one theory for why Google Catalogs has been in beta for a couple of years is that it may be merely a way for Google to test OCR on a large scale for various other purposes. Getting into Google Catalogs is so cheap and easy, though, that you might as well do it.

Figure 14-1:
The Google
Catalogs
Consumer
Electronics
page.

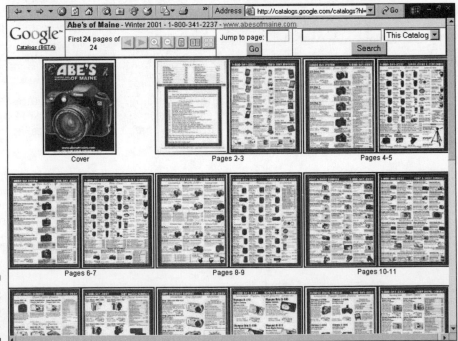

Figure 14-2:
Inside a
catalog.

Figure 14-3:
Viewing a catalog page.

Froogle

Froogle (www.froogle.com) is Google's product directory, and late in 2003, the Google folks began to incorporate it into the main Google site. They have added a Shopping? Try link onto the main page and are also experimenting with providing Froogle results and links to Froogle results on some search-results pages.

Getting into Froogle is easy. Although the instructions (look for the Information for Merchants link at the bottom) say that Froogle will take five to ten days to respond, it will probably send you instructions within minutes of signing up.

The system is entirely free. Froogle displays products in search results and channels traffic to your site at no cost whatsoever. (If you want to advertise on Froogle's search-results pages, you have to use Google AdWords; see Chapter 15 for details.)

Working with Froogle is also simple. You have to submit a *datafeed* file — a simple text file containing the product data, which I discuss later in this chapter. But because Froogle doesn't display a lot of information about each product (see Figure 14-4), it doesn't require much information from you: a link to the information page on your site, a link to an image of the product, the name and description, a price, and a category.

Yahoo! Shopping

You can get into Yahoo! Shopping (shopping.yahoo.com) two ways. You can either use Yahoo!'s shopping-cart system — Yahoo! Store (store.yahoo.com) — as your site's e-commerce system, or you can buy your way in. You're paying either way:

✔ If you use Yahoo!'s shopping cart, you pay the monthly fee (which starts at $49.95, plus a small sum per product listed) and a small commission on each sale that is derived from Yahoo! Shopping.

✔ If you don't use the Yahoo! shopping cart, you have to pay a per-click charge each time someone clicks a link to your site.

These are the free listings.

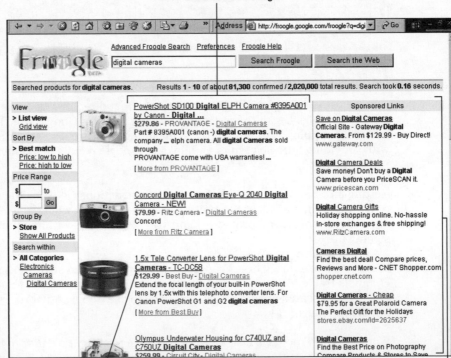

Figure 14-4: Search at Froogle, and you'll find pictures, a little information, and links to retailers' Web sites.

Links take you directly to the merchant's Web site.   These are paid, Google AdWord listings.

(Personally I don't care for Yahoo! Store, having used it for one of my sites. It's overly complicated to use and lacks many useful features. Much better products are on the market, but none get you into Yahoo! Shopping, of course.)

Yahoo! Shopping works a little differently from Froogle. Yahoo! does a product search, rather than a merchant search. While Froogle provides lots of individual matches from individual merchants, Yahoo! finds the product (see Figure 14-5) and then, when you click the link to the product page, finds merchants that sell the product (see Figure 14-6).

So how much is all this going to cost? That depends on the product category. Unlike some systems, Yahoo! charges a fixed fee per click that varies among categories; other systems charge a fee that is dependent on bidding, like the PPC systems. (See Chapter 15 for more on PPC systems.)

This link takes you to a product page, not a merchant.

Figure 14-5:
Yahoo!
Shopping is
product-
centric,
taking you
to product
pages, not
merchants.

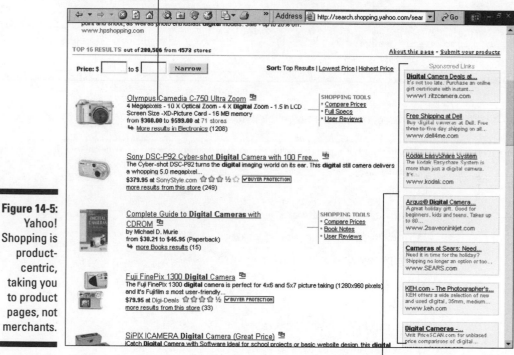

These are ads from Overture.

Figure 14-6:
You can find
links to
merchants
on the
product
page.

For instance, here are a few click prices:

Apparel	$0.19
Beauty	$0.25
Books	$0.19
Computers and Software	$0.38
Computers and Software > Desktop	$0.44
Computers and Software > Software	$0.38
DVD and Video	$0.25
Electronics	$0.38
Electronics > Digital Cameras	$0.50
Flowers, Gifts and Registry	$0.25
Flowers, Gifts and Registry > Flowers	$1.25
Toys and Baby Equipment	$0.25
Video Games	$0.25

Shopping.com

Shopping.com (found on the Web at shopping.com, of all places) is also a pretty important (that is, popular) shopping directory. It also charges by the click, and each category has a minimum rate. For instance, the following list shows a few minimum CPCs (cost per clicks):

Books	$0.05
Cables and Connectors	$0.10
Computers	$0.30
Drive Cases	$0.10
Furniture	$0.05
Graphics and Publishing Software	$0.05
Kitchen	$0.05

Figure 14-7 shows the Digital Cameras page, a subcategory of Electronics.

Figure 14-7:
The Shopping.com directory.

Remember, these are *minimums;* your mileage may vary (and almost certainly will). Unlike with Froogle and Yahoo! Shopping, the higher your bid in a system such as Shopping.com, the higher you'll initially appear on the product page. However, at Shopping.com, a site visitor can sort the product page by price, store name, and store rating, so as soon as a visitor sorts the page, most of the benefit of the higher bid price is lost. Bids are placed per category, by the way, not per product.

As with most shopping directories, you can provide a datafeed file to Shopping. com. But it also has another service, by which it grabs the information from your Web site for you. This costs $75 to set up and a $50 per month fee, but the directory will crawl your Web site every day.

Shopping.com was formed by a merger of DealTime and Epinions, the most popular product-comparison sites on the Web. Two separate sites, Shopping. com and Epinions.com, now exist; getting into Shopping.com gets you into both sites. It's worth noting that Epinions listings often rank well in search engines.

PriceGrabber and PrecioMania

PriceGrabber (www.pricegrabber.com) and its Spanish-language hermano PrecioMania (www.preciomania.com) claim to send over a billion dollars in customer referrals each month. True or not (how do you measure a referral, anyway?), PriceGrabber is a significant shopping directory in its own right, because it feeds data to various other shopping directories.

This system works two ways. You can pay per click for traffic sent to your Web site, as with most of the other shopping directories, or you can use the Price-Grabber Storefronts system and let PriceGrabber take the order and send the information to you to ship the product. (It charges 7.5 percent.)

BizRate

BizRate (shop.bizrate.com) is another popular system/per-click site. As with Shopping.com, BizRate charges a minimum fee per category, typically $0.10 to $0.30, with the actual rate dependent on bidding. Again, merchants with the highest bid are listed first, until the visitor re-sorts the list.

Figure 14-8 gives the BizRate take on digital cameras — and, no, I'm not necessarily dropping any hints here, although my birthday *is* coming up.

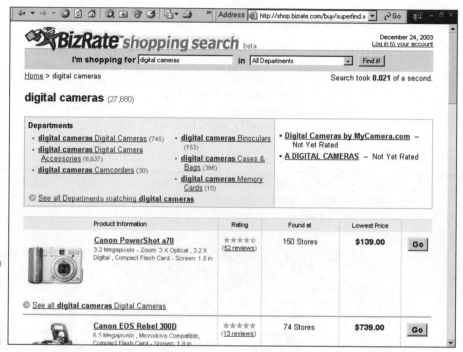

Figure 14-8:
The BizRate shopping directory.

NexTag

NexTag (www.nextag.com), yet another popular site, is also a PPC site with a category minimum and bidding for position. You don't pay a setup fee, but you do have to fund your account before you can get started. That's the norm with all these PPC shopping directories, but NexTag's $250 minimum to start is a little high.

NexTag is one of the few shopping systems that lists not only tangible products but also services. If your business sells auto insurance or long-distance telephone service, for instance, you can be listed at NexTag.

You can load data into a Web-form system if you have only a few products. If you have more, you'll want to use a datafeed file. NexTag will take any datafeed file; if you create one for Yahoo! Shopping, for instance, you can use the same one for NexTag. Just send the Yahoo! one to your NexTag account manager, and he or she will handle it.

Price Watch

Price Watch (www.pricewatch.com) isn't well known outside of geek circles. Many people in the computer business use Price Watch to buy their hardware after checking pricing at the site — the site is limited to computers, peripherals, and accessories. This is a crude system (as shown in Figure 14-9) that appeals to UNIX geeks in particular. It's fast and has no graphics on the search page (or even on the results pages in most cases).

The Price Watch folks claim to serve over 200 million pages each month, so if you have products in their categories, you may want to look into working with them. However, they don't necessarily make that easy. Contact them (you can find a contact page somewhere in the About area) and see if they get back to you!

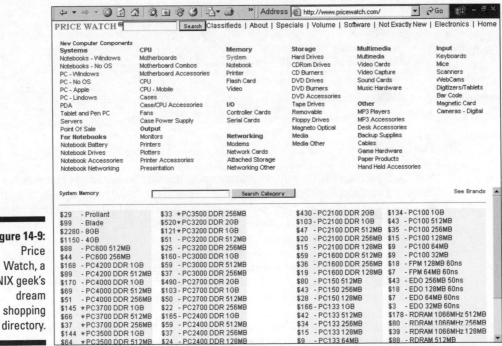

Figure 14-9: Price Watch, a UNIX geek's dream shopping directory.

PriceSCAN

PriceSCAN (www.pricescan.com) got off to a good start — it was one of the earliest shopping or price-comparison directories — but it seems to have been superseded by the other systems I've mentioned. However, PriceSCAN has one great advantage over most of them: As with Froogle, you can list your products for free. The directory does sell advertising, but the price comparisons are intended to be unbiased by fees or PPCs. E-mail the site at vendors@ pricescan.com, and who knows, someone might even respond.

More Shopping Services

Yep, there's more, plenty more. Here's a quick rundown of some other places you can list your products:

- ✔ **StreetPrices.com** (www.streetprices.com): A PPC site that claims to get 200,000 visitors each month, generating $90 million per month in "sales leads" (whatever that means). It charges from $0.45 to $0.55 cents per click.

- ✔ **iBuyernet.com** (www.ibuyernet.com): Is there anyone home? Who knows? This site doesn't seem very interested in signing up new merchants.

- ✔ **Ask Jeeves Shopping** (ask.pricegrabber.com), **Dogpile** (dogpile.pricegrabber.com), **MetaCrawler** (metacrawler.pricegrabber.com), **and PricingCentral.com:** All these systems use PriceGrabber; get in there, and you're in here, too.

- ✔ **Lycos Shopping** (shop.lycos.com): Uses BizRate.

- ✔ **mySimon** (www.mysimon.com) **and Shopper.com** (www.Shopper.com): Combined, these are very important sites, but because they don't make it easy for the average store owner to work with them, I've put them in the "more stuff" category. Owned by CNET, these systems don't have automated feeds set up for merchants. You need to contact them directly for information about how you can work with them (and they may take a couple of months to get back to you!). They have a variety of programs, from simple PPC text links (generally from 15 cents to 50 cents per click) to featured advertising positions.

- ✔ **AOL Shopping** (webcenter.shop.aol.com): A very exclusive property; if you want to work with AOL Shopping, you have to negotiate directly.

✔ **MSN Shopping** (`eshop.msn.com`): Not quite as exclusive as AOL, but if you want to be in MSN Shopping, you still have to negotiate directly.

✔ **Kelkoo** (`www.kelkoo.com`): Don't forget about shopping directories outside the United States. Kelkoo is one of the better-known systems in Europe.

Third-Party Merchant Sites

I want to quickly mention yet another type of listing you can get for your products: third-party merchant sites. I don't go into great detail here, because this is one step over the line between being in a search directory and being sold on another Web site.

You may want to consider selling your products on the major e-commerce sites, which consist of both auction and retail sites:

✔ With the auction sites, you sell your products, yep, at an auction and handle the transactions yourself.

✔ With the retail sites, the product is placed into a directory, and if anyone buys it, the retail site handles the transaction, sends you the information so you can ship the product, and then, a little while later, sends you the money (bar its commission, of course).

Many merchants use the auction sites as a way to generate traffic to their Web sites. By placing links in the ads, you can bring new customers directly to your site, and by carefully using price reserves, you can ensure that any sales you make through an auction are not at a loss.

Check out the following sites to find out more about working with third-party retail sites:

✔ **Amazon.com zShops:** This is a retail site where people searching at Amazon may run across your products. See `www.zshops.com`.

✔ **Amazon Marketplace:** If you sell the same products Amazon sells, you can place links to your products from the same pages on which Amazon sells its products. (You've probably seen the *THIS ITEM ALSO AVAILABLE TO BUY* box on Amazon product pages.) You can also find information on this at the zShops site.

✔ **Half.com:** Owned by eBay, this is a huge retail-products site. See `halfbay.ebay.com`.

- ✔ **eBay:** This is the world's most popular e-commerce site, with billions of dollars of products being sold here. See `www.ebay.com`.

- ✔ **Amazon Auctions:** It's not Amazon's core business, but it's worth checking out: `auctions.amazon.com`.

- ✔ **Yahoo! Auctions:** Did you even know Yahoo! had auctions? Well, it does. See `auctions.yahoo.com`.

Creating Data Files

Before you sign up with the shopping directories, you probably need a data file (often called a *datafeed*) containing information about your products. This is a simple text file, though carefully formatted using the correct layout. A datafeed allows you to quickly upload hundreds, even thousands, of products into the directories within minutes.

Although the datafeed file can be a simple text file, creating it is a little difficult for some people. Of course, if you have geeks on your staff, they can handle it for you. The ideal situation is one in which all your product data is stored in a database that is managed by capable, knowledgeable people who know how to export to a text file in the correct format. All you do is give them the data-file specification from the shopping directory, and they know exactly what to do. If that's your situation, be happy. If not, pay attention, and I'll help you.

I'm going to explain how to format your data using a spreadsheet program, which is probably the simplest way. If you have a large number of products, you may already have your data in some kind of database format. Unfortunately, you may need to manipulate your data — clean it up — before you can use it. I've noticed over the last couple of decades that, for some reason, data is usually a mess, whether the data files were created by small companies or large. The files are often badly formatted — for example, the text files contain the data, but the fields are improperly *delimited* (separated).

I suggest that you use a spreadsheet program to create your data file. Creating the file in a text editor is difficult and error prone, especially if you have a lot of products. Also, remember that each shopping directory is a little different, requiring different information. The spreadsheet file is your source file, from which you can create the various text files as needed.

You may already have a spreadsheet program; Microsoft Excel is hiding on millions of computers around the world, unknown to their owners. (It's part of Microsoft Office.) Or you may have Microsoft Works, which also includes a spreadsheet program. Various other database programs are available — StarOffice and AppleWorks contain spreadsheets, too. You don't need a terribly complicated program, because the work you do with the file is pretty simple. However, you want to use a program that can have multiple sheets open at once and allows you to link from a cell in one sheet to a cell in another.

You can also use a database program to manage all this data. It's just simpler in some ways to use a spreadsheet. Of course, you may already have your data in a database, especially if you have a lot of products.

The data you need

Take a look at the type of data you're going to need for your data file. Froogle, Google's shopping directory, requires the following data:

- **product_url:** A link to the product page on your Web site
- **name:** The name of the product
- **description:** A description of the product
- **price:** The price
- **image_url:** A link to the image file containing a picture of the product
- **category:** The category in which you want to place the product

Each service is different, of course. Here's the data that can be included in Yahoo! Shopping:

- **code:** An SKU (Stock Keeping Unit) or other kind of identifier
- **product_url:** A link to the product page on your Web site
- **name:** The name of the product
- **price:** The price
- **merchant-category:** Your own product category, based on how you categorize products on your site — for instance, Electronics and Camera > Television and Video > VCR
- **shopping-category:** The Yahoo! Store category under which the product will be placed
- **description:** A description of the product
- **image_url:** A link to the image file containing a picture of the product
- **isbn:** If the product is a book, the ISBN number
- **medium:** If your products are music or videos, the medium (CD, DVD, VHS, 8mm, and so on)
- **condition:** The product's condition (new, like new, very good, good, and so on)

- ✔ **classification:** A product type, such as new, overstock, damaged, returned, refurbished, and so on

- ✔ **availability:** Information about the product's availability

- ✔ **ean:** The European Article Number (EAN), a number used for barcoding products

- ✔ **weight:** The weight of the product

- ✔ **upc:** The Universal Product Code (UPC) number, another barcoding system

- ✔ **manufacturer:** The manufacturer's name

- ✔ **manufacturer-part-no:** The manufacturer's part number

- ✔ **model-no:** The product's model number

Don't worry — only five of these fields are absolutely required. As you can see, some fields are the same in both the Froogle and Yahoo! systems. (For details, you need to check the particular systems into which you want to load the data.)

Here's my suggestion. Begin by creating a spreadsheet file containing *all* the data you have about your products. At the very least, include this information:

- ✔ Product name

- ✔ Product description

- ✔ Product price

- ✔ Product category

- ✔ A URL pointing to the product's Web page on your Web site

- ✔ A URL pointing to the image file containing a picture of the product, on your site

You also want to include any other information you have — ISBN numbers, SKUs, EANs, media types, and so on. And keep the file clean of all HTML coding; you just want plain text, with no carriage returns or special characters in any field.

Formatting guidelines

Some of you may have problems with the product URL. If your site is a framed site, as I discuss in Chapter 6, you've got a problem because you can't link directly to a product page. But even if you don't have a framed site, you might have a problem or two. I discuss that in a minute.

Each shopping directory varies slightly, but datafeed files typically conform to the following criteria:

- ✔ They are plain text files. That is, don't save them in a spreadsheet or database format; save them in an ASCII text format. Virtually all spreadsheet programs have a way to save data in such a format.

- ✔ The first line in each file contains the header, with each field name — product_url, name, description, price, and so on — generally separated by tabs.

- ✔ Each subsequent line contains information about a single product; the fields match the headers on the first line.

- ✔ The last line of the file may require some kind of marker, such as *END*.

- ✔ In most cases, you can't include HTML tags, tabs within fields (tabs are usually used to separate fields), carriage returns, new line characters within fields, and so on. Just plain text.

Creating your spreadsheet

Take a look at Figure 14-10. This is a simple spreadsheet file containing a number of data fields; it's an example data file from Froogle. Each row in the spreadsheet is a product, and each cell in the row — each field — is a different piece of information about the product.

Although the final product will be a text file, you want to save the spreadsheet file in a normal spreadsheet file format. When you're ready to upload data to a shopping directory, *then* you save it as a text file.

	A	B	C	D	E
1	code	product-url	name	price	shopping-category
2	p12-x	http://www.yourstore123.com/1.html	American Pride Polo Shirt	25	Apparel
3	w345	http://www.yourstore123.com/2.html	Women's Overalls	39.95	Apparel
4	f45	http://www.yourstore123.com/3.html	Carrot Cake	29.95	Flowers, Gifts and Registry > Gourmet and F
5	f46	http://www.yourstore123.com/4.html	Apple Pie	19.99	Flowers, Gifts and Registry > Gourmet and F
6	hg202	http://www.yourstore123.com/5.html	Replacement Blade of Cof	12.95	Home, Garden and Garage > Appliances
7	12kn	http://www.yourstore123.com/6.html	PowerMax Juicer	129.95	Home, Garden and Garage > Appliances > S
8	f235	http://www.yourstore123.com/7.html	Soft Recliner	399.99	Home, Garden and Garage
9	p3002-x12	http://www.yourstore123.com/8.html	Litter box - Gray	14.95	Home, Garden and Garage
10	3exe345	http://www.yourstore123.com/9.html	Handheld power drill	89.95	Home, Garden and Garage

Figure 14-10: A sample datafeed spreadsheet.

Getting those product URLs

To do this spreadsheet business right, you need the URL for each product's Web page. If you don't have many products, this is easy — just copy and paste from your browser into the spreadsheet. If you have thousands of products, though, it might be a bit of a problem! If you're lucky and you have a big IT budget or some very capable but cheap geeks working for you, you don't need to worry about this. Otherwise, here's a quick tip that might help.

Many companies have a source data file that they use to import into an e-commerce program. For this to be useful to you, you have to figure out what page number the e-commerce program is assigning to each product. For instance, one e-commerce system creates its URLs like this:

```
http://www.yourdomain.com/customer/product.php?productid=
        18507
```

Notice that the `productid` number is included in this URL. Every product page uses more or less the same URL — all that changes is the `productid` number. So here's one simple way to deal with this situation. Suppose you have a data file that looks similar to the one in Figure 14-11, in which you have a product ID or code in one column, and an empty column waiting for the URL pointing to the product page.

	File Edit View Insert Format Tools Data Window Help		_ & x
	A	B	C	D
1	code	product-url	name	price	shopping-categ
2	803341		American Pride Polo Shirt	25	Apparel
3	803342		Women's Overalls	39.95	Apparel
4	803343		Carrot Cake	29.95	Flowers, Gifts
5	803344		Apple Pie	19.99	Flowers, Gifts
6	803345		Replacement Blade of Cof	12.95	Home, Garden
7	803346		PowerMax Juicer	129.95	Home, Garden
8	803347		Soft Recliner	399.99	Home, Garden
9	803348		Litter box - Gray	14.95	Home, Garden
10	803349		Handheld power drill	89.95	Home, Garden

Figure 14-11: Where do you get the URL from?

Start by copying the blank URL — a URL without the product ID in it, as shown in Figure 14-12 — into all the URL fields. Some spreadsheet programs try to convert the URL to an active link, one you can click to launch a browser. You might want to leave the URL in that format so later you can test each link. (But working with these active links is often a nuisance because it may be hard to select a link without launching the browser.)

Next, you create a macro or use a programmable keyboard that will, with a single keystroke, copy the number in the code field and paste it onto the end of the matching URL. (I love my programmable keyboard! It has saved me hundreds of hours. I use an old Gateway Anykey programmable keyboard, which you can buy at eBay.)

Figure 14-12:
Place a
blank URL in
the column
and then
copy the
product
code from
the code
column to
the end of
the URL.

| | File   Edit   View   Insert   Format   Tools   Data   Window   Help | | _ ₤ × |
	A	B	C	D
1	code	product-url	name	price	shopping-categ
2	803341	http://www.yourdomain.com/customer/product.php?productid=	American Pride Polo Shirt	25	Apparel
3	803342	http://www.yourdomain.com/customer/product.php?productid=	Women's Overalls	39.95	Apparel
4	803343	http://www.yourdomain.com/customer/product.php?productid=	Carrot Cake	29.95	Flowers, Gifts
5	803344	http://www.yourdomain.com/customer/product.php?productid=	Apple Pie	19.99	Flowers, Gifts
6	803345	http://www.yourdomain.com/customer/product.php?productid=	Replacement Blade of Cof	12.95	Home, Garden
7	803346	http://www.yourdomain.com/customer/product.php?productid=	PowerMax Juicer	129.95	Home, Garden
8	803347	http://www.yourdomain.com/customer/product.php?productid=	Soft Recliner	399.99	Home, Garden
9	803348	http://www.yourdomain.com/customer/product.php?productid=	Litter box - Gray	14.95	Home, Garden
10	803349	http://www.yourdomain.com/customer/product.php?productid=	Handheld power drill	89.95	Home, Garden

If you don't have a programmable keyboard (and you should have one!), the spreadsheet you're using may have a built-in macro program that allows you to program actions onto a single keystroke (MS Excel does, for instance). Another option is to use a macro program that you download from a share-ware site. If you have only 20 or 30 products, programmable keyboards and macros don't matter too much. If you have a few thousand products, it's worth figuring out how to automate keystrokes!

Creating individual sheets

After you have all your data in one sheet of the spreadsheet file, you can create a single sheet for each system to which you plan to upload data: one for Froogle, one for Yahoo! Shopping, and so on. (A *sheet* is a spreadsheet page, and all good spreadsheet programs allow you to have multiple sheets.)

Remember, each system requires different information, under different headings, and in a different order. For instance, suppose you're selling books. Yahoo! Shopping wants pretty much all the information you've got, including the books' ISBN numbers. Froogle, on the other hand, doesn't care about the ISBN number. Froogle provides just a little information — an image, a title, a description, and a price — expecting the searcher to click over to the merchant's site for more detailed information. (I suspect that Froogle will eventually add data fields. ISBN numbers, for instance, are useful for tracking down books.)

So you need to link information from the original sheet to each individual sheet. You don't want to actually copy this information. Say that you have five shopping directories you're working with, and after you've finished everything, you discover that you made a few mistakes. If you *copied* the data, you have to go into each sheet and correct the cells. If you *linked* between cells, you can just make the change in the original sheet, and the other five update automatically.

Here's how this works in Excel. I will assume you have two sheets, one named Yahoo! (which contains data for Yahoo! Shopping) and one named Original (containing all your product data). And you want to place the information from the *productid* column in the Original sheet into the Yahoo! sheet, under the column named *code*. Here's how you do it in Microsoft Excel:

1. **Click the Yahoo! tab at the bottom of the window to open the Yahoo! sheet.**

2. **Click cell 2 in the *code* column.**

   In this example, this cell is A2, as shown in Figure 14-13.

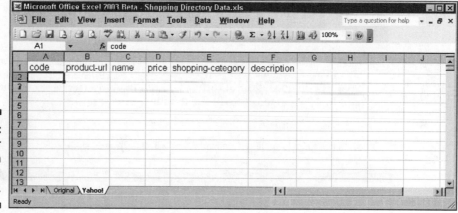

Figure 14-13: The cursor on cell A2 in the Yahoo! sheet.

3. **Press the = (equal) key to begin placing a formula into the cell.**

4. **Click the Original tab at the bottom of the page to open the Original sheet.**

5. **Click cell 2 in the *productid* column.**

   In this example, this cell is again A2, as shown in Figure 14-14.

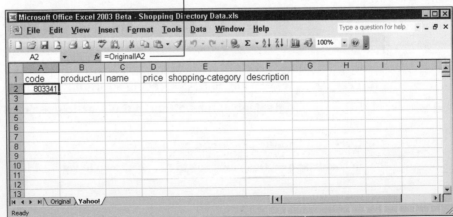

Figure 14-14:
The cursor
on cell A2 in
the Original
sheet.

6. **Press Enter.**

   The program jumps back to cell 2 in the *code* column of the Yahoo!
   sheet, places the data from the Original sheet into that cell, and then
   moves down to the cell below.

7. **Click cell 2 and then look in the formula box at the top of the window.**

   You see this formula (or something similar): =Original!A2, as shown in
   Figure 14-15.

   This means, "Use the data from cell A2 in the sheet named Original." You
   haven't copied the data; rather you're linking to the data, so that if the
   data in A2 changes, so will the data in this cell.

Here's the formula pulling data from Cell A2 in the Original sheet.

Figure 14-15:
Cell A2 in
the Yahoo!
sheet
contains
=Original
!A2.

8. **With cell 2 in the *code* column of the Yahoo! sheet selected, press Ctrl+C or choose Edit⇨Copy from the main menu to copy this data into the Clipboard.**

9. **Press the down arrow (↓) to select the cell below.**

10. **Hold the Shift key and press PgDn multiple times, until the cursor has selected as many cells as there are products.**

    For instance, if you have 1,000 products, you want the last selected cell to be cell 1001 (remember, the first cell contains the header, *code*).

11. **Press Ctrl+V or choose Edit⇨Paste from the main menu to paste the formula into all these cells.**

    The cursor jumps to cell 2 again, and data from the Original sheet — from the appropriate cells — now appears in the cells below cell 2.

12. **Press the Esc key to stop copy mode.**

If you go to the Original sheet and change data in the *productid* column, the cells are now linked. Change data in a *productid* cell, and it changes in the appropriate *code* cell, too.

Repeat this process for all the columns you need and for all the different sheets you need, and you're ready to export your text files.

Creating and uploading your data files

After you've created your sheets, you can export the text files you need to give to the shopping directories. Each spreadsheet program works a little differently. With some programs, you may find an Export command, and in Microsoft Excel, you use the Save As command. Here's how to export the text files from Excel:

1. **Save the spreadsheet file in its original spreadsheet file format, to make sure that any changes you've made are stored in the original file.**

2. **Click the tab for the sheet you want to export to a text file.**

    That sheet is selected.

3. **Choose File⇨Save As from the main menu to open the Save As dialog box.**

4. **In the Save As box, select the appropriate file type from the Save As Type drop-down menu.**

    In most cases, this option is *Text (Tab delimited)(*.txt)*, but it may be something different depending on the shopping directory you're working with; check the directory's data-file specifications.

5. **Provide a filename in the Name field.**

   For example, use Yahoo! if you're submitting to Yahoo!, and so on.

6. **Click OK, and you see a message box saying that you can't save the entire file; that's okay, all you want to do is save the selected sheet, so click Yes.**

7. **Now you see a message box telling you that some features can't be saved as text. That's okay, you don't want to save anything fancy, just text, so click Yes.**

   That's it, you've saved the file. It's still open in Excel, with the other sheets, so I suggest that you close the file. (Excel will ask again if you want to save the file — you can just say No.)

   If you want to export another text file, reopen the original spreadsheet file and repeat these steps.

If you want, you can open the file in a text editor like Notepad to see what it really looks like.

After you've created the text file, you're ready to upload it to the shopping directory. Each directory works a little differently, so refer to the directory's instructions.

These data files expire. They last only one month at Froogle, for example. Check each system carefully and remember to upload the latest data file before it expires or when you have any important changes.

Chapter 15

Pay Per Click — Overture, Google AdWords, and More

. . . .

In This Chapter

▶ Pay-per-click basics

▶ Figuring out how much a click is worth

▶ Creating ads that are acceptable

▶ Automating pay-per-click campaigns

. . . .

Here's a quick way to generate traffic through the search engines: Pay for it. Pay-per-click (PPC) campaigns provide a shortcut to search engine traffic, and many companies, particularly large companies with large marketing budgets, are going directly to PPC and bypassing the search engine optimization stage totally.

In this chapter, you examine these PPC programs, discover both their advantages and disadvantages, and find out how and where to employ them.

Defining PPC

If you use pay-per-click advertising, you'll pay each time someone clicks on one of your ads. PPC ads of various kinds have actually been used on the Web for years, but it's only the last couple of years that the medium has really taken off on the search engines.

Take a look at Figure 15-1, which shows search results at Google, and Figure 15-2, which shows results for the same search at Yahoo!. As you can see, many of the search results on these pages are actually ads. They are placed mainly based on pricing. (Google AdWords, as their PPC ads are known, is a special case, as I explain in a moment.) In other words, rather than going through all the trouble of optimizing your site and getting links from other sites into your site — the things that are explained in most of the rest of this book — you can simply buy your way to the top of the search engines! Maybe.

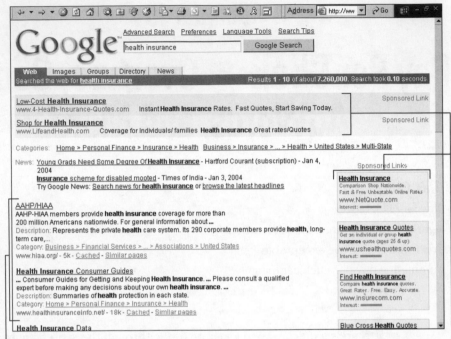

Figure 15-1: Pay-per-click placements in Google.

These are the "real," non-paid search results.   These results are pay-per-click ads.

Here is how it all works:

1. **You register with a PPC system, provide a credit card number, and load your account.**

2. **You create one or more ads — providing a title, body text, and link to the page to which you want to direct visitors.**

3. **You associate keywords with each ad.**

4. **You bid on each keyword.**

In general, when you bid on a keyword, you are bidding on a position. In Figure 15-3, you can see a list of keywords in the Overture PPC system. The very first entry shows how much you are willing to bid on the keywords *academic software.* In other words, if someone searches for *academic software,* you're willing to pay $1.51 if that person clicks on your ad. And, in this case, because the other people bidding on the term are not willing to pay that much, Overture will list your ad at the top. You can see how much others are willing to bid in the Top 5 Max Bids column.

These are the pay-per-click ads.

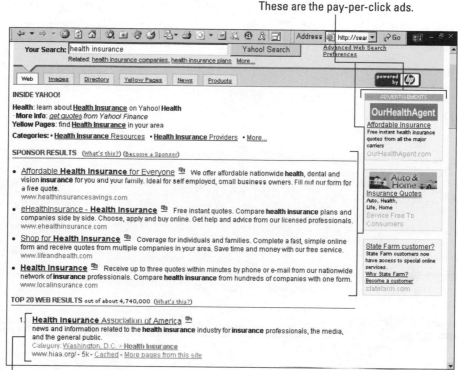

Figure 15-2:
Pay-per-
click place-
ments in
Yahoo!.

These are the non-paid ads, way down here.

In most PPC systems, the top bid gets the top position. Google's system is a little more complicated (and because of this, Google is actually a little more difficult to use, because you can never be sure exactly what position your ad will be). When Google has to position your ad for a particular search result, it chooses the ad position partly based on your bid price, but also partly on the *click rate* or *click-through rate,* the frequency with which people have clicked on your ad in the past. You may bid more than someone else, but because your ad has a low click-through rate in the past, it may still be placed below the lower bidder. As Google puts it, "The most relevant ads rise to the top. . . . Your ad can rise above someone paying more if it is highly relevant for a specific keyword."

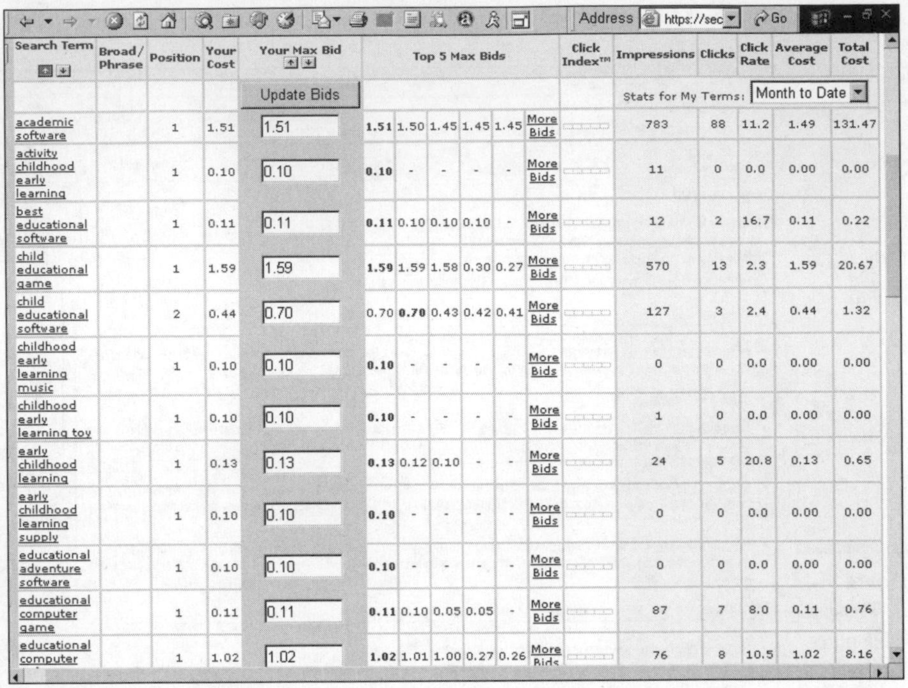

Search Term	Broad/Phrase	Position	Your Cost	Your Max Bid	Top 5 Max Bids						Click Index™	Impressions	Clicks	Click Rate	Average Cost	Total Cost
				Update Bids								Stats for My Terms: Month to Date ▾				
academic software		1	1.51	1.51	1.51	1.50	1.45	1.45	1.45	More Bids		783	88	11.2	1.49	131.47
activity childhood early learning		1	0.10	0.10	0.10	-	-	-	-	More Bids		11	0	0.0	0.00	0.00
best educational software		1	0.11	0.11	0.11	0.10	0.10	0.10	-	More Bids		12	2	16.7	0.11	0.22
child educational game		1	1.59	1.59	1.59	1.59	1.58	0.30	0.27	More Bids		570	13	2.3	1.59	20.67
child educational software		2	0.44	0.70	0.70	0.70	0.43	0.42	0.41	More Bids		127	3	2.4	0.44	1.32
childhood early learning music		1	0.10	0.10	0.10	-	-	-	-	More Bids		0	0	0.0	0.00	0.00
childhood early learning toy		1	0.10	0.10	0.10	-	-	-	-	More Bids		1	0	0.0	0.00	0.00
early childhood learning		1	0.13	0.13	0.13	0.12	0.10	-	-	More Bids		24	5	20.8	0.13	0.65
early childhood learning supply		1	0.10	0.10	0.10	-	-	-	-	More Bids		0	0	0.0	0.00	0.00
educational adventure software		1	0.10	0.10	0.10	-	-	-	-	More Bids		0	0	0.0	0.00	0.00
educational computer game		1	0.11	0.11	0.11	0.10	0.05	0.05	-	More Bids		87	7	8.0	0.11	0.76
educational computer		1	1.02	1.02	1.02	1.01	1.00	0.27	0.26	More Bids		76	8	10.5	1.02	8.16

Figure 15-3: Bidding on keywords at Overture.

The big question, of course, is how much should you bid? Here are a few things to consider:

✔ You must understand how much a click is really worth to you; most companies do not know this. I discuss this issue a little later in this chapter.

✔ The higher your position, the more traffic you are likely to get.

✔ In general, if you're not in the first three positions, there's a good chance your ad won't be seen often and will get *dramatically* lower click-throughs. Google, for instance, syndicates their top three AdWords to sites such as AOL, and Yahoo! displays the top three (sometimes four) Overture results at the top of their search results.

✔ Sometimes you may want to take position three, because you want to be in the first three, yet position one is just too expensive.

✔ Other times, you may notice that position one is just $0.01 more than you're already paying; it may be worth paying the extra $0.02 to leap frog the current bidder, just to boost your click-through.

✔ There's always a minimum bid level; $0.10 on Overture, for instance, and $0.03 on Enhance.

WARNING!

Overture and Google AdWords, and some of the tier 2 systems (see the section, "The three PPC tiers," later in this chapter), automatically adjust your bid price so that you only pay $0.01 above the lower bidder. Say, for instance, you have bid $3.50 for a keyword phrase, while the next highest bidder has only bid $2.99. You will be charged $3.00 for a click. If the next bidder raises his bid to $3.01, you'll be charged $3.02, and so on. However, note that some smaller systems don't do this, so you have to watch your bids carefully or you may pay significantly more than you need to for a position.

The two types of ads

Note that most tier 1 and tier 2 PPC systems (see "The three PPC tiers," later in this chapter) now have two types of ads: search engine ads and contextual or content match ads. The first are the search engine placements you've already seen. *Contextual* or *content match ads* are ads placed on Web sites other than search engines. For instance, go to Amazon.com and search for something, and you'll likely come across ads similar to those shown in Figure 15-4.

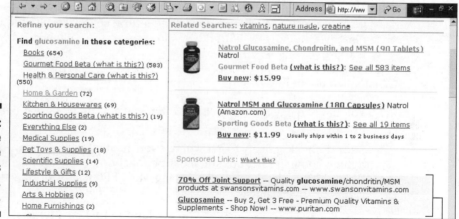

Figure 15-4: Google AdSense placements at Amazon.com.

These are ads from the Google AdWord's system.

In fact, anyone can sign up to run these ads on their Web site through Google's AdSense program (www.google.com/adsense) if they'd like to make money by running ads on their site. Sign up for this program, and Google examines your pages to see what ads are most appropriate for your page content. You place a little bit of code in your pages that pulls ads from the AdWords program, and Google automatically places ads into your page each time the page is loaded into a browser. If someone clicks on the ad, you earn a little bit of the click price.

From the PPC advertiser's perspective, though, you should understand that these ads are probably not as effective as the ads placed on the search engines. Some advertisers claim that people who click on these content ads are less likely to buy your product, for instance, than those who click on the same ad at the search engine. Unfortunately, most PPC networks will not let you know at which sites your ads were displayed, or the specific metrics of content ads versus the standard ads. However, you can generally turn off content ads if you wish, as many advertisers do.

Pros and cons

What's good about a PPC campaign?

- It's a much quicker way to begin generating traffic to your Web site — hours or days, compared to weeks or months through *natural search,* as unpaid search results are often known in the business.

- It's much more reliable. With a natural search, you may put huge effort (read, expense) and not do well; with PPC you'll get what you pay for. If you're willing to bid high enough, you'll get the traffic.

- It's more stable. A site can do well in natural search results today, then disappear tomorrow. With PPC, as long as you're willing to pay, your site is there.

What's bad about PPC?

- You have to pay for every click, which can add up to a great deal of money.

- Sticker shock is likely to get worse over the next year or two; 2003 saw a huge boom in PPC, but still most people don't even know what PPC is. Wait and see what happens to pricing when PPC is as well known as other forms of advertising.

- PPC doesn't always work, as you see later in this chapter — it's not possible for every company to buy clicks at a price that is low enough to be profitable.

- Many people don't click on sponsored search results, as they don't trust them — perhaps 20 percent of all searchers, possibly more — so you're missing part of the market.

Ideally, PPC should be one part of an overall marketing campaign — it should be combined with the other techniques in this book. Many companies spend huge sums on PPC, yet totally ignore natural search, which could often be managed for a fraction of the sum.

The three PPC tiers

The PPC companies are *networks;* that is, they place ads on multiple search sites. Yahoo!, for instance, owns one of the two big PPC companies, Overture, which places ads not only on the Yahoo! and Overture Web sites, but also on MSN, AltaVista, CNN, InfoSpace, Juno, NetZero, Dogpile, ESPN, and many others.

The other major service, Google's AdWords service, appears on Google, of course, but also on AOL, Ask Jeeves, EarthLink, CompuServe, Netscape, Excite . . . even on the Amazon.com Web site. In fact, Google has a service called AdSense, which allows virtually any Web site to carry Google PPC ads.

I think of the PPC market as being split into the following three tiers:

- ✔ **Tier 1:** Tier 1 comprises two companies, Yahoo!'s Overture and Google's AdWords. These two are responsible for more PPC placements than all the rest of the networks combined. They are also the most expensive. A click that costs $0.05 on a tier 2 or tier 3 network may cost $2.00 on Overture or AdWords.

- ✔ **Tier 2:** Tier 2 comprises a handful of smaller networks that may still channel decent traffic to you, and at much lower prices, such as Find-What (www.findwhat.com), Espotting Media (www.espotting.com), Enhance Interactive (www.enhance.com), and ePilot (www.epilot.com). They can't channel as much traffic to you as you would get by bidding for first position on Overture or AdWords, but in some cases, they *can* send as much traffic as you're getting on those two behemoths, simply because you can't afford the big guys' top price per click. In addition, the smaller engines don't have the same level of fraud protection as the bigger three.

  ePilot, for instance, places ads on YellowPages.com, Locate.com, Search Bug, and so on. They may be small, little known sites, but according to ePilot, the 100 or so systems they work with amount to almost 700 million searches a month. Enhance claims 1 billion searches throughout its network each month, on sites such as EarthLink, InfoSpace, and MSN.

  Note, however, that this situation may not last for long. The big PPC services have begun buying up the smaller fish; Sprinks.com, for instance, definitely one of the larger small fish, was bought by Google late in 2003.

✔ **Tier 3:** Finally, tier 3. There are many other PPC networks, too; hundreds, in fact, and some are little more than a scam, encouraging the unwary to pay a setup fee with little real hope of ever getting any traffic. (You can find a huge list of PPC systems, almost 600 at the time of writing, at `payperclicksearchengines.com`.) On the other hand, there are many that can generate a little traffic for you each month; the problem, however, is that you'll spend a huge amount of time managing these tier 3 companies. In general, it's not worth working with the tier 3 company directly; rather, it's possible to work with a company that will sell you clicks at a fixed rate, and then gather these clicks from a wide array of tier 3 PPC systems.

Where do these ads go?

Figures 15-1 and 15-2 show a couple of examples of ad placements. But placement does vary quite a bit from site to site. Take the `health insurance` search I did at Google, for instance. The first two ads were placed at the top of the search results, the first thing a searcher would see. Then ads are run down the right side of the page.

Do the same search at AOL, though, and you'll have the first four PPC ads at the top of the page, followed by a whole bunch of natural search results — that is, results that were not paid for — followed by another four Google AdWords PPC ads at the bottom of the page. At Ask Jeeves, the first four spots are reserved for ads they sell directly to advertisers, but following that they run *ten* of Google's AdWords ads, followed by ten natural search results. So ads run in different positions on different sites, and of course all this varies periodically; the general trend over the last year has been to stuff more and more ads into search results pages. Some small sites run nothing but paid ads in their search results.

In general, it's obvious that these placements are paid ads. In most cases, the ads are preceded by the words *sponsored links,* or *sponsored Web results,* or something similar, and in fact the Federal Trade Commission mandates some kind of indication that a placement is paid. Despite that, there's a definite movement afoot to make it less and less obvious that more and more ads are appearing. On Ask Jeeves recently, for instance, one of their SPONSORED CONTENT titles was such a light gray, on a white background, that it was almost illegible on a laptop screen. And in some cases, these ads are run without *any* notification that they are ads. You probably won't see that happen on the large search sites, or with ads being fed by Google AdWords and Overture, but some of the smaller ad networks evidently have lower standards.

By the way, the ads I've shown so far are simple text ads, but now the PPC companies are starting to allow advertisers to include, for instance, logos.

It may not work!

"Half the money I spend on advertising is wasted; the trouble is, I don't know which half."

—John Wanamaker, 1838–1922

John Wanamaker's store in Philadelphia — imaginatively named *Wanamaker's* — was probably the world's first department store. He later opened one in New York, and was eventually the Postmaster General, but he's probably best remembered for the preceding quote. (Come on, be honest, isn't that why you remember him?)

Wanamaker was almost certainly correct. Half (at least) of the money spent on advertising doesn't work (in the sense that the monetary value derived from the advertising is less — often considerably less — than the cost of the advertising). And back in Wanamaker's day, there was very little way to track advertising success. Even today, it's hard to know for sure if advertising works . . . except for direct mail and online ads. Because it is possible to track viewers' reactions to ads online in various different ways, it's possible to track results very carefully, which is how we know that billions of dollars were wasted on banner ads in the last few years of the last century!

And those days are being repeated, thanks to the latest online ad fad, pay-per-click search engine advertising. The boom in banner advertising in the years 1997 or so to 2000 was based on a simple principle; there was always some other idiot who would be willing to pay ridiculous advertising rates because he didn't know any better. Now the same thing is happening with pay-per-click ads.

Now, I'm not suggesting that you shouldn't use PPC advertising, or that some people aren't using it successfully — some definitely are. I'm just suggesting that you should be careful. In the days of the banner ad boom, companies were paying way too much for ads, often with little regard, it seemed, for the metrics; that is, the measurements, the payoff. And today, many people are paying too much for their clicks, and prices are on the way up.

Do *not* assume that, just because someone else is paying $1.50 per click for the keywords in which you are also interested, you should be paying $1.51. A few things to remember:

✔ As weird as it may seem, many companies are losing money on their clicks. I know one company that spends almost $300,000 a month on PPC advertising that has admitted to me that it probably loses money on the clicks, but claims that "we have to keep the leads coming in." (I'm sure many of you who spend your days working in corporate America will find this easy to believe.)

> ✔ Some companies don't care if they make money on a click; they regard it as merely part of the branding campaign — if a company is used to spending hundreds of millions of dollars on TV ads, for instance, it may not care too much about tracking the direct benefits of a few million spent on pay-per-click ads.
>
> ✔ Even if the company is making money on the clicks (I know another company spending $150,000 a month on very successful pay-per-click ads), that doesn't mean *you* can make money based on the same click payment.

The last point is essential to understand. Say Company A sells books about rodent racing, making $10 per book after paying production costs. Company B sells racing rodents, and it makes $200 for every racer it sells. The book company is out of luck; there's no way it can compete for clicks against Company B. Company B could pay $50 or $100 or more on clicks for every sale it makes; clearly Company A couldn't.

Ideally, before you begin a pay-per-click advertising campaign, you really should know what a click is worth to your company (in reality, this isn't always possible), so take a look at the next section's points related to the value of clicks.

Valuing Your Clicks

In order to calculate a *click value* — the maximum amount it's worth spending for a click — you have to work your way backwards from the end result, from the action taken by a visitor to your site.

The value of the action

Every commercial site has some kind of action that the site owner wants the site visitor to carry out: buy a product, pick up the phone and call the company, enter information into a form and request a quote, sign up to receive more information, and so on. You have to understand the value of this action.

Say you're selling a product. How much would you pay me if I brought you a sale? Perhaps you have a product that sells for $50, and it costs $25 to create (or buy) and ship to a customer. Your gross profit, then, is $25, so you could afford to spend up to $25 to get the sale without losing money.

However, the value of the click may actually be higher than this. Imagine, for a moment, that if you sell a product for $50, you have a one-third chance of turning the buyer into a regular customer, and you know that regular customers spend $50 with you every three months for 18 months on average. Thus, the lifetime value of your new customer is actually $150, not $25 ($25 per month for 18 months, divided by three).

Don't let some Internet geek convince you that you should take into consideration lifetime value. If you know you truly do have a lifetime customer value, that's fine, but many millions of dollars have been spent on online advertising based on the concept of an assumed lifetime value, when in fact there was little lifetime value beyond the first sale.

Of course, you may not be selling a product online. You may be gathering leads for your sales staff, or getting people to sign up for a catalog, or taking some other action that is not the end of the sales process but in some sense the beginning. This is more difficult to project, though if you are working in an established company, it's information you probably already know (or that someone in your organization knows). How much does your company pay for sales leads? Most medium to large companies know this number.

Your online conversion rate

Now you have to know your online conversion rate, which you may not know when you begin your pay-per-click campaign. If you have an established Web site that has been in business for a few months or years, then this is useful information that someone in the company should have. For every 1,000 people visiting your site, how many carry out the action you want (buy, call, sign up for more information, and so on)? How many visitors do you *convert* to customers or sales leads or subscribers (or whatever)?

Now, I said "for every 1,000 people," not "for every 100 people," for good reason. It may be a number below 1 percent. It may only be 7 or 8 out of every 1,000, for instance. I mention this because many people new to e-commerce do not realize that this is very much a numbers game, that very low conversion rates are common. Sure, there are businesses that convert a much higher proportion of their visitors; but there are also many businesses that convert 1 percent or less. One would expect that businesses that are trying to get people to fill in a form to get a quote for insurance or mortgage rates, for instance, would have much higher conversion rates than companies selling products. (One company in this business told me its conversion rate is around 30 percent, for instance.)

Remember that e-commerce is in many ways much closer to the direct-mail business than the retail store business. Although people often talk about online stores, they are really much more like online catalogs. In particular, they share the characteristic of low conversions. The success of direct-mail campaigns is often measured in fractions of a percent, as it often is online, too.

Figuring the click price

Coming back to the company selling a $50 product and making $25 per sale, you can assume that this company doesn't care about the lifetime value of the customer, as indeed many small companies don't. (Either most of their sales are one-off with little repeat business, or they can't afford to invest in lifetime-value customers anyway; they have to make money on every sale.)

You can also assume that this company has figured out that its conversion rate is around 2 percent; 1 visitor out of 50 buys the product. We know that each customer is worth a maximum of $25; how much is a visitor worth, then? Fifty cents ($25 divided by 50).

That is, $0.50 is the most the company could spend for each site visitor without losing money. (The company isn't actually *making* money, of course, and I've left out consideration of the cost of running the Web operation and other company overhead.) If this company discovers that it can buy clicks for $0.75 cents or a dollar, clearly it's going to lose money. If clicks are $0.25, and if these numbers hold true, then it stands to make a gross profit of $12.50 for every sale.

Different clicks = different values

The preceding is a simplification, of course. In fact, different visitors to your site may be more or less valuable to your company. If Visitor A goes to your site after being told by a friend that your site "sells the best rodent-racing handicap software on the Web," Visitor A is likely to be pretty valuable because she might buy several of your company's products or become a repeat customer. *Much* more valuable than Visitor B, who clicked on a link or banner ad that says something like "Ever Thought About Rodent Racing?" On the one hand, Visitor A went out of her way on the recommendation of a friend, presumably because she's interested in rodent-racing handicap software. On the other hand, Visitor B may simply be wondering what these idiots are talking about.

It's likely that search engine traffic is actually more valuable than the average value of your site visitor. Whether a click on a PPC ad or a natural search result, people who come to your site after searching for a particular keyword are likely to be more interested in your products and services than someone who simply stumbles across your site.

Some large companies spend huge amounts of money trying to analyze their traffic carefully — they want to know where every visitor comes from and exactly what each does. Unfortunately, it's difficult for small companies to do this, but at least you need to be aware of this issue when selecting keywords for your pay-per-click campaigns. Note also that the major PPC systems provide additional services that allow you to track results — systems that will help you see what people do when they arrive at your site. You will be able to see how many PPC visitors actually buy your products, for instance, which will give you a real solid idea of your site's click value.

They Won't Take My Ad!

One of the most frustrating things to deal with when working with a PPC network is having your ads dropped because they don't match the network's standard. Or, as often happens, because one of the company's editors *thinks* the ad doesn't match the network's standards, or even because your Web site is not acceptable. While some of the tier 2 networks are much less fussy, Overture and Google AdWords have very strict guidelines about what sort of Web page or Web site your ads can link to. Each network is different, but the following are the type of things that can kill your ad campaign on Overture or Google:

✔ Your site requires a password. Personally, I think if you're stupid enough to point an ad to a password-protected Web site, the PPC network should take your money and run; and affiliates must make clear in the ad that they are affiliates.

✔ Your site's content doesn't match the ad. Perhaps you have a very weak ad that simply doesn't provide much information about the subject area you are advertising around.

✔ Your ad contains abusive, objectionable, or threatening language.

✔ Your site appears to facilitate the use or distribution of illegal drugs. Overture, for instance, won't take ads for sites that sell kits intended to help people cheat on drug tests.

✔ The landing page specified in the ad must either contain content related to the ad, or have an obvious path to the related content.

✔ You used a trademarked term in your ad, but there's no content related to that product on your Web site.

✔ Your ad doesn't explain that the product you are selling on your site can only be shipped to a very limited area.

✔ Multilevel marketing sites are not allowed to use the terms *job* and *employment* on some PPC systems, but may use the terms *business opportunity* and *work*.

✔ You don't own the page you are linking to. If you are an affiliate, you must link to your own page, and then direct visitors to the retailer's site, for instance; and you can't use a redirect to automatically push visitors across.

✔ If the ad promises information that is not on the site, but will be delivered in some manner — by e-mail or snail mail, for instance — the ad must state that fact.

✔ The Web site must function in Internet Explorer.

✔ You're using a term that is not allowed for your business. For instance, a finance company may not bid on the word *car* at Overture.

✔ Auction sites may not bid on terms related to products not currently on sale at the site.

✔ The network believes that someone searching for the keywords you chose will not find your ad relevant.

✔ Your site contains content that may not be legal or is in some other way objectionable, or links to such a site.

✔ Your ads may not contain *superlatives* (biggest, best, greatest), ALL CAPS, or exclamation points.

✔ Your Web site disables the browser's Back button.

✔ Your Web site contains many broken links or is in some other way malfunctioning.

✔ The language used in your ad must match the language of the target Web site. If your ad is written in Spanish, it can't direct people to an English-language Web site.

✔ You can't put contact information, such as phone numbers and e-mail addresses, in an ad.

✔ Your site spawns a pop-up window when the visitor arrives.

Phew! This isn't all of it, either. What makes it all the more difficult is that the editors enforcing the rules often don't have a full understanding of the rules themselves. One Overture editor may tell you that *all* superlatives are banned; another might tell you that in some contexts they are okay. One ad I ran for a client used the term *largest warehouse,* which I was told was okay by one editor after having the ad killed by another. (It was okay, I was told, because it was a "secondary superlative" that didn't directly relate to the search term. That's one of the unwritten rules you just have to stumble across.) And in another ad, the term *our latest discounts* became a problem. "Other companies may have more recent discounts," I was told. After pointing out that the superlative referred to my clients' discounts, not everyone else's, they let it through. And when advertising a product in the city of Superior, Colorado, the ad was killed because the word *superior* is a superlative!

Check your ads carefully after they've been accepted. Editors may change things without telling you, sometimes turning your finely tuned prose into something significantly different.

Why are the PPC networks so fussy? Surely, if you're paying, who cares if your site is broken or if your ad isn't relevant to the keywords you chose? It's your money, after all. Well, the networks are trying to achieve two things here:

✔ They want as many of the ads as possible to be clicked on; they don't want to clutter up that valuable advertising space with irrelevant ads that nobody clicks on because the networks only get paid when a searcher clicks.

✔ They want to protect the search results' relevance. PPC ads now make up a significant proportion of search results (in many cases, in particular with the smaller PPC networks, 100 percent of the first screen of results seen by the searcher are paid ads), so it's as important for paid results to be relevant as it is for natural search results.

Automating the Task

Working with PPC campaigns can be rather tedious. Ideally, you've got to keep your eye on the rankings each day or your ad could slip. In very competitive markets, it may be necessary to check several times a day. You may be using half a dozen systems, too. If you are working with thousands of keywords (one client has 4,000–5,000 keywords to manage), that's a huge job. How do you handle all this without it getting totally out of control? Here are a few ideas:

✔ Many companies hire a full-time person, even two or three people, just to manage their PPC campaigns.

✔ Programs are available that help to automate PPC management across multiple systems; GoToast (www.gotoast.com) is one of the best known, but various products are available.

✔ Some companies hire a third party to manage their PPC campaigns.

There's no easy answer. The automation software may be a good idea if you have a significant PPC campaign — tens or hundreds of thousands of dollars a month, with thousands of keywords over multiple PPC networks. On the other hand, having used one of the major automation systems, I have to say it was complicated, buggy, and expensive — *not* something you would want to use for a simple PPC campaign.

Sometimes it's actually cheaper to hire someone to manage the PPC campaign. One client, spending $150,000 per month on PPC, switched from having another company manage its PPC campaign to doing it itself. I estimated that the employee in charge of the PPC program probably spent 2–3 hours a day managing the program, and after my client realized that it could hire a full-time person to manage the program for 25 percent of what it was paying for another company to manage the PPC campaign, switching was easy!

One strategy some companies use is this: They manage Google, Overture, and perhaps two or three of the other, more productive tier 2 systems themselves, in house, perhaps using software if they have a very big keyword list. Then they use a PPC management company, or software such as GoToast or BidRank, to buy them keywords from the smaller tier 2 and tier 3 PPC companies at a fixed price per click. For instance, you may agree to pay, say, $0.35 per click. The management company then uses dozens, maybe hundreds, of smaller systems to get those clicks for you, keeping the difference between what they actually pay for the clicks (perhaps $0.05) and your $0.35.

Part V
The Part of Tens

The 5th Wave   By Rich Tennant

"Good news, honey! No one's registered our last name as a domain name yet! Hellooo Haffassoralsurgery.com!"

In this part . . .

After you've got the basics of search engine optimization under your belt, this final part of the book gives you one last push in the right direction.

I talk about a number of myths and mistakes that are common in the search engine business. (No, most Web designers do not understand search engines, no matter what they say; and yes, you should start thinking about search engines before you build your site.)

This part also points you in the direction of some great information resources, places where you can find out more about search engine optimization or get info on a particular search engine technique. I also tell you about useful tools to help you in your endeavors, from programs that help you analyze the traffic coming to your Web site, to link checkers and search-rank tools.

Chapter 16

Ten-Plus Ways to Keep Up-to-Date and Track Down the Details

. . . .

In This Chapter

▶ Keeping up-to-date with search engine technology

▶ Finding detailed information for particular projects

▶ Getting information directly from the search engines

▶ Finding people to help you

. . . .

The naysayers said it couldn't be done, that a book about search engine optimization couldn't be written because the technology is changing so quickly. That's not entirely true — the basics really don't change, such as creating pages that the search engines can read, picking good keywords, getting lots of links into your site, and so on.

But some details *do* change. Which are the most important search engines? What tricks are the search engines really clamping down on? Why did your site suddenly drop out of Google (as many thousands did in the fall/winter of 2003)?

You may also need more detailed information than I can provide in this book. Perhaps you have a problem with dynamic pages, and you need to know the details of URL rewriting for a particular Web server. You need to know where to go to find more information. In this chapter, I provide you with resources that you can use to keep up-to-date and track down the details.

Let Me Help Some More

Visit my Web site at www.SearchEngineBulletin.com. I point you to important resources, provide links to all the Web pages listed in this book (so you can just click instead of typing them), and provide important updates — for instance, I let you know what's going on with Microsoft's new MSNBot search engine and the effect of Yahoo! dumping Google search results and using its own.

I also provide consulting services, including phone consultations. I can examine a company's online strategy not just from the perspective of search engines, but also from a wider view; I've been working online for 20 years now, and have experience in Web design, e-commerce and online transactions, traffic conversion, non-search-engine traffic generation, and so on. An hour or two of advice can often save a company from the huge expense of going down the wrong path!

Current Wisdom

The technical editor on this book, Micah Baldwin, has tremendous experience in the SEO field, and he is posting a bunch of "do it yourself" resources and links to such resources at his company's Web site, `www.currentwisdom.com`, to help people carry out simple search engine optimization tasks themselves.

The Search Engines Themselves

One of the best ways to find information about the search engines is by using carefully crafted search terms at the search engines themselves. Say you want to find detailed information about dealing with session IDs (see Chapter 7). You could go to Google and search for `search engine session id`. Or perhaps you know a little about session ids, and you know that you need to use something called `mod_rewrite`. Go to a search engine and search for `mod_rewrite` or `mod rewrite` (the former is the correct term, while many people talk of mod rewrite in the vernacular).

It's amazing what you can find if you dig around for a little while. A few minutes research through the search engines can save you many hours of time wasted through inefficient or ineffective SEO techniques. I suggest you read the bonus chapter posted at `www.dummies.com/go/seo`, which explains various techniques for searching at Google. A good understanding of how to use the search engines can pay dividends.

Google's Webmaster Pages

Google is happy to tell you what it wants from you and what it doesn't like. No, it won't tell you exactly how it figures out page ranking, but good information is there nonetheless. It's a good idea to review the advice pages Google provides for Webmasters. You can find them at the following URLs.

✔ **Google Webmaster Guidelines:** `www.google.com/webmasters/guidelines.html`

✔ **Google Information for Webmasters FAQ:** `www.google.com/webmasters/faq.html`

Yahoo!'s Search Help

Yahoo!'s search engine is the world's second most important, so perusing the Yahoo! Search Help area may be a good use of your time. You find information about how to use the system and how to work with it to get your pages indexed at `help.yahoo.com/help/us/ysearch/index.html`.

MSN's SEO Tips

At the time of writing, MSN is using search results from Yahoo!, so take a look at Yahoo!'s Search Help. By the time you read this, MSN may have dumped Yahoo!, though. MSN has a very general Search Engine Optimization Tips page, which perhaps will have more specific information once the change occurs: `www.submit-it.com/subopt.htm`.

Teoma/Ask Jeeves' FAQ

One more for you. You can find out what Teoma/Ask Jeeves thinks in its Site Submit Program FAQ (`ask.ineedhits.com/faq.asp`).

Search Engine Watch

The Search Engine Watch site gives you a great way to keep up with what's going on in the search engine world. This site provides a ton of information about a very wide range of subjects related not only to search engine optimization, but also the flip side of the coin; subjects related to searching online. In fact, perhaps its greatest weakness is that it provides *so much* information; it's really intended for search engine optimization experts, rather than the average Webmaster or site manager. The site is divided into a free area and a paid-subscription area.

Danny Sullivan, who founded Search Engine Watch, has been in this business for years, and he really knows his stuff. (In fact, Search Engine Watch was one of the very first sources of information on this subject.) He's also very much plugged into the SEO community — he is perhaps one of the best known people in the business — so he has an inside track to information that is otherwise hard to find. Visit his site at www.searchenginewatch.com.

Google's Newsgroups

When you have a specific, detailed question about search engine optimization, where do you go? You can ask thousands of other people, many with extensive experience, by posting a question to a newsgroup devoted to search engine optimization. There are a number of great discussion groups where you may find the answer to your question already posted somewhere in an existing conversation, or you can post a question to start a conversation of your own.

Google hosts a newsgroup that is widely distributed across the Internet through many newsgroup services. If you know how to use newsgroups — if you already have a newsreader — check to see if your provider subscribes to google.public.support.general. If not, ask if they will. Or read the newsgroup through Google Groups, a free, Web-based newsgroup distribution service provided by Google itself:

```
groups.google.com/groups?hl=en&group=google.public.support.general
```

A quick word of warning about this newsgroup, and any other discussion group about search engine optimization. Not all the information you read will be correct or even close to the truth. The search engine optimization business is rife with rumor, hype, and conjecture. Some of the information in the discussion groups is just plain wrong. How can you tell? The greater your knowledge of search engine optimization, the more likely you are to have a feel for whether the advice makes sense. And one good thing about the discussion groups is that they are, to some degree, peer reviewed. Do other people agree with the advice? Do many people disagree, even disagree vehemently? If you're unsure how valid someone's advice or claim is, checking the reactions of other people in the discussion can help you determine the accuracy of the advice.

WebMaster World

WebMaster World (www.webmasterworld.com) is a very good discussion group, with many knowledgeable people. It'll cost ya, though: $89 for six months, or $150 for a year.

Pandia

Pandia Search Central (www.pandia.com) is a great resource site with information about search engines, from how to use search engines to how to rank well. The site also provides tutorials and links to all sorts of useful sites.

1HelpYouServices.com

A huge amount of information is available at www.ihelpyouservices.com/forums in about three dozen discussion groups, from those related to general search engine information, such as link popularity and page content, to those dedicated to specific search systems.

HighRankings.com

Hosted by a search engine optimization consultant, HighRankings.com is a pretty busy forum (free this time), with discussions covering a wide range of subjects. Check it out at www.highrankings.com/forum.

The Yahoo! Search Engine Optimization Resources Category

This is a good place to find a variety of resources related to search engine optimization: companies, online services, information resources, and so on. Check it out at:

```
dir.yahoo.com/Computers_and_Internet/Internet/World_Wide_Web/Site_Announcement_
                and_Promotion/Search_Engine_Optimization__SEO_/
```

The Open Directory Project Search Categories

Of course the Open Directory Project also has a number of useful search categories:

- ✔ dmoz.org/Computers/Internet/Searching
- ✔ dmoz.org/Computers/Internet/Searching/Search_Engines
- ✔ dmoz.org/Computers/Internet/Searching/Directories
- ✔ dmoz.org/Computers/Internet/Searching/Search_Engines/ Specialized

You might also visit www.resource-zone.com, where you can find forums hosted by Open Directory Project editors who may be able to help you.

Chapter 17

Ten Myths and Mistakes

In This Chapter

▶ Common mistakes made by site developers

▶ Harmful myths

▶ Problems that hurt your search engine rank

A lot of confusion exists in the search engine world; a lot of myths and a lot of mistakes. In this chapter, I quickly run through a few of the ideas and omissions that can hurt your search engine positions.

Myth: It's All about Meta Tags and Submissions

This is the most pervasive and harmful myth of all, one held by many Web designers and developers. All you need to do, many believe, is code your pages with the right meta tags — the KEYWORDS and DESCRIPTION tags, and things like the REVISIT-AFTER and CLASSIFICATION meta tags — and then submit your site to the search engines. I know Web designers who tell their clients that they are search engine experts, then follow nothing more than this procedure.

It's completely wrong, for various reasons. Most meta tags aren't particularly important (see Chapter 5), or aren't used by the search engines at all. Without keywords in the page content, the search engines won't index what you need them to index (see Chapters 4 and 5). And submitting to search engines doesn't mean they will index your pages (see Chapter 9).

Myth: Web Designers and Developers Understand Search Engines

I'm a geek. I've worked in software development for over 20 years; I still work closely with software developers (these days mostly Web-software developers); I build Web sites for my clients (so I work with developers and designers on these sites); my friends are developers and designers . . . and I'm telling you now that most developers and designers do *not* understand the search engines to any great degree.

Most Web-development companies these days tell their clients that they know how to handle the search engines, and even that they are experts. In most cases, that's simply not true, any more than it's true that I'm an expert in neurosurgery. This makes it very hard for business owners when they hire a Web-development team, of course, though perhaps this book will help. It will give you an idea of the sorts of questions you should ask your developers to figure out if they really *do* understand search engine requirements.

Myth: Multiple Submissions Improve Your Search Position

As far as the major search engines go, multiple submissions, even automated submissions, don't help. Someone recently told me that he was sure it did help, because his position improved in, for instance, the Open Directory Project when he frequently resubmitted. This is completely wrong — in the case of the Open Directory Project, there's no way it could possibly help, as they don't accept automated submissions anyway, and all entries have to be reviewed by a human editor.

As you just read, submitting to the search engines — requesting that they index your pages — often doesn't get your page indexed anyway. Far more important is a link campaign to get plenty of links to your site (see Chapters 12 and 13).

Multiple submissions to smaller search engines may help, it's true. But it won't help with the major systems.

Mistake: You Don't Know Your Keywords

This is also a major problem — the vast majority of Web sites are created without the site owners or developers really knowing what keywords are important. (That's okay, perhaps, because most sites are built without any idea of using keywords in the content anyway.) At best, the keywords have been guessed at. At worst — the majority of the cases — nobody's thought of the keywords at all.

Don't guess at your keywords. Do a proper keyword analysis (see Chapter 4). I can almost guarantee two things will happen. You will find that some of your guesses were wrong — people aren't often using some of the phrases you thought would be common. And you'll also discover very important phrases you had no idea about.

Mistake: Too Many Pages with Database Parameters and Session IDs

This is a surprisingly common problem. Many, many sites, in particular sites built by big companies with large development teams, are created these days in such a manner that the search engines won't read them. Search engines don't like database parameters or session IDs in a URL (see Chapter 6).

A large chain of electronics stores' Web site currently has fewer than 100 pages indexed by Google, for instance, and most of those are Adobe Acrobat files or pop-up ads ("Free Shipping!"), or links to dynamic pages that won't appear when a searcher clicks a link in the search results. Yet this is a company selling many thousands of products — it should (could) have thousands, perhaps tens of thousands, of pages indexed by Google.

Mistake: Building the Site and Then Bringing in the SEO Expert

Most companies approach search engine optimization as an afterthought. They build their Web site, and then think, "Right, time to get people to the site." You really shouldn't begin a site until you have considered all the different ways you are going to create traffic to the site. That's like starting to build a road without knowing where it needs to go; if you're not careful, you'll get halfway there and realize "there" is in another direction.

In particular, though, you shouldn't start building a Web site without an understanding of search engines. Most major Web sites these days are built by teams of developers who have little understanding of search engine issues. These sites are launched, and then someone decides to hire a search engine consultant. And the search engine consultant discovers all sorts of unnecessary problems. Good business for the consultant, expensive fixes for the site owner. In addition, Web developers usually don't enjoy working with search marketing experts. They think that all the search engine experts want to do is make the site ugly or remove the dynamism. This is the furthest from the truth, and a Web developer who refuses to work with an SEO expert may just be worried for his or her job.

Myth: $25 Can Get Your Site a #1 Position

There's a lot of background noise in the search engine business, companies claiming to be able to get your site into thousands of search engines, and rank your site well, for $25 a month . . . or a $50 flat fee . . . or $75 a month . . . or whatever.

The truth is that it's more complicated than that, and most people I've spoken to who have used such services have been very disappointed. They often don't get into the major search engines at all, and even if they get included in the index, they don't rank well. Search engine ranking is sometimes very easy — but other times it's complicated, time consuming, and tedious. Most of the offers you'll see streaming into your Inbox in spam e-mail messages, or displayed in banner ads on the Web, are not going to work.

Myth: Bad Links to Your Site Will Hurt Its Position

Another common myth is that getting links to your site from "bad neighborhoods" (such as link farms, or Web sites unrelated to your site's theme) will hurt your search engine position. This isn't exactly so. It won't help, but it won't hurt, either, unless it is obvious that you are actively interacting with link farms or FFA (Free For All) link pages.

If bad links did hurt your site, you could assassinate your competition by linking to their sites from every lousy link farm and FFA you could find. So the search engines can't use such links to downgrade your site.

Mistake: Your Pages Are "Empty"

This one is a huge problem for many companies; the pages have nothing much for the search engines to index. In some cases, the pages have little or no text that a search engine can read because the words on the page are embedded into images. In other cases, all the words may be real text, but there are very few words . . . and what words there are, are not the right keywords.

Remember, search engines like — need — content. And to a search engine, *content* means text that it can read and index. And whenever you provide text to a search engine, it should be the text that does the most for you, text that will help you be found in the search results. And the more content, the better.

Next time you do a search at a major search engine, keep your eyes peeled for search results that don't say much: the description says *Copyright 2004,* for instance (or, worse, *Copyright 1997*), or *All Rights Reserved,* or perhaps something like *Home · About BMC · Products · Testimonials · Links · E-mail BMC.* These are pages with insufficient content.

Myth: Pay per Click Is Where It's At

Pay per click (PPC; see Chapter 15) can be a very important part of a Web site's marketing strategy. It's reliable, predictable, and relatively easy to work with. But it's not the only thing you should be doing. In fact, many companies cannot use PPC because the clicks are too expensive for their particular business model (and click prices are likely to keep rising as search marketing continues to be the hot Internet marketing topic).

The growth in pay per click has been partly caused by the lack of search engine optimization knowledge. Companies build a site without thinking about the search engines, and then don't hire professional expertise to help them get search engine traffic, so they fall back on PPC. Many companies are now spending hundreds of thousands of dollars on PPC; they could complement their PPC campaigns with natural search engine traffic for a small fraction of that cost.

The wonderful thing about PPC advertising and SEO is that the two work hand in hand. Want to know if a word is important enough to optimize for? Get a hundred clicks from your favorite search engine through PPC and look at the conversion rates and ROI (Return on Investment). Want to expand your PPC keyword list? No problem, look at the words that people are already using to find you as a baseline, and grow your list from these words. (For example, if they are using *rodent racing* to find you, why don't you buy the words *mouse rodent racing, rat rodent racing,* and so on?) Many companies are using PPC profitably; just don't assume it's the only way to go.

Chapter 18

Ten-Plus Useful Tools for Search Engine Optimization

*I*n this chapter, I describe a number of useful tools that you can employ in a variety of ways during a search engine optimization campaign, from finding out how well your site ranks in the search engines, to analyzing potential link partners, from seeing what a search engine sees, to seeing how people are arriving at your Web site.

Checking Your Site Rank

How do you know how well your site ranks in the search engines? You can go to a search engine, type a keyword phrase, and see just what happens. If you're not on the first page, check the second, if you're not there, check the third. Then go back and do it for 50 search terms on several search engines. It's going to take a while.

Luckily there's help. Many programs are available that will check your search engine position for you. You tell the program which keywords you're interested in, which search engines you want to check, and the Web site you're looking for in the search results, and leave it to do its work.

Note, however, that most search engines don't like these automated tools. In fact, Google even mentions one of the most popular of these tools, WebPosition Gold (see Figure 18-1), as "unauthorized software." If Google notices a computer using one of these tools excessively, it may ban search queries from that computer . . . if it can identify the computer by IP number, that is. (The problem for Google is that computers accessing the Internet through many ISPs have different IP numbers each time they log on, making it impossible for Google to know which IP number to block.)

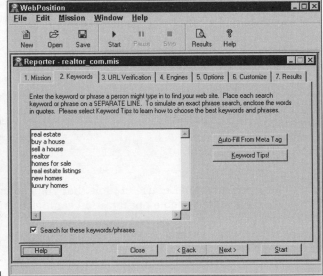

Figure 18-1: WebPosition Gold, being set up to check a page's rank in the search engines.

On the other hand, Google provides an authorized way to send queries of this kind by using various software programs and services, such as Digital Point's free Keyword Tracker tool (`www.digitalpoint.com/tools/keywords`). You sign up for a Google API (Application Program Interface) key at `www.google.com/apis`, and you can then use the key with these programs and services.

You can see a typical keyword report, showing positions for each keyword in a large variety of different search engines — in this case produced by Web-Position Gold — in Figure 18-2. Many tools do site ranking, though, such as WebCEO (`www.webceo.com`), Position Vision (`www.positionvision.com`), and so on.

real estate listings	1	1	NA	NA	www.realtor.com/
real estate listings	2	1	NA	NA	www.realtor.com/FindHome/USMapHome.asp
new homes	3	1	NA	NA	www.realtor.com/
new homes	41	5	NA	NA	www.realtor.com/FindHome/USMapHome.asp
luxury homes	Not in first 60.	Not in first 6.	NA	NA	No pages found.

Google					
Keyword	**Position**	**Page**	**Last Position**	**Change**	**URL**
real estate	1	1	NA	NA	www.realtor.com/
buy a house	Not in first 60.	Not in first 6.	NA	NA	No pages found.
sell a house	Not in first 60.	Not in first 6.	NA	NA	No pages found.
realtor	1	1	NA	NA	www.realtor.com/
realtor	2	1	NA	NA	www.realtor.com/FindHome/USMapHome.asp
realtor	8	1	NA	NA	www1.realtor.com/ASPContent/whyreal.asp
realtor	10	1	NA	NA	nar.realtor.com/
realtor	14	2	NA	NA	ca.realtor.com/
realtor	16	2	NA	NA	netscape.realtor.com/FindReal/RedirAddress.asp
realtor	28	3	NA	NA	prudential.realtor.com/illinois/nbselil.asp
realtor	30	3	NA	NA	netscape.realtor.com/Bacico/AllAbout/Realtors/Why.asp
realtor	37	4	NA	NA	houseandhome.aol.realtor.com/FindReal/RedirAddress.asp
homes for sale	1	1	NA	NA	www.realtor.com/
homes for sale	2	1	NA	NA	www.realtor.com/FindHome/USMapHome.asp
homes for sale	30	3	NA	NA	ca.realtor.com/
homes for sale	53	6	NA	NA	remax.realtor.com/defaultREMAX.asp?gate=remax
real estate listings	1	1	NA	NA	www.realtor.com/
new homes	10	1	NA	NA	www.realtor.com/
new homes	11	2	NA	NA	www.realtor.com/
luxury homes	Not in first 60.	Not in first 6.	NA	NA	No pages found.

LookSmart					
Keyword	**Position**	**Page**	**Last Position**	**Change**	**URL**
real estate	3	1	NA	NA	www.realtor.com/
buy a house	Not in first 60.	Not in first 4.	NA	NA	No pages found.
sell a house	Not in first 60.	Not in first 4.	NA	NA	No pages found.

Figure 18-2: A page-rank report generated by WebPosition Gold.

Checking for Broken Links

Link checkers are always handy, whether you're interested in optimizing your site for the search engines or not. After you've created a few pages, you should run a link check to make sure you didn't make any mistakes in your links. Again, many, many link checkers are available, including paid services such as LinkAlarm (linkalarm.com), that will automatically check links on your site and send you a report. I'm currently using a little Windows program called Xenu's Link Sleuth, shown in Figure 18-3 (home.snafu.de/tilman/xenulink.html) — it's free, which is always nice! (The creator of Link Sleuth requests that if you like the program, support some of his favorite causes.) This program is very quick — it can check tens of thousands of links in a few minutes — and it's very easy to use. It produces a report, displayed in your Web browser, showing the pages containing broken links; click a link, and it opens the page so you can take a look. You can use the program to check both internal and external links on your site. Note also that your Web design software package may include a built-in link checker.

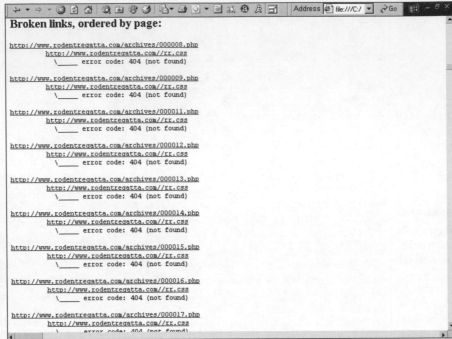

Figure 18-3:
A report
created by
Xenu's Link
Sleuth; it
checked
over 17,000
links in less
than ten
minutes.

Google Toolbar

The Google Toolbar (`toolbar.google.com`) is a great little tool. I mainly use it for two purposes: for searching Google without having to go to the Google site first, and for seeing if a Web page is in Google's cache (click the i button and then click Cached Snapshot of Page), as discussed in Chapter 1. But it contains a number of other neat tools, such as the ability to search Dictionary.com (type the word you want to check into the text box and then select Dictionary from the Search Web drop-down list — see Figure 18-4).

Figure 18-4:
The Google
Toolbar.

The toolbar also has the PageRank indicator (discussed in Chapter 12), which can be useful when evaluating a potential link partner; a pop-up blocker; a way to search Google for pages similar to the one you're viewing; and a link to Google Zeitgeist.

Google Zeitgeist

Google Zeitgeist (www.google.com/press/zeitgeist.html) is worth perusing now and then, particularly if you are looking for an online business and want to know the types of things people search for, or to see how current events affect searches. Google Zeitgeist is an analysis of what people are searching for, when, and where. You can find the most popular brand-name searches, charts showing how searches peak for particular keywords during news events or in response to TV shows (Iraq, SARS, and so on), the most popular searches for particular men, women, and fictional characters, the most popular movie searches in Australia, the most popular brands in Italy, and so on (see Figure 18-5). This is a wealth of information that can give you a feel for what people are really searching for. (Did you know the number of searches for recipes jumps dramatically in October and November? Or that in France, the TV reality show *Greg le Millionaire* got only a fraction of the searches for *Star Academy?*)

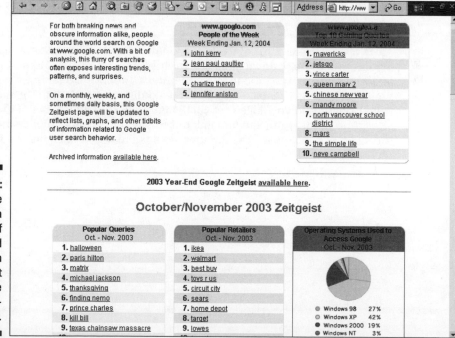

Figure 18-5:
Google Zeitgeist, a wealth of background information about what people are searching for.

There are other, similar tools. Wordtracker, for instance, will periodically send you a free report of the top 500 searches (with or without sexually explicit terms), and Ask Jeeves has a service that shows you the top "advancing" search terms — the ones that are growing most quickly (`sp.ask.com/docs/about/jeevesiq.html`). Yahoo! Buzz (`buzz.yahoo.com`) can be interesting, too. Last, but not least, the Lycos 50 is published weekly by Aaron Schatz at `50.lycos.com`. The interesting thing about the Lycos 50 is that Aaron uses it to predict what will be hot or not.

Alexa Toolbar

The Alexa Toolbar (`download.alexa.com`) can be handy, too. I sometimes use it to assess the traffic of Web sites I may want to work with. For instance, if someone approaches you trying to sell advertising space on their site, how do you know if it's a good deal? So many sites get almost no traffic, that it may not be worth the expense.

The Alexa Toolbar can give you a very general idea of whether the site gets any traffic at all; you can view traffic details for the site, such as the traffic rank, an estimate of the number of visitors to the site out of every million Internet users, and so on. Reportedly, Alexa's numbers are pretty good for the world's most popular sites, but very inaccurate for the average site. However, you can still get a general feel. If the site is ranked 4,000,000, you can bet it doesn't get much traffic at all. If the site is ranked 4,000, it's far more popular.

Alexa also provides a list of the most popular sites in thousands of categories, a good way to track down affiliates, for instance, or link partners. And it has an interesting search function; use the Alexa Toolbar to search Google, and you'll get different results. Sites are ranked differently, though the data comes from Google, and you'll also get small images of the home page of the top few sites. And point at the Site Info link to see site information such as how long the site has been online, the number of sites linking to it, similar sites, and so on (see Figure 18-6).

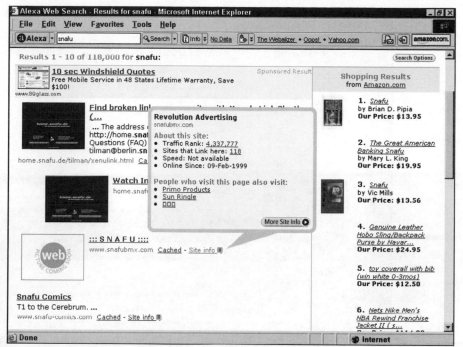

Figure 18-6:
Searching
from the
Alexa
Toolbar.

Finding Links

Being able to produce a list of pages linking back to a Web site is extremely
useful (and a great way to impress a boss or client). I use a link analysis tool
(generally LinkSurvey — www.antssoft.com) to find out how many links are
pointing to a client's site in comparison with competitors' sites, and also to
find out who in particular is linking to competitors — a good start in a link
campaign. This tool, shown in Figure 18-7, lets me view the link pages in the
program itself, though it will also export to an Excel spreadsheet for further
manipulation.

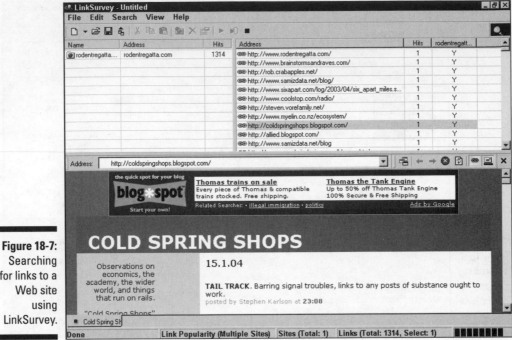

Figure 18-7:
Searching
for links to a
Web site
using
LinkSurvey.

Seeing What the Search Engines See

I admit I don't often use this type of tool, but it's interesting now and then. Some utilities will read a Web page and display the content of the page in the manner in which a search engine is likely to see it (see Figure 18-8). When looking at a competitor's pages, you can sometimes see things that aren't visible to the site visitor but that have been placed on the page for the benefit of the search engines. When viewing your pages, you may want to check that all the links are readable by the search engines (these tools generally provide a list of readable links).

Here are a couple of these utilities:

✔ **Sim Spider:** www.searchengineworld.com/cgi-bin/sim_spider.cgi

✔ **Delorie:** www.delorie.com/web/ses.cgi

You can also search for terms such as search engine simulator or searchbot simulator.

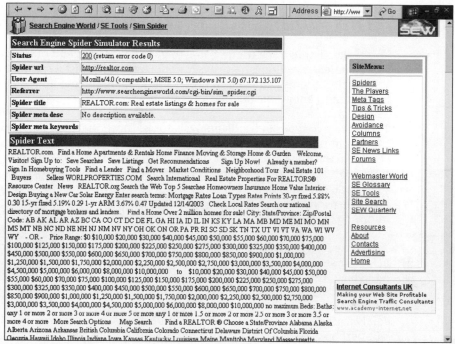

Figure 18-8:
The results
from Search
Engine
World's Sim
Spider.

Another great way to check a site is to use a text-mode browser, such as Lynx, to visit your site. If your site can't be seen in Lynx, it will have problems ranking in any search engine. You can find a Lynx simulator at www.delorie.com/web/lynxview.html.

Finding Your Keyword Density

As I explain in Chapter 5, you don't need to get too hung up on keyword density. You can analyze to the nth degree, and everyone has a different opinion as to exactly what the density should be. But it's sometimes interesting to check your pages for keyword density, and many tools are available to help you do so. WebPosition Gold, mentioned earlier in this chapter, has a built-in density tool, and you can find various online tools, as well, such as the following:

✔ **Search Engine World's Keyword Density Analyzer:** www.searchengineworld.com/cgi-bin/kwda.cgi

✔ **KeywordDensity.com:** www.keyworddensity.com

Analyzing Your Site's Traffic

You really should track traffic going to your site. At the end of the day, your search engine position isn't terribly important — it's just a means to an end. What really counts is the amount of traffic coming to your site. And it's important to know *how* people get to your site, too.

There are two types of traffic-analysis tools: those that read server logs, and those that tag your Web pages and track traffic using a program on another server. In the first case, the tool analyzes log files created by the Web server — the server adds information each time it receives a request for a file. In order to use the tag systems, you have to add a little piece of code to your Web pages — each time a page from your site is requested, the program is, in effect, informed of the fact.

You quite likely have a traffic-analysis tool already installed on your site — ask your server administrator how to view your logs. Otherwise, you can use a tag-based traffic-analysis tool; in general, you'll have to pay a monthly fee for such a service.

Analysis tools show you all sorts of interesting and often useless information. But perhaps the most important things you can find are

- Which sites are sending visitors to your site?
- Which search engines are sending visitors to your site?
- What keywords are people using to reach your site?

You may find that people are reaching you with keywords you hadn't thought of, or perhaps unusual combinations of keywords that you hadn't imagined. This doesn't replace a real keyword analysis, though (see Chapter 4), as you'll only see the keywords used by people who found you, not the keywords used by people who *didn't* find you but were looking for products or services like yours.

Unfortunately, most traffic-analysis tools are really not very good. Some don't provide much information, but the ones that do provide a lot of information are often way too complex and confusing. One log-based system I really like is ClickTracks (www.clicktracks.com). ClickTracks, shown in Figure 18-9, was created by someone who worked for one of the top log tools companies, but who felt the popular tools just throw statistics at people, instead of providing useful, easy-to-understand information. This is a very cool tool that uses tables and images of your Web site to make understanding your logs very easy. ClickTracks also has a tag-based tool that you can use for a monthly fee.

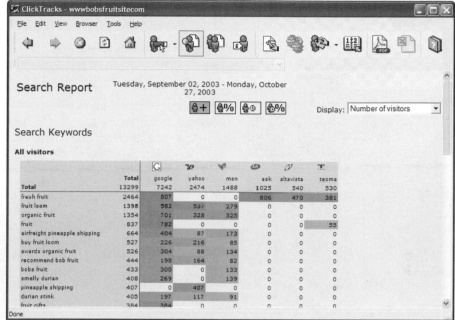

Figure 18-9:
Log analy-
sis from
ClickTracks.

More Tools

If you're looking for more tools, try these sites:

- ✔ **Search Engine World:** www.searchengineworld.com/misc/tools.htm
- ✔ **SEO Help:** www.seo-help.com/seo-reference/seo-resources.html
- ✔ **Pandia SEO:** www.pandia.com/optimization

Don't Forget the Search Engines

Don't forget that you can find just about anything through the search engines themselves. If you have some kind of tedious procedure to work through, chances are someone has built a program to automate the procedure. So head to your favorite search engine and spend a little time tracking it down!

Part VI
Appendix

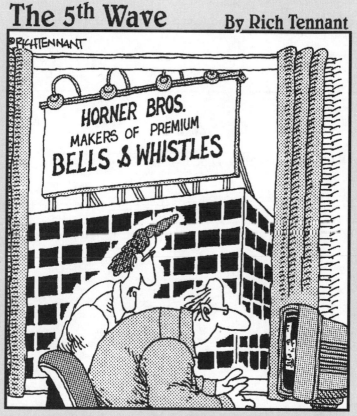

The 5th Wave — By Rich Tennant

HORNER BROS.
MAKERS OF PREMIUM
BELLS & WHISTLES

"As a web site designer I never thought I'd say this, but I don't think your site has enough bells and whistles."

In this part . . .

In this Appendix, you find information on copyright laws.

Appendix

Staying Out of Copyright Jail

∙ ∙

*I*n Chapter 8, I describe several sources of content for your Web site. Because you can get into trouble if you take *copyrighted* materials without permission, I feel it's important to cover a few copyright basics.

Many people think that they're allowed to take and use pretty much anything they find, especially if it can be found on the Internet. Search for usa today, for instance, and you'll discover thousands of sites that have copied articles from that newspaper. Although you *can* do this and *may* get away with it, you should be aware that you *don't* have the right to do this. It is, to put it bluntly, plagiarism. It's illegal, and the owner of the material has the right to sue you. Whether it's text, images, sounds, or whatever, if someone else created it, you don't own it!

I summarize copyright law in Chapter 8, and this appendix goes into a little more detail about the four exceptions I describe:

- ✔ If it's really old, you can use it.
- ✔ If the guvmint created it, you can use it.
- ✔ If it's "donated," you can use it.
- ✔ It's only fair — *fair use* explained.

If It's Really Old, You Can Use It

In some cases in which you find old works that would be appropriate for your site, you can simply take content and do what you want with it. In the old days, copyrights didn't last very long, a real contrast with the situation today.

Copyright is currently intended to allow the creator to profit from a work, and his worthless children to live a life of drunkenness and unmerited indolence. (Luckily for my kids, computer books have a very short life.) For works created after January 1, 1978, . . . well, you can forget the details for them because you probably won't be alive when copyright expires on such works. (I will. Having done research for a book I'm going to call *Live Forever or Die Trying,* I've learned a few tricks.) Let's just say, by way of example, that the copyright on a work created on January 1, 1978, by a 19-year-old writer who manages to live to 89, will expire in the year 2118. (No, that's not a joke.)

The situation for works created before 1978 gets complicated because the law kept changing and seems to have been intended to confuse. I'm not going to go into details — it makes my head hurt just to think about. It all depends on whether you are Uruguayan, are quick on your toes, were 28 on January 1, 1964, and have a Swiss-born mother. However . . .

Anything copyrighted — and by that I mean either published or registered with the U.S. Copyright Office — *after January 1, 1964,* is out of bounds for the foreseeable future (at least until 2059).

Works copyrighted *between 1921 and December 31, 1963,* may have lost copyright protection, depending on whether the copyright holder renewed it. (In those days, works had to be registered with the U.S. Copyright Office and renewed to get the full term of protection; as I mentioned before, registration, at any point, is no longer necessary.) If it was renewed, the work may still be protected. Thus *most* works published between these dates have actually lost copyright protection (renewals being relatively rare) — the problem is figuring out *which* works.

If you really want to use a particular work, you can figure all this out. You need to contact the Copyright Office to see if the work was renewed, though unfortunately this means you have to do the work yourself at its offices in Washington, D.C., or pay $75 per hour for a manual search. (See www.copyright.gov for more information.)

Works copyrighted *before 1921* are not copyright protected anymore. You can take 'em and use 'em for whatever you want.

Does this help you? If you have a site selling cell phones, it almost certainly does not help you. If you have a site related to Victorian poetry, travelogues, or herbal medicine, it may be useful. (I have a friend who republishes old school books, many of which are now copyright-free.)

This is a very quick rundown of copyright law, which should be sufficient for most people's purposes. However, there are many details I haven't covered — titles, short phrases, and slogans can't be copyrighted, for instance. (Be careful, though — a title can be *trademarked.* Just try publishing a book with *For Dummies* in the title and see what happens!) For the full details, visit the U.S. Copyright Office Web site: www.copyright.gov. And www.unc.edu/~unclng/public-d.htm condenses all this complexity into a simple little chart.

Before I move on, a word of warning: Be careful before you take something you think is old enough to be out of copyright. Make sure you're using a copy of the original, not a modified version, because those modifications may be protected! You can freely copy and use Charles Dickens' *Great Expectations,* but if someone has taken the original, edited it, and added notes, you can't use that. Nor can you use a version that has been translated in recent years because the translation will be copyrighted.

If the Guvmint Created It, You Can Use It

This is a good example of your tax dollars at work. The U.S. government spends many millions of dollars creating *content.* This content is not copyright protected. Thus you can take the full text of a government report and publish it on your Web site. Yep, that's right, as amazing as it may seem, you can take, for instance, all the tax forms and instructions you want, or videos created by the EPA, and post them on your site.

However, some rare exceptions exist. A government department may hold donated materials that were originally copyright protected, and continue to hold the copyright. It may commission a private individual or company to create a work or publish the work under another arrangement, and that person or company may hold the copyright. And works created by the National Technical Information Service or the United States Postal Service may be copyright protected.

If It's "Donated," You Can Use It

Sometimes people simply give away their work — they "donate" it in one of two ways. In some cases, a work may be given to the public domain, which means the author relinquishes all rights to the work. In other cases, the author may simply allow the use of the work, but retain copyright. For instance, sometimes you see statements such as the one on the copyright chart at `www. unc.edu/~unclng/public-d.htm`:

> "Chart may be freely duplicated or linked to for nonprofit purposes. No permission needed. Please include Web address on all reproductions of chart so recipients know where to find any updates."

The author has allowed anyone to use the chart under certain conditions: The use must be "nonprofit" (although this term is rather ambiguous, you can assume that at the very least it means you can't print the chart and sell it), and the address of the original chart should be included.

It's Only Fair — Fair Use Explained

You can copy parts of a copyrighted work and use them on your site, under an exclusion known as *fair use*. The only problem with fair use is that one man's fair use is another man's plagiarism. In other words, there are no hard and fast rules as to what *fair use* means.

I'm not going to explain this. In fact, I'm going to take some copyright-free text directly off the U.S. Copyright Office Web site and save myself a few moments:

> "Under the fair use doctrine of the U.S. copyright statute, it is permissible to use limited portions of a work including quotes, for purposes such as commentary, criticism, news reporting, and scholarly reports. There are no legal rules permitting the use of a specific number of words, a certain number of musical notes, or percentage of a work. Whether a particular use qualifies as fair use depends on all the circumstances. See FL 102, Fair Use, and Circular 21, Reproductions of Copyrighted Works by Educators and Librarians."

The fair use exception isn't, in most cases, terribly useful for most people, because you can't just take huge gobs of the work and drop them into your site. However, you can weave quotes from copyrighted works (make sure that you properly cite your sources) into original material you've written.

Index

Notes

Notes

Notes

Notes

FOR DUMMIES®

The easy way to get more done and have more fun

PERSONAL FINANCE

0-7645-5231-7

0-7645-2431-3

0-7645-5331-3

Also available:

Estate Planning For Dummies
(0-7645-5501-4)

401(k)s For Dummies
(0-7645-5468-9)

Frugal Living For Dummies
(0-7645-5403-4)

Microsoft Money "X" For Dummies
(0-7645-1689-2)

Mutual Funds For Dummies
(0-7645-5329-1)

Personal Bankruptcy For Dummies
(0-7645-5498-0)

Quicken "X" For Dummies
(0-7645-1666-3)

Stock Investing For Dummies
(0-7645-5411-5)

Taxes For Dummies 2003
(0-7645-5475-1)

BUSINESS & CAREERS

0-7645-5314-3

0-7645-5307-0

0-7645-5471-9

Also available:

Business Plans Kit For Dummies
(0-7645-5365-8)

Consulting For Dummies
(0-7645-5034-9)

Cool Careers For Dummies
(0-7645-5345-3)

Human Resources Kit For Dummies
(0-7645-5131-0)

Managing For Dummies
(1-5688-4858-7)

QuickBooks All-in-One Desk Reference For Dummies
(0-7645-1963-8)

Selling For Dummies
(0-7645-5363-1)

Small Business Kit For Dummies
(0-7645-5093-4)

Starting an eBay Business For Dummies
(0-7645-1547-0)

HEALTH, SPORTS & FITNESS

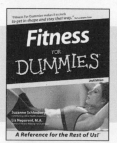

0-7645-5167-1

0-7645-5146-9

0-7645-5154-X

Also available:

Controlling Cholesterol For Dummies
(0-7645-5440-9)

Dieting For Dummies
(0-7645-5126-4)

High Blood Pressure For Dummies
(0-7645-5424-7)

Martial Arts For Dummies
(0-7645-5358-5)

Menopause For Dummies
(0-7645-5458-1)

Nutrition For Dummies
(0-7645-5180-9)

Power Yoga For Dummies
(0-7645-5342-9)

Thyroid For Dummies
(0-7645-5385-2)

Weight Training For Dummies
(0-7645-5168-X)

Yoga For Dummies
(0-7645-5117-5)

Available wherever books are sold.
Go to www.dummies.com or call 1-877-762-2974 to order direct.

WILEY

FOR DUMMIES®

A world of resources to help you grow

HOME, GARDEN & HOBBIES

0-7645-5295-3

0-7645-5130-2

0-7645-5106-X

Also available:

Auto Repair For Dummies
(0-7645-5089-6)

Chess For Dummies
(0-7645-5003-9)

Home Maintenance For Dummies
(0-7645-5215-5)

Organizing For Dummies
(0-7645-5300-3)

Piano For Dummies
(0-7645-5105-1)

Poker For Dummies
(0-7645-5232-5)

Quilting For Dummies
(0-7645-5118-3)

Rock Guitar For Dummies
(0-7645-5356-9)

Roses For Dummies
(0-7645-5202-3)

Sewing For Dummies
(0-7645-5137-X)

FOOD & WINE

0-7645-5250-3

0-7645-5390-9

0-7645-5114-0

Also available:

Bartending For Dummies
(0-7645-5051-9)

Chinese Cooking For Dummies
(0-7645-5247-3)

Christmas Cooking For Dummies
(0-7645-5407-7)

Diabetes Cookbook For Dummies
(0-7645-5230-9)

Grilling For Dummies
(0-7645-5076-4)

Low-Fat Cooking For Dummies
(0-7645-5035-7)

Slow Cookers For Dummies
(0-7645-5240-6)

TRAVEL

0-7645-5453-0

0-7645-5438-7

0-7645-5448-4

Also available:

America's National Parks For Dummies
(0-7645-6204-5)

Caribbean For Dummies
(0-7645-5445-X)

Cruise Vacations For Dummies 2003
(0-7645-5459-X)

Europe For Dummies
(0-7645-5456-5)

Ireland For Dummies
(0-7645-6199-5)

France For Dummies
(0-7645-6292-4)

London For Dummies
(0-7645-5416-6)

Mexico's Beach Resorts For Dummies
(0-7645-6262-2)

Paris For Dummies
(0-7645-5494-8)

RV Vacations For Dummies
(0-7645-5443-3)

Walt Disney World & Orlando For Dummies
(0-7645-5444-1)

Available wherever books are sold. Go to www.dummies.com or call 1-877-762-2974 to order direct.

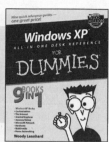

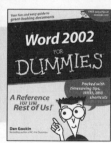

FOR DUMMIES®

Helping you expand your horizons and realize your potential

INTERNET

0-7645-0894-6

0-7645-1659-0

0-7645-1642-6

Also available:

America Online 7.0 For Dummies
(0-7645-1624-8)

Genealogy Online For Dummies
(0-7645-0807-5)

The Internet All-in-One Desk Reference For Dummies
(0-7645-1659-0)

Internet Explorer 6 For Dummies
(0-7645-1344-3)

The Internet For Dummies Quick Reference
(0-7645-1645-0)

Internet Privacy For Dummies
(0-7645-0846-6)

Researching Online For Dummies
(0-7645-0546-7)

Starting an Online Business For Dummies
(0-7645-1655-8)

DIGITAL MEDIA

0-7645-1664-7

0-7645-1675-2

0-7645-0806-7

Also available:

CD and DVD Recording For Dummies
(0-7645-1627-2)

Digital Photography All-in-One Desk Reference For Dummies
(0-7645-1800-3)

Digital Photography For Dummies Quick Reference
(0-7645-0750-8)

Home Recording for Musicians For Dummies
(0-7645-1634-5)

MP3 For Dummies
(0-7645-0858-X)

Paint Shop Pro "X" For Dummies
(0-7645-2440-2)

Photo Retouching & Restoration For Dummies
(0-7645-1662-0)

Scanners For Dummies
(0-7645-0783-4)

GRAPHICS

0-7645-0817-2

0-7645-1651-5

0-7645-0895-4

Also available:

Adobe Acrobat 5 PDF For Dummies
(0-7645-1652-3)

Fireworks 4 For Dummies
(0-7645-0804-0)

Illustrator 10 For Dummies
(0-7645-3636-2)

QuarkXPress 5 For Dummies
(0-7645-0643-9)

Visio 2000 For Dummies
(0-7645-0635-8)

Available wherever books are sold. Go to www.dummies.com or call 1-877-762-2974 to order direct.